Table of Contents

Introduction

This book is a hands-on guide to designing, building, and testing microcontroller-based devices. Microcontrollers, or single-chip computers, are ideal for projects that require computer intelligence, but don't need the overhead of a complete personal computer with disk drives, keyboard, and full-screen display.

Why the 8052-BASIC?

This book focuses on the 8052-BASIC microcontroller, which is easy to use, full featured, and inexpensive to work with. The on-chip BASIC-52 programming language enables you to write, run, and test your programs quickly. With over 100 commands, instructions, and operators, BASIC-52 is more capable than other microcontroller BASICs. And, as a member of the 8051 microcontroller family, the 8052-BASIC has a standard, popular architecture.

The ideas and applications presented here are not limited to the 8052-BASIC, however. If your favorite chip is a different one, you can adapt the circuits and programs to it. The schematics and program listings in this book include comments and explanations to help you apply the ideas, whether or not you are using the 8052-BASIC.

What's Inside?

This is not just a textbook that presents information but glosses over the details of how to apply it. Inside, you'll find practical information, including the following:

- Complete circuit schematics and parts lists—so you can easily build the circuits yourself.

- Design theory—for example, why use this particular component? or how can I expand or modify the circuit shown?

- Example program listings—for easy testing and use of the circuits.

- Construction and debugging tips—to help you get the circuits up and running without problems.

The appendices include a complete list of sources to help you find the components and additional information you need for your projects.

Because microcontroller projects involve both circuit design and programming, I cover both the hardware and software aspects. The book begins with an introduction to microcontrollers, and to the 8052-BASIC chip in particular. Next are basic circuits to get you started programming and interfacing to the chip, along with the reasons behind the component and design choices, and construction details for prototyping. To the basic circuits, I show how to add switches, keypads, displays, and other input/output interfaces.

A programming reference describes each of BASIC-52's keywords, with specific tips for trouble-free programming in BASIC-52.

You'll also find out how to add these to your system:

- Sensors, for detecting detect and measuring physical properties.

- Clock/calendar functions, for keeping track of seconds, minutes, hours, days, months, and years, and to trigger alarms at particular times.

- Control of AC power, switch matrices, stepper and continuous motors, and gain of an op amp.

- Programmable wireless links, for situations where stringing wires isn't practical or convenient.

A chapter on assembly-language interfacing shows how to add assembly-language programs for faster program execution, how to add your own commands the BASIC-52 programming language, and how to use the 8052-BASIC as a development system for an all-assembly-language project.

The final chapters cover other options for 8052-BASIC systems, including how to store BASIC-52 in external memory rather than in the 8052's internal ROM, and a review of related products, including BASIC compilers, 8052-BASIC circuit boards, and development software for more convenient and possibly cheaper project development.

Your Feedback Is Welcome

This book is the result of requests from readers of my articles in *ComputerCraft* magazine and its successor, *The MicroComputer Journal.* I've expanded the coverage of several topics, including programming of EPROMs and other devices, display options, sensors, and programming tips.

Thanks to everyone who responded to my articles with comments, questions, criticisms, and suggestions, and who, in doing so, helped to make this book as useful as it can be. As always, I welcome your comments on this work.

Jan Axelson
10-94

Introduction

1

Microcontroller Basics

This chapter introduces you to the world of microcontrollers, including definitions, some history, and a summary of what's involved in designing and building a microcontroller project.

What's a Microcontroller?

A microcontroller is a computer-on-a-chip, or, if you prefer, a single-chip computer. *Micro* suggests that the device is small, and *controller* tells you that the device might be used to control objects, processes, or events. Another term to describe a microcontroller is *embedded controller*, because the microcontroller and its support circuits are often built into, or embedded in, the devices they control.

You can find microcontrollers in all kinds of things these days. Any device that measures, stores, controls, calculates, or displays information is a candidate for putting a microcontroller inside. The largest single use for microcontrollers is in automobiles—just about every car manufactured today includes at least one microcontroller for engine control, and often more to control additional systems in the car. In desktop computers, you can find microcontrollers inside keyboards, modems, printers, and other peripherals. In test equipment, microcontrollers make it easy to add features such as the ability to store measurements, to create and store user routines, and to display messages and waveforms. Consumer products that use microcontrollers include cameras, video recorders, compact-disk players, and ovens. And these are just a few examples.

A microcontroller is similar to the microprocessor inside a personal computer. Examples of microprocessors include Intel's 8086, Motorola's 68000, and Zilog's Z80. Both microprocessors and microcontrollers contain a central processing unit, or CPU. The CPU executes instructions that perform the basic logic, math, and data-moving functions of a computer. To make a complete computer, a microprocessor requires memory for storing data and programs, and input/output (I/O) interfaces for connecting external devices like keyboards and displays.

In contrast, a microcontroller is a single-chip computer because it contains memory and I/O interfaces in addition to the CPU. Because the amount of memory and interfaces that can fit on a single chip is limited, microcontrollers tend to be used in smaller systems that require little more than the microcontroller and a few support components. Examples of popular microcontrollers are Intel's 8052 (including the 8052-BASIC, which is the focus of this book), Motorola's 68HC11, and Zilog's Z8.

A Little History

To understand how microcontrollers fit into the always-expanding world of computers, we need to look back to the roots of microcomputing.

In its January 1975 issue, Popular Electronics magazine featured an article describing the Altair 8800 computer, which was the first microcomputer that hobbyists could build and program themselves. The basic Altair included no keyboard, video display, disk drives, or other elements we now think of as essential elements of a personal computer. Its 8080 microprocessor was programmed by flipping toggle switches on the front panel. Standard RAM was 256 bytes and a kit version cost $397 ($498 assembled). A breakthrough in the Altair's usability occurred when a small company called Microsoft offered a version of the BASIC programming language for it.

Of course, the computer world has changed a lot since the introduction of the Altair. Microsoft has become an enormous software publisher, and a typical personal computer now includes a keyboard, video display, disk drives, and Megabytes of RAM. What's more, there's no longer any need to build a personal computer from scratch, since mass production has drastically lowered the price of assembled systems. At most, building a personal computer now involves only installing assembled boards and other major components in an enclosure.

A personal computer like Apple's Macintosh or IBM's PC is a general-purpose machine, since you can use it for many applications—word processing, spreadsheets, computer-aided design, and more—just by loading the appropriate software from disk into memory. Interfaces to personal computers are for the most part standard ones like those to video displays, keyboards, and printers.

But along with cheap, powerful, and versatile personal computers has developed a new interest in small, customized computers for specific uses. Each of these small computers is dedicated to one task, or a set of closely related tasks. Adding computer power to a device can enable it to do more, or do it faster, better, or more cheaply. For example, automobile engine controllers have helped to reduce harmful exhaust emissions. And microcontrollers inside computer modems have made it easy to add features and abilities beyond the basic computer-to-phone-line interface.

In addition to their use in mass-produced products like these, it's also become feasible to design computer power into one-of-a-kind projects, such as an environmental controller for a scientific study or an intelligent test fixture that ensures that a product meets its specifications before it's shipped to a customer.

At the core of many of these specialized computers is a microcontroller. The computer's program is typically stored permanently in semiconductor memory such as ROM or EPROM. The interfaces between the microcontroller and the outside world vary with the application, and may include a small display, a keypad or switches, sensors, relays, motors, and so on.

These small, special-purpose computers are sometimes called single-board computers, or SBCs. The term can be misleading, however, since the computer doesn't have to be on a single circuit board, and many types of computer systems, such as laptop and notebook computers, are now manufactured on a single board.

New Tools

To design and build a computer-controlled device, you need skills in both circuit design and software programming. The good news is that a couple of recent advances have simplified the tasks involved.

One is the introduction of microcontrollers themselves, since they contain all of the elements of a computer on a single chip. Using a microcontroller can reduce the number of components and thus the amount of design work and wiring required for a project. The 8052-BASIC microcontroller even includes its own programming language, called BASIC-52.

The other development is personal computers themselves. A desktop computer can help tremendously by serving as a *host system* for writing and testing programs. As you are developing a project, you can use a serial link to connect the host system to a *target system*, which contains the microcontroller circuits you are testing. You can then use the personal computer's keyboard, video display, disk drives, and other resources for writing and testing programs and transferring files between the two systems.

Project Steps

Putting together a microcontroller project involves several steps:

1. Define the task
2. Design and build the circuits
3. Write the control program
4. Test and debug

Sometimes the steps won't follow exactly in this order. You may begin writing your program before you build the circuits, or you may build and test some of the circuits before you start programming. But however you go about it, each of the above steps is part of the process. To see what's involved in each step, let's look at each in more detail.

Defining the Task

Every project begins with an idea, or a problem that needs a solution. For example, How can I monitor light intensity at different locations and times of day to find the best location for a solar collector? Or how can I automate the process of drilling printed-circuit boards? Or how can I create a computer-controlled, animated display for a store window?

Once you know what you want to accomplish, you need to determine whether or not your idea is one that requires a computer at all. In general, a computer is the way to go when the circuits must make complex decisions or deal with complex data. For example, a simple AND gate can easily decide whether or not two inputs are both valid logic highs, and will change its output accordingly. But it would require many small-scale chips to build a circuit that stores a series of values representing sensor outputs and the times they occurred, and displays the information in an easily understandable form.

This type of application is where microcontrollers come in handy. Inside, microcontrollers are little more than a carefully designed array of logic gates and memory cells, but modern fabrication processes allow thousands of these to fit on a single chip. Since the basic functions of a microcontroller—performing arithmetic, logic, data-moving, and program branching functions—are common ones that are useful in many applications, it's practical to design and market a chip that performs these functions. The user accesses the abilities of the microcontroller by writing a program that performs the desired functions.

On the other end of the scale, how do you know if an idea is suitable for a microcontroller, or whether you should use a full desktop computer? If your design requires users to enter or view complex commands, data, or graphical information, or if you need large amounts of data or program storage, then a system with keyboard, full-screen display, and disk drives makes sense. For simpler designs, a microcontroller with perhaps a keypad, small display, and solid-state memory (no disk drives) can often do the job, with less expense and smaller size.

In fact, recently the two extremes have been meeting. Some 32-bit microcontrollers are as capable as desktop systems, and notebook-size computers are available with solid-state, diskless storage. Also, expansion cards, other hardware, and software are now available for those who want to use desktop computers for monitoring and control tasks. So there's something for everyone.

The 8052-BASIC chip described in this book is perfect for many simpler applications, especially control and monitoring tasks. Because the chip is easy to use, it's a good way to learn about microcontrollers and computers in general. Although you can't do the most complex projects with it, you can do a lot, at low cost and without a lot of hassle.

Designing and Building

When you're ready to design and build the circuits for a project, there are several ways to proceed. You can design your circuits from scratch, using manufacturers' data books as guides; you can follow a tested design (a kit or project presented in a magazine for example); or you can buy an assembled single-board computer, adding only the interfaces and programming your application requires. This book presents designs that you can build yourself, but you can also use a kit or assembled board as a base if you wish.

Choosing a chip. Does it matter which microcontroller chip you use? All microcontrollers contain a CPU, and chances are that you can use any of several devices for a specific project.

Within each device family, you'll usually find a selection of family members, each with different combinations of options. For example, the 8052-BASIC is a member of the 8051 family of microcontrollers, which includes chips with program memory in ROM or EPROM, and with varying amounts of RAM and other features. You select the version that best suits your system's requirements.

Microcontrollers are also characterized by how many bits of data they process at once, with a higher number of bits generally indicating a faster or more powerful chip. Eight-bit chips are popular for simpler designs, but 4-bit, 16-bit, and 32-bit architectures are also available. The 8052-BASIC is an 8-bit chip.

Power consumption is another consideration, especially for battery-powered systems. Chips manufactured with CMOS processes usually have lower power consumption than those manufactured with NMOS processes. Many CMOS devices have special standby or "sleep" modes that limit current consumption to as low as a few microamperes when the circuits are inactive. Using these modes, a data logger can reduce its power consumption between samples, and power up only when it's time to take data.

The 8052-BASIC chip is available in both NMOS and CMOS versions. The original 8052-BASIC was an NMOS chip, offered directly from Intel. (Intel's term for its NMOS process is HMOS.) Although Intel never offered a CMOS version directly, Micromint became a source by ordering a batch of CMOS 8052's with the BASIC-52 programming language in ROM. The CMOS version, the 80C52-BASIC, has maximum power consumption of 30 milliamperes, compared to 175 milliamperes for the NMOS 8052-BASIC.

All microcontrollers have a defined instruction set, which consists of the binary words that cause the CPU to carry out specific operations. For example, the instruction *0010 0110* tells an 8052 to add the values in two locations. The binary instructions are also known as operation codes, or opcodes for short. The opcodes perform basic functions like adding, subtracting, logic operations, moving and copying data, and controlling program branching.

Control circuits often require reading or changing single bits of input or output, rather than reading and writing a byte at a time. For example, a microcontroller might use the eight bits of an output port to switch power to eight sockets. If each socket must operate independently of the others, a way is needed to change each bit without affecting the others. Many microcontrollers include bit-manipulation (also called Boolean) opcodes that easily allow programs to set, clear, compare, copy, or perform other logic operations on single bits of data, rather than a byte at a time.

Options for storing programs. Another consideration in circuit design is how to store programs. Instead of using disk storage, most microcontroller circuits store their programs on-chip. For one-of-kind projects or small-volume production, EPROM has long been the most popular method of program storage. Besides EPROMs, other options include EEPROM, ROM, nonvolatile (NV), or battery-backed, RAM, and Flash EPROM. The program memory may be in the microcontroller chip, or a separate component.

To save a program in **EPROM**, you must set the EPROM's data and address pins to the appropriate logic levels for each address and apply special programming voltages and control signals to store the data at the selected address. The programming process is sometimes called *burning* the EPROM. You erase the contents by exposing the chip's quartz window, and the circuits beneath it, to ultraviolet energy.

Some microcontrollers contain a one-time-programmable, or field-programmable, EPROM. This type has no window, so you can't erase its contents, but because it's cheaper than a windowed IC, it's a good choice when a program is finished and the device is ready for quantity production.

Several techniques are available for programming EPROMs and other memory chips. With a manual programmer, you flip switches to toggle each bit and program the EPROM byte by byte. This is acceptable for short programs, but quickly becomes tedious with a program of any length. Computer control simplifies the job greatly. With an EPROM programmer that connects to a personal computer, you can write a program at your keyboard, save it to disk if you wish, and store the program in EPROM in a few easy steps. Data sheets for EPROMs rarely specify the number of erase and reprogramming cycles a device is guaranteed for, but a typical EPROM should endure 100 erase/program cycles, and usually many more.

EEPROMs are much like EPROMs except that they are electrically erasable—no ultraviolet source is required. Limitations of EEPROMs include slow speed, high cost, and a limited number of times that they can be reprogrammed (typically 10,000 to 100,000).

ROMs are cost-effective when you need thousands of copies of a single program. ROMs must be factory-programmed and once programmed, can't be changed.

NVRAM typically includes a lithium cell, control circuits, and RAM encapsulated in a single IC package. When power is removed from the circuit, the lithium cell takes over and preserves the information in RAM, for 10 years or more. You can reprogram an NVRAM n infinite number of times, with the only limitation being battery life.

Flash EPROM is electrically erasable, like EEPROM, but most Flash devices erase all at once, or in a few large blocks, rather than byte-by-byte like EEPROM. Some Flash EPROMs require special programming voltages. As with EPROMs, the number of erase/program cycles is limited.

The 8052-BASIC uses two types of program memory. An 8-kilobyte, or 8K, on-chip ROM stores the BASIC-52 interpreter. For storing the BASIC-52 programs that you write, the BASIC-52 language has programming commands that enable you to save programs in external EPROM, EEPROM, or NVRAM.

Other memory. Most systems also require a way to store data for temporary use. Usually, this is RAM, whose contents you can change as often as you wish. Unlike EPROM, ROM, EEPROM, and NVRAM, the contents of the RAM disappear when you remove power the chip (unless it has battery back-up).

Most microcontrollers include some RAM, typically a few hundred bytes. The 8052-BASIC has 256 bytes of internal RAM. A complete 8052-BASIC system requires at least 1024 bytes of external RAM as well.

I/O options. Finally, input/output (I/O) requires design decisions. Most systems require interfaces to things like sensors, keypads, switches, relays, and displays. Most microcontrollers have ports for interfacing to the world outside the chip. The 8052-BASIC uses many of its ports for accessing external memory and performing other special functions, but some port bits are available for user applications, and you can easily increase the available I/O by adding support chips.

Writing the Control Program

When it's time to write the program that controls your project, the options include using machine code, assembly language, or a higher-level language. Which programming language you use depends on things like desired execution speed, program length, and convenience, as well as what's available in your price range.

Machine code. The most fundamental program form is machine code, the binary instructions that cause the CPU to perform the operations you desire.

Assembly language. One step removed from machine code is assembly language, where abbreviations called mnemonics (memory aids) substitute for the machine codes. The mnemonics are easier to remember than the machine codes they stand for. For example, in the 8052's assembly language, the mnemonic *CLR C* means clear the carry bit, and is easier to remember than its binary code (*11000011*).

Since machine code is ultimately the only language that a CPU understands, you need some way of translating assembly-language programs into machine code. For very short programs, you can *hand assemble,* or translate the mnemonics yourself by looking up the machine codes for each abbreviation. Another option is to use an *assembler*, which is software that runs on a desktop computer and translates the mnemonics into machine code. Most assemblers provide other features, such as formatting the program code and creating a listing that shows both the machine-code and assembly-language versions of a program side -by-side.

Higher-level languages. A disadvantage to assembly language is that each device family has its own set of mnemonics, so you have to learn a new vocabulary for each family you work with. To get around this problem, higher-level languages like C, Pascal, Fortran, Forth, and BASIC follow a standard syntax so that programs are more portable from one device to another. The idea is that with minor changes, you can use a language like BASIC to write programs for many different devices. In reality, each language tends to develop many different dialects, depending on the chip and the preferences of the language's vendor, so porting a program to a different device isn't always effortless. But there are many similarities among the dialects of a single language, so, as with spoken language, a new dialect is easier to learn than a whole new language.

Higher-level languages also simplify programming by allowing you to do in one or a few lines what would require many lines of assembly code to accomplish.

Interpreters and **compilers** are two forms of higher-level languages. An interpreter translates a program into machine code each time the program runs, while a compiler translates only once, creating a new, executable file that the computer runs directly, without re-translating.

As a rule, interpreters are very convenient for shorter programs where execution speed isn't critical. With an interpreted language, you can run your program code immediately after you write it, without a separate compile or assembly step. A compiler is a good choice when a program is long or has to execute quickly. A single language like BASIC may be available in both interpreted and compiled versions.

Each device family requires its own interpreter or compiler to translate the higher-level code into the machine code for that device. In other words, you can't use QuickBASIC for IBM PCs to program an 8052 microcontroller—you need a compiler that generates program code for the 8052.

Compared to an equivalent program written in assembly language, a compiled program usually is larger and slower, so assembly language is the way to go if a program must be as fast or as small as possible. A higher-level language also may not offer all of the abilities of assembly code, though you can get around this by calling subroutines in assembly language when necessary.

BASIC-52 is an interpreted language, but BASIC compilers for the 8052 are also available. In fact, you can have the best of both worlds by testing your programs with the BASIC-52 interpreter, and compiling the finished product for faster execution and other benefits of the compiled version.

Testing and Debugging

After you've written a program, or a section of one, it's time to test it and as necessary, find and correct mistakes to get it working properly. The process of ferreting out and correcting mistakes is called debugging. Easy debugging and troubleshooting can make a big difference in how long it takes to get a system up and running. As with programming, you have several options here as well.

Testing in EPROM. One way is to burn your program into EPROM, install the EPROM in your system, run the program, and observe the results. If problems occur (as they usually will) you modify the program, erase and reburn the EPROM, and try again, repeating as many times as necessary until the system is operating properly.

Development systems. Another option is to use a development system. A typical development system consists of a monitor program, which is a program stored in EPROM or other memory in the microcontroller system, and a serial link to a personal computer. Using the abilities of the monitor program, you can load your program from a personal computer into RAM (instead of the more permanent EPROM) on the microcontroller system, then run the program, modify it, and retry as often as necessary until the program is working properly.

Most development systems also allow single-stepping, setting breakpoints, and viewing and changing the data in memory. In single-stepping, you run the program one step at time, pausing after each step, so you can more easily monitor what the circuits and program are doing at each step. A breakpoint is a program location where the program stops executing and waits for a command to continue. You can set breakpoints at critical spots in your program. At any breakpoint, you can view or change the contents of memory or perform other tests.

Simulators. Another development tool is a simulator, which is software that runs on a desktop computer and uses the video display to demonstrate what would happen if a specific microprocessor or microcontroller were to run a particular program. You can look "inside" the simulated chip, observe the contents of internal memory, and single-step or set breakpoints to stop program execution at a desired program location or condition. In this way, you can get a program working properly before you commit it to EPROM. One drawback to simulators is that they can't mimic all features of the chip of interest, especially interrupt-response and timing characteristics.

Emulators. An in-circuit emulator (ICE) is hardware that replaces the microprocessor in question by plugging into the microprocessor's socket on the device you want to test. Like a simulator, an emulator lets you control program execution and monitor what happens at each program step. Microprocessor emulators typically are expensive. A ROM emulator is a lower-cost option that simulates an EPROM (using RAM, for example) for program storage, and usually provides the abilities of a development system as well.

The 8052-BASIC's development system. The 8052-BASIC system and a personal computer form a complete development system for writing, testing, and storing programs. The personal computer's keyboard and screen make it easy to write and run programs and view the results.

BASIC-52 has many built-in debugging features that make it easy to test programs. You can run a program immediately after writing it, without having to assemble, compile, or program an EPROM. You can use a `STOP` statement and `CONT` (continue) command to set breakpoints and resume executing your program. You can use `PRINT` statements to display variables as the program runs. And, if you wish, you can use your personal computer for writing programs off-line and uploading and downloading them to the 8052-BASIC system.

2

Inside the 8052-BASIC

This chapter introduces you to the 8052-BASIC chip, including the kinds of projects you can do with it, what equipment, materials, and skills you need in order to design and build an 8052-BASIC project, and a pin-by-pin look at the chip and its abilities.

Possibilities

The 8052-BASIC microcontroller is an easy-to-use, low-cost, and versatile computer-on-a-chip. It's ideal for projects that require more than an assortment of logic gates, but less than a complete desktop computer system with a full keyboard, display, and disk drives. If you're interested in doing more with computers than simply running applications programs, the 8052-BASIC gives you a chance to design and build a system from the ground up.

With a few support chips and a program stored in memory, you can use the 8052-BASIC to sense, measure, and control processes, events, or conditions. Here are just a few examples of the uses you can put it to:

- data collection
- machine control
- test equipment
- wired and wireless links for communications and control

The 8052-BASIC is actually two products in one: it's an 8052 microcontroller, with the BASIC-52 programming language on-chip. To begin using the 8052-BASIC, you need a minimum circuit consisting of the 8052-BASIC and some support components, plus a personal computer. This book contains specific instructions for use with "IBM-compatible," or MS-DOS, computers, but you can use any computer that has an RS-232 serial port and communications software to go with it. Figure 2-1 shows the basic setup.

With an 8052-BASIC circuit connected by a serial link to a personal computer, you have a complete development system with these abilities:

• You can write and run BASIC programs. You use the keyboard, video display, and other resources of the personal computer to type and view the programs and commands that the 8052-BASIC system executes. BASIC-52 is an interpreted language whose programs do not require an additional assembling or compiling step. You can run programs or execute commands immediately after you write them.

• You can use BASIC-52's programming functions to permanently store your programs in EPROM or other nonvolatile memory. You don't need a separate EPROM programmer.

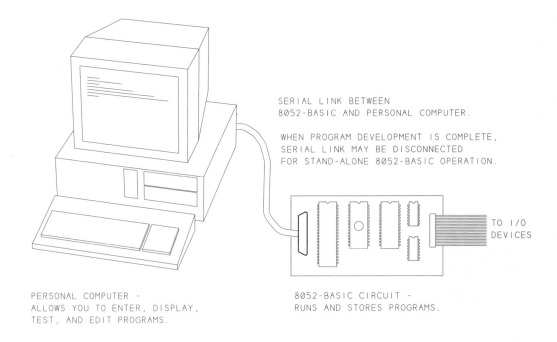

SERIAL LINK BETWEEN
8052-BASIC AND PERSONAL COMPUTER.

WHEN PROGRAM DEVELOPMENT IS COMPLETE,
SERIAL LINK MAY BE DISCONNECTED
FOR STAND-ALONE 8052-BASIC OPERATION.

TO I/O
DEVICES

PERSONAL COMPUTER -
ALLOWS YOU TO ENTER, DISPLAY,
TEST, AND EDIT PROGRAMS.

8052-BASIC CIRCUIT -
RUNS AND STORES PROGRAMS.

Figure 2-1 Setup for working with the 8052-BASIC.

- You can also store programs on your personal computer's disk. You can write or edit programs on your personal computer, and then upload them to the 8052-BASIC system.

- To the basic circuits, you can add displays, switches, keypads, relays, and other components, depending on the needs of your project.

- After program development, you can disconnect the link to the personal computer and let the 8052-BASIC system run its stored program on its own.

Limits

No single product is ideal for every use. These are some of the limitations to the 8052-BASIC:

- Program execution can be slow, compared with programs that run on more powerful computers, or programs written in assembly language. A typical program line in BASIC-52 takes several milliseconds to execute. Because of this, there are some tasks that BASIC-52 just can't handle—for example, detecting and responding to an interrupt within a few microseconds. But for many control, monitoring, and other tasks, BASIC-52 is fine. For example, a weather station that senses conditions once per minute and stores or displays the results doesn't need super-fast response. And, if necessary, you can call an assembly-language routine for a portion of a program where speed is critical.

  Even if you write your programs in assembly language, C, or another language, you can use the 8052-BASIC system as a development system that enables you to upload your program to memory, run the program, and test and debug your programs and circuits.

- Another limitation of the 8052-BASIC is that a complete project requires additional components. If you're looking for a true single-chip solution, the 8052-BASIC isn't it. Even a minimal system requires an external RAM chip, and most systems also have an external EPROM or other non-volatile memory. The serial link and other optional functions also use some of the on-chip timers and input/output ports, so these may not be available for other uses.

  Still, the 8052-BASIC lets you to do a lot with a little. When needed, you can easily add chips to expand the input/output ports, timers, and other functions.

- And finally, don't expect BASIC-52 to have the abilities of *QBasic, Visual Basic* or other BASIC programming languages that you may use on your personal computer. BASIC-52 is more capable than many other single-chip BASICs. It includes features like loops, subroutines, string handling, and even floating-point math for handling fractional quantities. But there are some primitive aspects to the language. For example, the on-line editing functions are limited. Once you write a program line, you can change it only by retyping from the beginning. The limitations are understandable, because the entire programming language has to fit in the 8052's 8 kilobytes of ROM. Fancy editing and other features just aren't feasible in this small space.

There are solutions here as well. You can get around many of the editing limitations by writing and editing programs off-line, using your personal computer and text editor, and then uploading to the 8052-BASIC system. And, there are software and hardware products that enhance BASIC-52 and make it easier to use, especially for longer, more complex programming jobs.

What You Need

To use the 8052-BASIC chip, you need the following equipment, materials, and skills:

Components

The 8052-BASIC chip and supporting components are widely available. Appendix A lists sources for the components used in the circuits described in this book.

Power Supply

You'll need a regulated +5-volt power supply to power the circuits. Output capability of at least 500 milliamperes is recommended for general experimenting. The power supply can be powered by batteries or AC line voltage, but it must have a regulated output between 4.75 and 5.25 volts.

Construction Materials

To build the circuits, you'll need circuit-construction materials and the skills to use them. Wire-wrapping is an effective, quick way to build the circuits described, but if you prefer, you can use point-to-point soldering or design and make a printed-circuit board, or use any method that you're comfortable with. Another option is to buy one of the available kits or prebuilt 8052-BASIC boards. You can then use this book as a guide to using and expanding the abilities of your board. Appendix A lists board suppliers and books on project-construction techniques.

Documentation

Using just the information in this book, you can build and begin using your system. For serious experimenting, two additional references are recommended: programming and hardware manuals. For programming, you have two choices: Intel's *BASIC-52 User's Manual,* or Systronix's *BASIC-52 Programming.* Each of these describes the BASIC-52 programming language in detail. The Intel manual includes a few schematics, while Systronix's version has more programming examples and is better organized in general. Intel's *Embedded Microcontrollers* data book is a hardware reference that describes the 8052 chip, including electrical specifications and timing requirements. It also includes an assembly-language reference. Appendix A tells where to get these.

Other useful documentation includes data sheets for the other components in your projects. For a small charge, many component vendors will send along data sheets for the parts you order.

Host Computer

To program the 8052-BASIC, you connect its circuits to a host computer, using an RS-232 asynchronous serial port and terminal-emulation software. The computer can be any type, as long as it has a serial port and appropriate software.

The serial port is the same connector where you plug in an external modem, serial printer, serial mouse, or other RS-232 serial device.

Terminal-emulation software is the same type of software that you may use for modem communications with an on-line BBS. Examples for MS-DOS computers are Datastorm

Table   2-1.   Differences among 8051-family chips.

Chip	Program Memory		Ram (bytes)	Timers
	Type	kilobytes		
8051	ROM	4	128	2
8052	ROM	8	256	3
8031	none	-	128	2
8032	none	-	256	3
8751	EPROM	4	128	2
8752	EPROM	8	256	3

• 80C51, 80C52, 80C31, and so on are CMOS versions of above.
• 80C51FA/B/C add more versatile timers and an enhanced serial channel.
• 8052-BASIC has the BASIC-52 programming language in ROM.
• Packages include 40-pin DIP, 40-lead PLCC, and 44-pin QFP.

Technologies' *Procomm Plus* and the Terminal accessory in Microsoft Windows. At minimum, the software must enable you to do the following: set the baud rate and other communications parameters, serially transmit the characters that you type at the keyboard, and display the characters received at the serial port. Also useful, but not essential, is the ability to upload and download text files from your disk, over the serial link. If you don't have a favorite communications program, look in shareware catalogs or the file areas of online services or BBS's, where you can try out the offerings for a small disk-copying or downloading charge.

Test Equipment

Some basic test equipment will help you monitor, test, and troubleshoot your circuits. Minimum requirements include a multimeter capable of reading volts, ohms, and milliamperes. Just about any basic meter will do for this. A logic probe is convenient, but not essential, for monitoring logic levels and transitions. Best of all, an oscilloscope lets you view the actual waveforms on one or more channels.

Knowledge

This book assumes that you have a basic knowledge of electronic circuits, including digital logic. It does not assume that you know a lot about computer programming and computer circuits. Appendix A lists some books that cover the basics, if you want to review or learn these. Appendix C is a review of hexadecimal, binary, and decimal number systems.

The 8051 Family

At the core of the 8052-BASIC is an 8052 microcontroller, a member of the 8051 microcontroller family. Intel Corporation introduced the 8051 in 1980. Since that time, 8051-family chips have been used as the base of thousands of products. Many other companies, including Philips, Siemens, Dallas Semiconductor, OKI, Fujitsu, and Harris-Matra now also make 8051-family chips. Some companies have expanded the 8051 family by offering compatible chips with additional features.

Table 2-1 summarizes the differences among popular 8051-family chips. The 8052 is an enhanced 8051, with an extra timer and more RAM and ROM. The 8031 and 8032 are identical to the 8051 and 8052, except that the ROM area is unused, and program code must be stored in an external EPROM or other memory chip.

The 8052, like other 8051-family chips, is available in NMOS and CMOS versions. Figure 2-2 shows the pinout of the 8052 and 8052-BASIC, and Table 2-2 describes the pin functions.

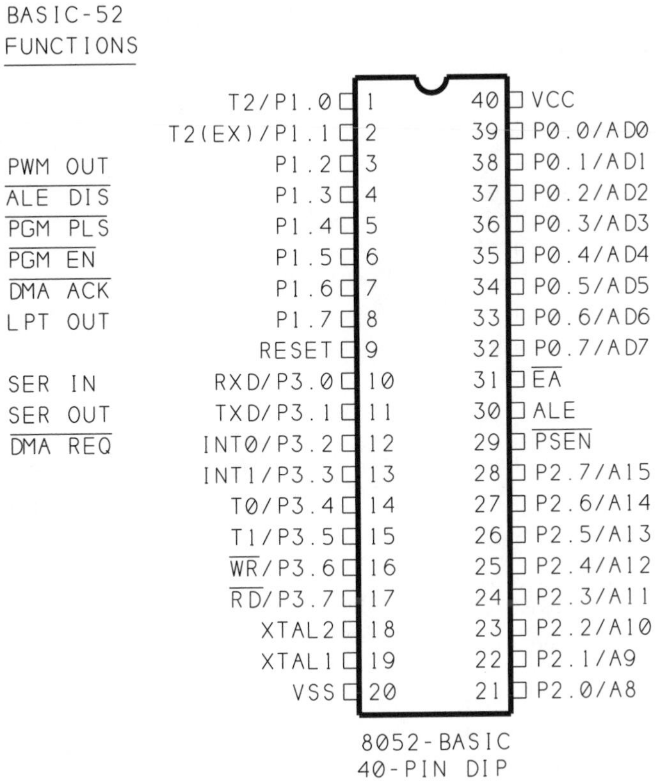

```
BASIC-52
FUNCTIONS
```

```
                       T2/P1.0 ▯ 1        40 ▯ VCC
                  T2(EX)/P1.1 ▯ 2         39 ▯ P0.0/AD0
     PWM  OUT         P1.2 ▯ 3            38 ▯ P0.1/AD1
     ALE  DIS         P1.3 ▯ 4            37 ▯ P0.2/AD2
     PGM  PLS         P1.4 ▯ 5            36 ▯ P0.3/AD3
     PGM  EN          P1.5 ▯ 6            35 ▯ P0.4/AD4
     DMA  ACK         P1.6 ▯ 7            34 ▯ P0.5/AD5
     LPT  OUT         P1.7 ▯ 8            33 ▯ P0.6/AD6
                     RESET ▯ 9            32 ▯ P0.7/AD7
     SER  IN       RXD/P3.0 ▯ 10          31 ▯ EA
     SER  OUT      TXD/P3.1 ▯ 11          30 ▯ ALE
     DMA  REQ     INT0/P3.2 ▯ 12          29 ▯ PSEN
                  INT1/P3.3 ▯ 13          28 ▯ P2.7/A15
                    T0/P3.4 ▯ 14          27 ▯ P2.6/A14
                    T1/P3.5 ▯ 15          26 ▯ P2.5/A13
                    WR/P3.6 ▯ 16          25 ▯ P2.4/A12
                    RD/P3.7 ▯ 17          24 ▯ P2.3/A11
                     XTAL2 ▯ 18           23 ▯ P2.2/A10
                     XTAL1 ▯ 19           22 ▯ P2.1/A9
                       VSS ▯ 20           21 ▯ P2.0/A8
```

```
8052-BASIC
40-PIN DIP
```

Figure   2-2   Pin functions of the 8052 and 8052-BASIC microcontrollers.

Elements of the 8052 and 8052-BASIC

These are the major elements of the 8052, plus the enhancements included in the 8052-BA-SIC:

CPU

The CPU, or central processing unit, executes program instructions. Types of instructions include arithmetic (addition, subtraction), logic (AND, OR, NOT), data transfer (move), and program branching (jump) operations. An external crystal provides a timing reference for clocking the CPU.

ROM

ROM (read-only memory) is the read-only memory that is programmed into the chip in the manufacturing process. In the 8052-BASIC, the ROM contains the BASIC-52 interpreter program that the 8052 executes on boot-up. As far as the hardware is concerned, this is the only difference between the ordinary 8052 and the 8052-BASIC.

Table 2-2. (page 1 of 2) Pin functions of the 8052 microcontroller and 8052-BASIC additions.

Pin	Symbol	Input/Output	8052 Function	8052-BASIC Additions Symbol	Function
1	P1.0 T2	I/O	Port 1, bit 0; Timer 2 external input		
2	P1.1 T2(EX)	I/O	Port 1, bit 1; Timer 2 external reload/capture		
3	P1.2	I/O	Port 1, bit 2	PWM	Pulse-width-modulated output
4	P1.3	I/O	Port 1, bit 3	$\overline{\text{ALE DIS}}$	Address latch disable
5	P1.4	I/O	Port 1, bit 4	$\overline{\text{PGM PLS}}$	Program pulse
6	P1.5	I/O	Port 1, bit 5	$\overline{\text{PGM EN}}$	Programming voltage enable
7	P1.6	I/O	Port 1, bit 6	$\overline{\text{DMA ACK}}$	DMA acknowledge
8	P1.7	I/O	Port 1, bit 7	LPT	Line printer out
9	Reset	Input	Reset system		
10	P3.0 RXD	I/O	Port 3, bit 0 Serial receive	SER IN	Serial port in
11	P3.1 TXD	I/O	Port 3, bit 1 Serial transmit	SER OUT	Serial port out
12	P3.2 $\overline{\text{INT0}}$	I/O	Port 3, bit 2 External interrupt 0	$\overline{\text{DMA}}$ $\overline{\text{REQ}}$	DMA request
13	P3.3 $\overline{\text{INT1}}$	I/O	Port 3, bit 3 External interrupt 1		
14	P3.4 T0	I/O	Port 3, bit 4 Timer 0 external input		
15	P3.5 T1	I/O	Port 3, bit 5 Timer 1 external input		
16	P3.6 $\overline{\text{WR}}$	I/O	Port 3, bit 6 Write strobe for external memory		
17	P3.7 $\overline{\text{RD}}$	I/O	Port 3, bit 7 Read strobe for external memory		
18	XTAL1	Input	Inverting oscillator amplifier (crystal)		
19	XTAL2	Output	Inverting oscillator amplifier (crystal)		
20	VSS	Input	Circuit ground		

Table 2-2. (page 2 of 2)

Pin	Symbol	Input/ Output	8052 Function	8052-BASIC Additions (none on pins 21-40)
21	P2.0 A8	I/O	Port 2, bit 0 Address bit 8	
22	P2.1 A9	I/O	Port 2, bit 1 Address bit 9	
23	P2.2 A10	I/O	Port 2, bit 2 Address bit 10	
24	P2.3 A11	I/O	Port 2, bit 3 Address bit 11	
25	P2.4 A12	I/O	Port 2, bit 4 Address bit 12	
26	P2.5 A13	I/O	Port 2, bit 5 Address bit 13	
27	P2.6 A14	I/O	Port 2, bit 6 Address bit 14	
28	P2.7 A15	I/O	Port 2, bit 7 Address bit 15	
29	$\overline{\text{PSEN}}$	Output	Program store enable Read strobe for external program memory	
30	ALE	Output	Address latch enable	
31	$\overline{\text{EA}}$	Input	External access enable for program memory	
32	P0.7 AD7	I/O	Port 0, bit 7 Address/data bit 7	
33	P0.6 AD6	I/O	Port 0, bit 6 Address/data bit 6	
34	P0.5 AD5	I/O	Port 0, bit 5 Address/data bit 5	
35	P0.4 AD4	I/O	Port 0, bit 4 Address/data bit 4	
36	P0.3 AD3	I/O	Port 0, bit 3 Address/data bit 3	
37	P0.2 AD2	I/O	Port 0, bit 2 Address/data bit 2	
38	P0.1 AD1	I//O	Port 0, bit 1 Address/data bit 1	
39	P0.0 AD0	I/O	Port 0, bit 0 Address/data bit 0	
40	Vcc	Input	Supply voltage	

RAM

RAM (random-access memory) is where programs store information for temporary use. Unlike ROM, the CPU can write to RAM as well as read it. Any information stored in RAM is lost when power is removed from the chip. The 8052 has 256 bytes of RAM. BASIC-52 uses much of this for its own operations, with a few bytes available to users.

I/O Ports

I/O (Input/Output) Ports enable the 8052 to read and write to external memory and other components. The 8052 has four 8-bit I/O ports (Ports 0-3). As the name suggests, the ports can act as inputs (to be read) or outputs (to be written to). Many of the port bits have optional, alternate functions relating to accessing external memory, using the on-chip timer/counters, detecting external interrupts, and handling serial communications. BASIC-52 assigns alternate functions to the remaining port bits. Some of these functions are required by BASIC-52, while others are optional. If you don't use an alternate function, you can use the bit for any control, monitoring, or other purpose in your application.

Accessing external memory. The largest alternate use of the ports has to do with accessing external memory. Although the 8052 is a single-chip computer, a complete 8052-BASIC system requires additional components. It must have external RAM in addition to the 8052's internal RAM, and most systems also have EPROM, EEPROM, or battery-backed RAM for permanent storage of BASIC-52 programs.

Accessing this external memory uses all of Ports 0 and 2, plus bits 6 and 7 of Port 3, to hold data, addresses, and control signals for reading and writing to external memory. Data here refers to a byte to be read or written, and may be any type of information, including program code. The address defines the location in memory to be read or written.

During a memory access, Port 0's eight pins (AD0-AD7) first hold the lower byte of the address, followed by the data to be read or written. This method of carrying both addresses and data on the same signal lines is called a *multiplexed address/data bus*. It's a popular arrangement that many devices use, since it requires fewer pins on the chip, compared to giving each data and address line its own pin. Port 2's eight lines hold the higher byte of the address to be read or written to. These lines make up the high address bus (A8-A15). Together, the 16 address lines can access 64 kilobytes (65,536 bytes) of memory, from 00000000 00000000 to 11111111 11111111 in binary, or 0000h to FFFFh in hexadecimal.

Besides pins to hold the data and addresses, the 8052 must also provide control signals to initiate the read and write operations. Control signals include $\overline{WR}$ (write), $\overline{RD}$ (read), $\overline{PSEN}$ (program store enable), and ALE (address latch enable). Some of the address lines may also function as control signals that help to select a chip during a memory access.

Code and data memory. To understand the operation of the control signals, you need to know a little about how the 8052 distinguishes between two types of memory: data and code, or program, memory. By using different control signals for each type of memory, the 8052 can access two separate 64K areas of memory, with each addressed from 0000h to FFFFh, and each using the same data and address lines.

The 8052 accesses code memory when it executes an assembly-language program or subroutine. Code memory is read-only; you can't write to it. The only instructions that access code memory are read operations. Code memory is intended for programs or subroutines that have been previously programmed into ROM or EPROM. The 8052 strobes, or pulses, $\overline{PSEN}$ when it accesses external code memory. Accesses to internal code memory (the BASIC-52 interpreter in ROM) do not use $\overline{PSEN}$ or any external control signals.

Data memory is read/write memory, usually RAM. Instructions that read data memory strobe $\overline{RD}$, and instructions that write to data memory strobe $\overline{WR}$. The term *data memory* may be misleading, because it can hold any information that is accessed with instructions that strobe $\overline{RD}$ or $\overline{WR}$. In fact, BASIC-52 programs are stored in data memory, not code memory as you might think. This is because the 8052 does not execute the BASIC programs directly. Instead, the BASIC-52 interpreter program reads the BASIC programs as data and then translates them to machine code for execution by the 8052.

If you don't need all of the available memory space, you can combine code and data memory in a single area. With combined memory, $\overline{WR}$ controls write operations, and $\overline{PSEN}$ and $\overline{RD}$ are logically ANDed to create a read signal that is active when either $\overline{PSEN}$ or $\overline{RD}$ is low. Combined data/code memory is handy if you want the flexibility to store either BASIC or assembly-language programs in the same chip, or if you want to be able to upload assembly-language routines into RAM for testing.

ALE is the final control signal for accessing external memory. It controls an external latch that stores the lower address byte during memory accesses. When the 8052 reads or writes to external memory, it places the lower address byte on AD0-AD7 and strobes ALE, which causes the external latch to save the lower address byte for the rest of the read or write cycle. After a short delay, the 8052 replaces the address on AD0-AD7 with the data to be written or read.

Timers and Counters. The 8052 has three 16-bit timer/counters, which make it easy to generate periodic signals or count signal transitions. BASIC-52 assigns optional functions for each of the timer/counters.

Timer 0 controls a real-time clock that increments every 5 milliseconds. You can use this clock to time events that occur at regular intervals, or as the base for clock or calendar functions. Timer 1 has several uses in BASIC-52, including controlling a pulse-width-modulated output (PWM) (a series of pulses of programmable width and number); writing to a line printer or other serial peripheral (LPT); and generating pulses for EPROM programming ($\overline{\text{PGM PULSE}}$). Timer 2 generates a baud rate for serial communications at SER IN and SER OUT. These are all typical applications for timer/counters in microcontroller circuits.

If you don't use the optional timer functions, you can program the timers for other applications. In addition to timing functions, where the timer increments at a defined rate, you can use the timers for event counting, where the timer increments on an external trigger and measures the time between triggers. If you use the timers for event counting, T2, T2(EX), T0, and T1 detect transitions to be counted.

The serial port. The 8052's serial port automatically takes care of many of the details of serial communications. On the transmit side, the serial port translates bytes to be sent into serial data, including adding start and stop bits and writing the data in a timed sequence to SER OUT. On the receive side, the serial port accepts serial data at SER IN and sets a flag to indicate that a byte has been received. BASIC-52 uses the serial port for communicating with a host computer.

External interrupts. $\overline{\text{INT0}}$ and $\overline{\text{INT1}}$ are external interrupt inputs, which detect logic levels or transitions that interrupt the CPU and cause it to branch to a predefined program location. BASIC-52 uses $\overline{\text{INT0}}$ for its optional direct-memory-access (DMA) function.

Programming functions. BASIC-52's programming commands use three additional port bits ($\overline{\text{ALEDIS}}$, $\overline{\text{PGM PULSE}}$, and $\overline{\text{PGM EN}}$) to control programming voltages and timing for storing BASIC-52 programs in EPROM or other nonvolatile memory.

Additional Control Inputs

Two additional control inputs need to be mentioned. A logic high on RESET resets the chip and causes it to begin executing the program that begins at 0 in code memory. In the 8052-BASIC chip, this program is the BASIC-52 interpreter. $\overline{\text{EA}}$ (external memory access) determines whether the chip will access internal or external code memory in the area from 0 to 1FFFh. In BASIC-52 systems, $\overline{\text{EA}}$ is tied high so that the chip runs the BASIC interpreter in internal ROM on boot-up.

Power Supply Connections

And, finally, the chip has two pins for connecting to a +5-volt DC power supply (VCC) and ground (VSS).

That finishes our tour of the 8052-BASIC chip. We're now ready to put together a working system.

3

Powering Up

This chapter presents a circuit that enables you to start using the 8052-BASIC chip. You can write and run programs and experiment with the BASIC-52 programming language. Later, you can add non-volatile memory for permanent program storage and interfaces to displays, keypads, and whatever else your projects require.

About the Circuit

Figure 3-1 contains all of the components you need to get a BASIC-52 system up and running, plus a few optional extras for future use. Table 3-1 is a parts list for the circuit.

The circuit has five major components: the 8052-BASIC chip (U2), an address latch (U4), an address decoder (U6), static RAM (U7), and an RS-232 interface (U5). As I'll explain below, a few of the components aren't essential at this point, but I've included them to allow easy expansion later on.

The circuit configuration is a more-or-less standard design, similar to many other microcontroller circuits. When you understand this circuit, you're well on your way to understanding many others.

The following paragraphs explain the circuit operation, component by component. If you're impatient to get started, you can skim or skip over this section for now, and go straight to the construction details.

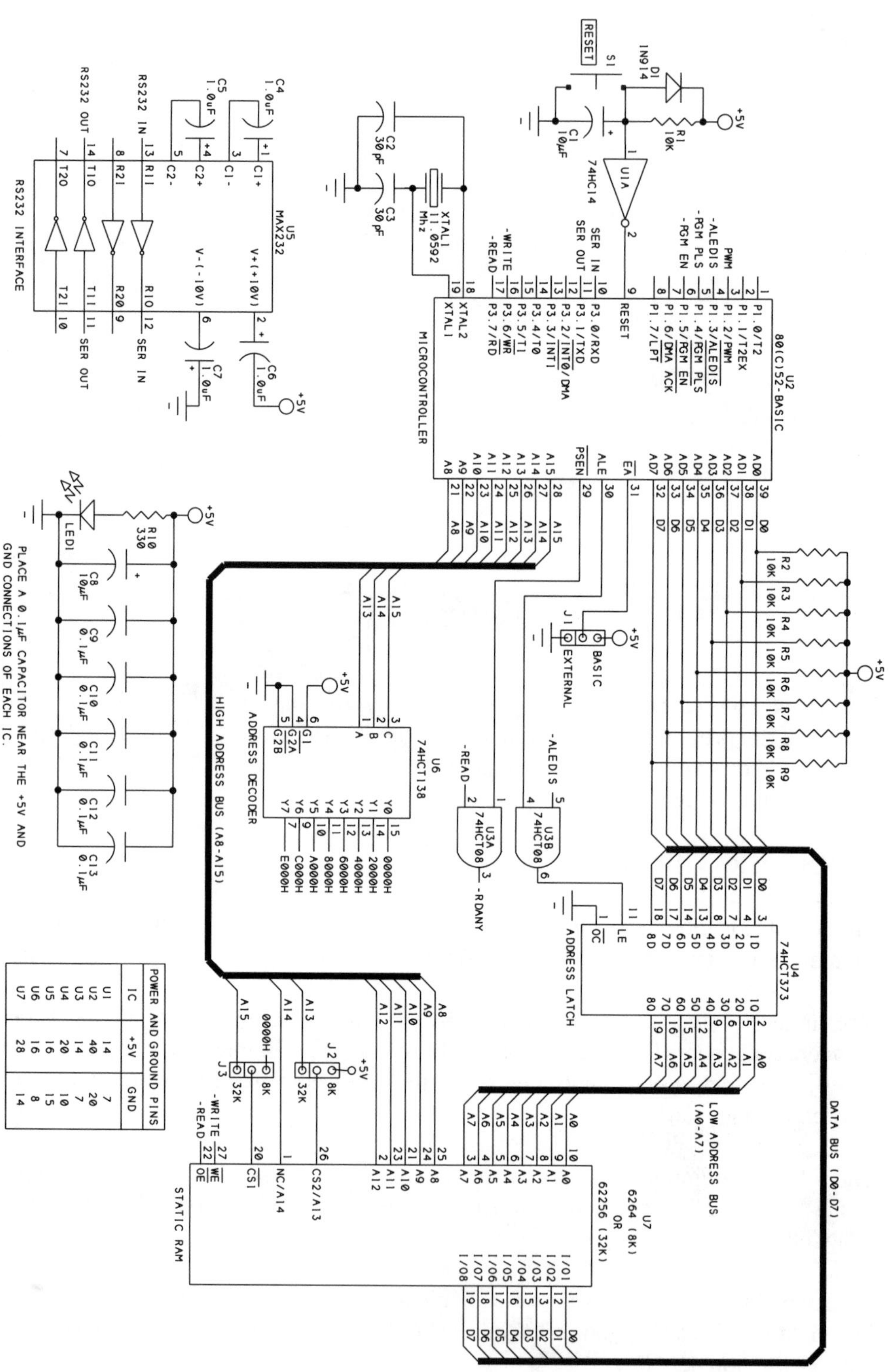

POWER AND GROUND PINS		
IC	+5V	GND
U1	14	7
U2	40	20
U3	14	7
U4	20	10
U5	16	15
U6	16	8
U7	28	14

Figure 3-1. Complete 8052-BASIC system for experimenting.

Table 3-1. Parts list for Figure 3-1's circuit.

Semiconductors

LED1	Light-emitting diode
U1	74HC14 quad inverting Schmitt trigger
U2	8052-BASIC or 80C52-BASIC microcontroller
U3	74HCT08 quad AND gate
U4	74HCT373 octal transparent latch
U5	MAX232, RS-232 driver/receiver
U6	74HCT138 3-to-8-line decoder
U7	6264 (8 kilobyte) or 62256 (32 kilobyte) static RAM, access time 250ns or less

Resistors (1/4-watt, 5% tolerance)

R1-R9	10,000-ohm
R10	330-ohm

Capacitors (16WVDC, 20% tolerance)

C1,C8	10-microfarad, aluminum or tantalum electrolytic
C2,C3	30-picofarad ,ceramic disc
C4-C7	1.0-microfarad,aluminum or tantalum electrolytic
C9-C13	0.1-microfarad, ceramic disc

Miscellaneous

J1-J3	SIP header, 3-terminal, and shorting block
S1	Switch, normally-open momentary pushbutton
XTAL1	11.0592-Mhz crystal

RS232 connector, IC sockets, perforated board, wire, solder, and other circuit-construction materials

The Microcontroller

U2 is the 8052-BASIC chip. The circuit is designed so that you can use either the NMOS version or the CMOS 80C52-BASIC.

$\overline{EA}$, the External Access Enable input (pin 31 of U2), connects to +5V. This causes the 8052 to run the BASIC-52 interpreter in ROM on boot-up. If $\overline{EA}$ is low, the 8052 ignores its internal ROM and instead accesses external program memory on boot-up. You can wire $\overline{EA}$ directly to +5V, or use a jumper as shown in the schematic, to allow you to bypass BASIC-52 and boot to an assembly-language program in external memory, as described in Chapter 13.

The crystal. XTAL1 is an 11.0592-Mhz crystal that connects to pins 18 and 19 of U2. This crystal frequency has two advantages. It gives accurate baud rates for serial communications, due to the way that the 8052's timer divides the system clock to generate the baud rates. Plus, BASIC-52 assumes this frequency when it times the real-time clock, EPROM programming pulses, and serial printer port.

However, you should be able to use any crystal value from 3.5 to 12 Megahertz. If you use a different value, you can use BASIC-52's XTAL operator to adjust the timing to match the frequency of the crystal you are using. The serial communications are reliable if the baud rate is accurate to within a few percent. The higher the crystal frequency, the faster your programs will execute, so most designs use either 11.0592 Mhz or 12 Mhz, which is the maximum clock frequency that the standard 8052 chip can use.

Capacitors C2 and C3 are 30 picofarads each, as specified in the 8052's data sheet. Their precise value isn't critical. Smaller values decrease the oscillator's start-up time, while larger values increase stability.

Reset circuit. A logic high on pin 9 of U2 resets the chip. On power up, pin 1 of U1 rises slowly from 0V to +5V as capacitor C1 charges through resistor R1. Inverter U1 has a Schmitt-trigger input, which has upper and lower switching thresholds that help to ensure a clean reset pulse at pin 9 of U2. On a logic gate that doesn't have a Schmitt-trigger input, the output may oscillate if a slowly changing input remains near the switching threshold. In contrast, at U1, when pin 1 reaches the upper switching threshold (about 2.8V), pin 2 switches from high to low, but won't go high again until pin 1 drops to the lower threshold of about 1.8V.

Pressing and releasing S1 resets the 8052-BASIC chip by discharging C1 and then allowing it to recharge, which brings RESET high, then low again

External Memory

The remaining connections to U2 have to do with reading and writing to external memory.

Read and write signals. To enable reading combined program and data memory, AND gate U3A's output is $\overline{\text{RDANY}}$. This signal is low when either $\overline{\text{READ}}$ or $\overline{\text{PSEN}}$ is low. Figure 3-1's circuit doesn't use $\overline{\text{RDANY}}$, but I've included U3A for future use. Writing to data memory is controlled by $\overline{\text{WRITE}}$. Code memory can't be written to.

AD0-AD7 connect to U4, a 74HCT373 octal transparent latch that stores the lower address byte during memory accesses. The chip contains a set of D-type latches that store logic states.

74HCT138
3-TO-8-LINE DECODER

INPUTS					OUTPUTS							
ENABLE			SELECT									
G1	G2A	G2B	C	B	A	Y0	Y1	Y2	Y3	Y4	Y5	Y6	Y7
L	X	X	X	X	X	H	H	H	H	H	H	H	H
X	H	X	X	X	X	H	H	H	H	H	H	H	H
X	X	H	X	X	X	H	H	H	H	H	H	H	H
H	L	L	L	L	L	**L**	H	H	H	H	H	H	H
H	L	L	L	L	H	H	**L**	H	H	H	H	H	H
H	L	L	L	H	L	H	H	**L**	H	H	H	H	H
H	L	L	L	H	H	H	H	H	**L**	H	H	H	H
H	L	L	H	L	L	H	H	H	H	**L**	H	H	H
H	L	L	H	L	H	H	H	H	H	H	**L**	H	H
H	L	L	H	H	L	H	H	H	H	H	H	**L**	H
H	L	L	H	H	H	H	H	H	H	H	H	H	**L**

74HCT373
OCTAL TRANSPARENT LATCH

OUTPUT CONTROL	LATCH ENABLE	DATA	OUTPUT
OC	LE	1D-8D	1Q-8Q
L	H	H	H
L	H	L	L
L	L	X	NO CHANGE
H	X	X	Z

L = LOGIC LOW
H = LOGIC HIGH
X = DON'T CARE
Z = HIGH IMPEDANCE

Figure 3-2. Truth tables for the 74HCT138 decoder and 74HCT373 octal transparent latch.

A latch-enable input (LE) controls whether the outputs are latched (stored), or not latched (immediately follow the inputs). Figure 3-2 shows the truth table for the chip. When pin 11 is high, 1Q-8Q follow 1D-8D. When pin 11 goes low, outputs 1Q-8Q will not change until pin 11 goes high again.

During each external memory access, 1Q-8Q store the low address byte, so the eight lines that connect to these outputs carry the label LOW ADDRESS BUS. AND gate U3B latches, or stores, U4's outputs only when both ALE and $\overline{\text{ALEDIS}}$ are high. During normal memory accesses, $\overline{\text{ALEDIS}}$ remains high, and ALE controls U4. $\overline{\text{ALEDIS}}$ disables the latches when BASIC-52 executes its programming commands. Figure 3-1's circuit doesn't use the programming commands, so ALE could control U4 directly, but again, I've included U3B for future use.

Because AD0-AD7 hold the data to be read or written during a memory access, the signals as a group carry the label DATA BUS. Each line of AD0-AD7 has a 10K pullup resistor. These are required for the programming functions, and are included for future use. You can use eight individual resistors, or a resistor network that contains eight resistors in a SIP or DIP package. In a bussed resistor network, one pin connects to one side of all of the resistors, so you have fewer connections to wire.

The remaining bus is the HIGH ADDRESS BUS (A8-A15), which consists of the upper eight address lines, and is not multiplexed.

Address decoding. U6 is a 74HCT138 3-to-8-line decoder. It functions as an address decoder for the 64K external memory space. Address decoding allows multiple chips to connect to the address and data buses, with each chip enabled only when it is selected.

Figure 3-2 shows a truth table for the decoder. The 8052-BASIC chip uses the three highest address lines (A13-A15) to generate a chip-select signal for each of eight 8K blocks in memory. This is by no means the only way to decode memory, but it's a common and flexible one. In the schematic, each output is labeled with the base, or bottom, address in the block it controls.

For example, when U2 reads or writes to an address between 0 and 1FFFh in external memory, A13, A14, and A15 are low, so pin 15 of U6 is low. For all other addresses, pin 15 is high. If we connect pin 15 to the chip-select input of an 8K RAM, the RAM will be enabled only when addresses from 0 to 1FFFh are accessed. (Remember that 8K, or 8 kilobytes, is 2000h, or 0 through 1FFFh, in hexadecimal.)

If you use a 32K RAM, you don't need U6 to decode its addressing. For all of the 32K RAM's addresses (0 to 7FFFh), A15 is low, and for all other addresses (7FFFh to FFFFh), A15 is high. This means that you can use A15 directly as a chip select, without additional decoding. U6 will come in handy later, however, even if you use a 32K RAM.

RAM choices. The minimal circuit includes just one memory chip, U7, which can be an 8K or 32K static RAM, or SRAM. BASIC-52 requires at least 1K of RAM, but I've used the larger capacities, since the extra room is useful and doesn't cost much more. The pinouts of the two chips are similar, with jumpers J2 and J3 routing the signals that vary.

The 8K chip has 13 address inputs (A0-A12), while the 32K chip has 15 (A0-A14). Eight data I/O pins (I/O1-I/O8) connect to the data bus and hold the bytes to be read or written.

The RAM has three control inputs whose functions match those of the 8052's control outputs. Pin 20 ($\overline{CS1}$, or Chip Select 1) enables U7 whenever the 8052 reads or writes to the chip, with the address decoding determining the address range of the chip.

Jumper J3 chooses the chip select for an 8K or 32K device. Some 8K RAMs have a second chip select (CS2), which is tied high (always selected) by J2. If you limit yourself to either 8K or 32K RAMs, you can eliminate J2 and J3 and wire the appropriate connections directly.

Pin 27 ($\overline{WE}$, or Write Enable) is driven by $\overline{WRITE}$, and is strobed low during each write to external data memory. Pin 22 ($\overline{OE}$, or Output Enable) is driven by $\overline{READ}$, and strobes low when either external data or code memory is read.

With an 8K RAM, each write cycle follows this sequence: The 8052 brings ALE high and places the address to be written to on AD0-AD7 and A8-A15. For addresses from 0 to 1FFFH, A13-A15 are low, so U7 is selected at its pin 20. After a short delay, the 8052 brings ALE low, which causes U7 to store the lower address byte. After another short delay, the 8052 replaces the address on AD0-AD7 with the data to be written. A low pulse at pin 27 ($\overline{WE}$) causes the RAM to write the data into the address specified by A0-A12.

Read cycles are similar, except that a pulse at pin 22 ($\overline{OE}$) causes the requested data to appear on AD0-AD7, where the 8052 reads it.

With a 32K RAM, the process is the same, except that A15 is the chip select and there are two more address lines on the chip.

Static RAM chips are rated by their read-access time, which is the maximum time the chip will require to place a byte on the data bus after a read is requested. With a crystal frequency of 12 Mhz or lower, an access time of 250 nanoseconds or less is fine for accessing external data or code memory. Access times and other timing characteristics are described in the timing diagrams in the data sheets for the 8052 and RAM.

When you use the 8052-BASIC, you don't have to worry about any of these specifics about the read and write cycles. If the circuit is wired correctly, and if all of the components are functioning as they should, reading and writing occur automatically in the course of executing BASIC-52 statements and commands. A single program line in BASIC-52 can cause dozens or more read and write operations to occur.

Logic families. Logic chips U3, U4, and U6 are HCT-family components, which have TTL-compatible inputs and CMOS-compatible outputs. This means that they can interface directly to either TTL or CMOS logic.

If HCT-family parts aren't available, there are alternatives. You may use an LSTTL chip (74LS08, 74LS138, 74LS373) for U3, U4, or U6. Or, if you use a CMOS 80C52-BASIC for U2, you may use an HCMOS 74HC08 or 74HC138 for U3 or U6. If U3 is a 74HC08 or 74HCT08, you may use a 75HC373 for U4. For U1, you may use a 74HC14 or 74LS14.

Table   3-2. Voltage specifications for different types of logic, powered at 5V.

Logic Type	Output		Input	
	0 (maximum)	1 (minimum)	0 (maximum)	1 (minimum)
TTL, including LSTTL most NMOS	0.4V	2.4V	0.8V	2.0V
HCTMOS	0.1V	4.9V	0.8V	2.0V
HCMOS	0.1V	4.9V	1.0V	3.5V
4000-series CMOS	0.1V	4.9V	1.5V	3.5V

Table 3-2 summarizes the input and output voltage specifications for different logic-device families. The main point to remember is that a TTL logic-high output voltage (and most NMOS high outputs) may be as low as 2.4V, which does not meet the minimum input-voltage requirement for HCMOS or 4000-series CMOS devices. To interface a TTL output to CMOS, use an HCTMOS device, which accepts TTL-logic inputs. Or, you may add a pull-up resistor to a TTL output to pull it near +5V.

Serial Interface

The final chip in the schematic is U5, a MAX232 driver/receiver, which is the popular single-chip solution for RS-232 interfaces. One side connects to the 8052's serial input and output on pins 10 and 11 of U1, and the other side sends and receives signals at standard RS-232 levels to a personal computer. Larger capacitor values for C4-C7 are fine, and the MAX232A version can use values as small as 0.1 microfarad. If you splurge on a MAX233, which has internal capacitors, you don't need C4-C7 at all.

Power Supply

A final essential component is the power supply. For the basic system, all you need is a regulated +5-volt supply. These are widely available from mail-order suppliers. An output capability of at least 500 milliamperes is recommended.

Capacitors C8-C13 provide power-supply decoupling. Digital devices draw current as they switch. Capacitors C9-C13 store energy that the components can draw quickly, without causing spikes in the supply or ground lines. C8 stores energy for quick recharging of C9-C13. The exact values aren't critical, but C9-C13 should be a type with good high-frequency response, such as ceramic, mica, or polystyrene.

LED1 and current-limiting resistor R10 are an optional power-on indicator.

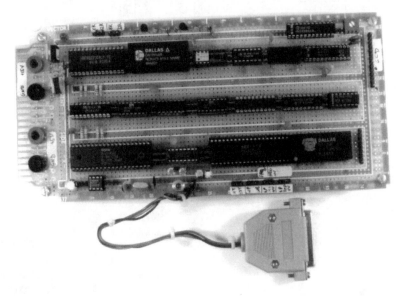

Figure   3-3.   This is the circuit board on which I wire-wrapped and tested many of the circuits in this book.

Circuit Construction

This circuit is intended for use as a flexible system for testing and experimenting, rather than a fixed, unchanging design for a single application. For this reason, I recommend building it with wire-wrapping or another construction method that allows easy changes and additions. Figure 3-3 shows an 8052-BASIC circuit wire-wrapped onto perfboard.

Reading the Schematic

In the schematic, I used a couple of different techniques to represent connections between pins and components. In the reset circuit, connections are drawn as direct point-to-point lines. For the address and data lines, I used buses for a neater, more compact schematic. When you wire these connections, use the signal labels as a guide. For example, the label D0 tells you to interconnect these points: pin 39 of U2, pin 3 of U4, pin 11 of U7, and one end of R2. Other connections are indicated by labels. For example, the $\overline{\text{WRITE}}$ label tells you to connect pin 16 of U2 and pin 27 of U7.

Another point to be aware of is the conventions used in the schematics and text of this book for indicating an active-low signal, or a signal that is valid, or enabled, when low. In this book, the schematics use a leading hyphen (-WRITE) , while the text uses an overscore ($\overline{\text{WRITE}}$). Their meanings are the same.

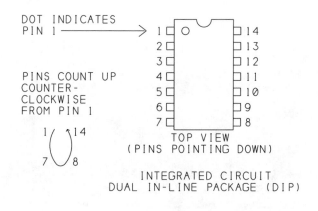

DOT INDICATES
PIN 1

PINS COUNT UP
COUNTER-
CLOCKWISE
FROM PIN 1

TOP VIEW
(PINS POINTING DOWN)

INTEGRATED CIRCUIT
DUAL IN-LINE PACKAGE (DIP)

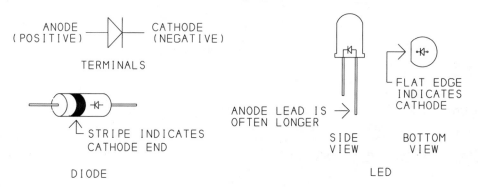

ANODE
(POSITIVE)   CATHODE
                    (NEGATIVE)

TERMINALS

STRIPE INDICATES
CATHODE END

DIODE

ANODE LEAD IS
OFTEN LONGER

FLAT EDGE
INDICATES
CATHODE

SIDE
VIEW

BOTTOM
VIEW

LED

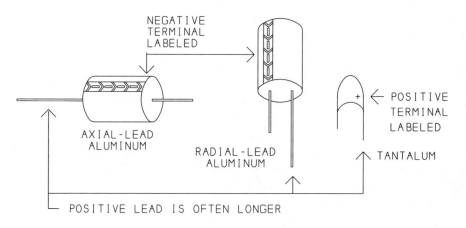

NEGATIVE
TERMINAL
LABELED

POSITIVE
TERMINAL
LABELED

AXIAL-LEAD
ALUMINUM

RADIAL-LEAD
ALUMINUM

TANTALUM

POSITIVE LEAD IS OFTEN LONGER

ELECTROLYTIC CAPACITORS

Figure 3-4. How to determine the correct orientation for ICs, diodes, LEDs, and electrolytic capacitors.

Construction Tips

These are some things to be aware of as you build the circuit:

- Choose a circuit board that has room for additions, at least 4 by 6 inches.

- A board with interleaved buses, such as Vector's 3677 series, allows easy, low-impedance connections to +5V and ground. Designate one bus as ground, and the other as +5V. For power and ground connections, wrap one end of the wire to the appropriate pin on the chip, and trim and solder the other end directly to the bus.

- To connect the power and ground buses to the +5V supply, use thick (AWG #22 or lower) wires, not #30 wire-wrap wires. You can solder the other ends of the wires to banana plugs or screw terminals, or clip your power-supply leads directly to the wires.

- The schematic doesn't show an ON/OFF switch for the circuit, but you can add a SPST toggle or slide switch in series with the connection to the +5V supply if you wish.

- Place C8 near where the +5V supply connects to the board. Mount decoupling capacitors C9-C13 so that each chip's +5V and GND pins are near a capacitor. In other words, space the capacitors evenly around the board; don't group them all in one area. Keep the wires or traces between the capacitor's leads and the IC's +5V and ground pins as short as possible.

- To minimize noise in the oscillator circuits, place XTAL1, C2, and C3 close to pins 18 and 19 of U2 and connect them with short wires. Wire the ground terminals of C2 and C3 directly to pin 20 of U2.

- When you wire the following components, correct orientation is required: C1, C4-C8, D1, LED1, and U1-U7. Figure 3-4 shows common polarity indicators for these components. Notice that C7's positive terminal connects to ground, and C6's negative terminal connects to +5V, since these capacitors connect to the MAX232's -10V and +10V outputs.

- As you wire the circuits, remember that everything on the wire-wrap or solder side of the board is a mirror image of the way it looks on the component side of the board. If pin 1 is in the upper left corner on the component side, it's in the upper right corner on the wire-wrap side (assuming that you flip the board over from side to side, not top to bottom).

- Labels on the wire-wrap side are helpful. You can place a dot of indelible ink near pin 1, or adhesive labels between the pins, or use prelabeled and punched plastic labels that slide onto the wire-wrap pins.

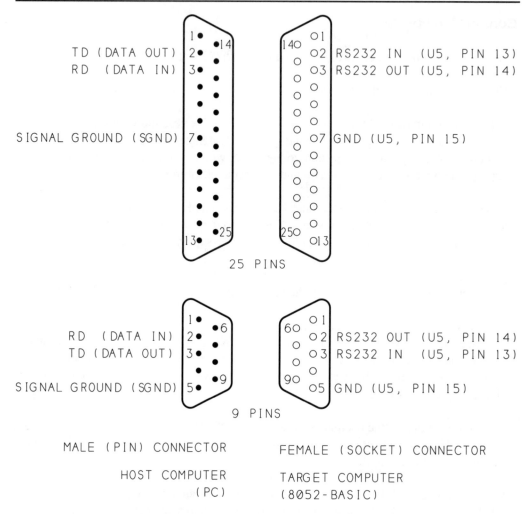

Figure   3-5.   Pin connections for 25-pin and 9-pin RS-232 connectors.

• Don't plug the ICs into their sockets until you've completed wiring all of the circuits.

Unused Gates

Two gates on U3 and five gates on U1 are unused. To prevent the unused CMOS inputs from floating and possibly drawing excessive currents, wire pins 9, 10, 12, and 13 of U3 to ground or +5V. Do the same for pins 3, 5, 9, 11, and 13 of U1. Don't forget to remove these connections if you later use the pins. If you are using LSTTL chips (74LS08, 74LS14), leave the unused inputs open.

Serial Connectors

Connections to RS-232 OUT and RS-232 IN depend on the type of serial connector you have on your personal computer or its serial cable.

Connectors vary, but two common ones are a male 25-pin or 9-pin D-connector. (The outer shell of a D-connector is roughly in the shape of a *D*.) For the 8052-BASIC system, you'll need a mating female 25-pin or 9-pin D-connector. The connection has just three wires. A solder-cup-type connector allows easy soldering of the wires.

Figure 3-5 shows the wiring for 9- and 25-pin connectors. A few computers require additional handshaking signals. BASIC-52 doesn't support these, but you can simulate them by connecting together pins 5, 6, 8, and 20 at the personal-computer end of the link. (Pin numbers are for a 25-pin connector.)

Powering Up

The first time you power up an untested circuit, it pays to be cautious. I recommend the following steps:

First Steps

Visually inspect the circuit. You don't have to spend a lot of time on this, but sometimes a missing or miswired wire or component or another problem will become obvious.

Install U1-U7 on the board, making sure that pin 1 on each is oriented correctly. Set J1 to BASIC, and set J2 and J3 to match the size of your RAM at U7.

With an ohmmeter, measure the resistance from +5V to ground, to be sure these aren't shorted together by mistake. The exact value you measure isn't critical, but if you read less than 100 ohms, something is miswired and you need to find and fix the problem before you continue.

If you suspect a problem, check the wiring of the power and ground connections, comparing the connections to those on the schematic. Be sure all components are oriented correctly. When all checks out, you're ready to boot up BASIC-52.

Booting BASIC-52

For the initial check, begin with everything powered down. I'll use the term *host computer,* or *host system,* to refer to the personal computer, and *target computer,* or *target system*, to refer to the 8052-BASIC circuits. Included are some specific tips for users of Datastorm's

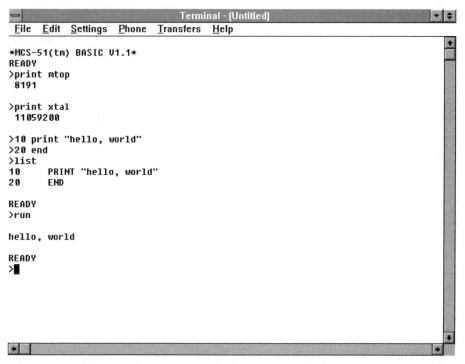

Figure 3-6. BASIC-52's sign-on message and a simple program, using the Windows Terminal accessory for communications.

Procomm Plus for DOS and Microsoft Windows 3.1's Terminal Accessory, but other communications software should have similar features and abilities.

Turn on the host computer and run your communications software. Configure the software for 8 data bits, no parity, and 1 stop bit. The baud rate you select isn't critical, since BASIC-52 automatically adjusts to what you are using. To start, use a rate of 9600 or less. Don't enable any handshaking or flow-control options such as XON/XOFF or RTS/CTS.

Select the appropriate serial, or COM, port, if necessary. If you're using an MS-DOS (IBM-compatible) computer, you must find a COM port and interrupt-request (IRQ) level that aren't being used by your modem, mouse, or another device. Because COM1 and COM3 often share an IRQ level, as do COM2 and COM4, you generally can't use COM1 and COM3 at the same time, or COM2 and COM4. If you have an external modem, you can unplug it and use its serial port.

In *Procomm Plus,* use the line/port setup menu (ALT+P) to configure. In the Windows Terminal, use the Settings menu. Cable together the serial ports of the host and target systems.

You're now ready to power up the target system. Turn on its power supply, and press the SPACE bar at the host's keyboard. You should see this BASIC-52 sign-on message and prompt:

```
*MCS-51(tm) BASIC V1.1*
READY
```

Figure 3-6 shows the sign-on message and a simple program, using Windows' Terminal accessory for communications.

Troubleshooting

If you don't see the prompt, it's time to troubleshoot. Getting the system to boot up the first time can be the most challenging part of a project, especially when serial communications are involved. Here are some things that may help you isolate the cause of the problem:

- Try again by pressing and releasing S1 and pressing the space bar. If you are using a 32K RAM for U7, BASIC-52 requires about 1 second to perform its memory check after a reset, before it will respond to the space bar. With an 8K RAM, the delay is a few tenths of a second (proportionately longer with slower crystals).

- Double-check the easy things. Are the communications parameters correct? Did you select the correct serial port? Are all ICs inserted?

- Verify that pin 9 of U2 goes high, then low, when you press and release S1.

- Check the power and ground pins of all ICs for proper voltages.

- Connect a logic probe to pin 10 of U2. When you press the space bar, you should see the logic level toggle as U2 receives the ASCII code for a space (20h). If not, you probably have a problem in the setup of your communications software or in the serial cabling.

- Verify that pin 30 of U2 is toggling (at 1/6 the crystal frequency, if you have an oscilloscope to measure). This indicates that the oscillator circuit is functioning.

- Verify that pins 21-28 and 32-39 of U2 toggle as BASIC-52 performs its memory check immediately after powering up or rebooting.

- If all else fails, recheck your wiring for missing or misrouted wires. Sometimes there's no alternative but to go through the schematic connection by connection, checking each with an ohmmeter.

Basic tests

When your system boots, you're ready for some basic tests. The BASIC-52 programming manual is a useful reference at this point.

In some ways, BASIC-52 is similar to BASIC compilers like Microsoft's *QuickBASIC*. Many of the keywords and syntax rules are similar. But BASIC-52 is closer to older interpreted BASICs like *GW-BASIC* or *BASICA*. You can type a statement or command and execute it immediately when you press ENTER, or you can type a series of statements and run them later as a program. When a line begins with a line number, BASIC-52 treats it as a program line rather than as a command to execute immediately.

Here are some quick tests and experiments you can do:

Memory Check

Type

```
PRINT MTOP
```

to learn the amount of external data memory that BASIC-52 detected on boot-up. With an 8K RAM, MTOP should be 8191, and with 32K, it should be 32,767. If you prefer hexadecimal notation, type

```
PH0. MTOP
```

(In PH0., be sure to include the period and use a zero, not the letter "O".)

Crystal Frequency

The special operator XTAL represents the value of the timing crystal that clocks the 8052-BASIC. The default value is 11059200, or 11.0592 Mhz. You can verify this by typing

```
PRINT XTAL
```

Most BASIC-52 statements don't use the XTAL operator, so it doesn't matter if the value isn't accurate. Exceptions are the real-time clock, programming commands, PWM output, and LPT output. For these, XTAL should match your crystal's frequency. To set XTAL for a 12Mhz crystal, type

```
XTAL=12000000
```

To verify, type

```
PRINT XTAL
```

Line Editing

After typing a few commands, you may discover some of BASIC-52's line-editing abilities. While typing a line, you can correct mistakes by deleting back to the mistake and retyping. In *Procomm Plus,* if you select VT100 terminal emulation (under Setup menu, Terminal Options), you can use either the DELETE or BACKSPACE key to delete. With the *Windows* terminal, you must use the DELETE key (not BACKSPACE). Many communications programs allow you remap the keyboard, so you can select whatever delete key you wish.

Once you press ENTER, you can't edit a line you've typed, unless you retype it from the beginning.

BASIC-52 treats upper and lower-case characters the same. In most cases, spaces are ignored, so you can include them or not as you wish.

Running a Program

Here is a very simple program to try:

```
10 FOR I=1 to 10
20 PRINT I
30 NEXT I
40 END
```

Enter each of the lines, including the line numbers. BASIC-52 automatically stores the program in RAM. To run the program, type RUN. You should see this:

```
1
2
3
4
5
6
7
8
9
10
```

To view the program lines, type

```
LIST
```

To erase the current program, type

```
NEW
```

To verify that the program no longer exists, type

```
LIST
```

You can change individual program lines by typing the line number, followed by a new statement:

```
10 FOR I=1 to 20
```

To erase a line, type the line number and press ENTER:

```
20
```

Getting Out of Trouble

Occasionally, a programming error may cause a program to go into an endless loop or crash the system. If it's an endless loop, you can exit it and return to the READY prompt by pressing CONTROL+C. If that doesn't work, your only choice is to press S1 to reset the 8052-BASIC system. Resetting will erase the program in RAM, so you'll have to re-enter it.

Simple Programs to Try

The following sections offer some short programs to try, to help you explore your system and become familiar with BASIC-52. Don't worry if you don't understand every line of the programs. Later chapters get into programming in more detail.

Reading Port 1

You can use BASIC-52 to read and write to Port 1 (pins 1-8) on the 8052-BASIC.

The command

```
PH0.PORT1
```

will display the hex value of the entire port. Listing 3-1 is a program that displays the value of each of the bits in the port.

Enter each line carefully. Be sure to include all of the punctuation shown. When you run the program, you should see a display like this:

```
PORT 1 Bit Values:
Bit 0 =  1
Bit 1 =  1
Bit 2 =  1
Bit 3 =  1
Bit 4 =  1
Bit 5 =  1
Bit 6 =  1
Bit 7 =  1
```

If a port pin is open, or unconnected, its internal pull-up resistor will cause it to read as 1. If you connect a jumper wire from a port pin to ground, or bring the pin low by driving it with a logic low output, it should read 0. Line 10 in Listing 3-1 brings all of Port 1's bits high, which enables them to be used as inputs.

Writing to Port 1

You can control the bits of Port 1 by writing to them. Listing 3-2 allows you to set or clear individual bits. Here's an example of what happens when you run the program:

```
Enter a bit to set or clear (0-2, 4-7) :7
Enter 1 to set, 0 to clear :0
Enter a bit to set or clear (0-2, 4-7) :3
Do not change bit 3!
```

The program doesn't allow you to change bit 3 (P1.3), because the 8052-BASIC circuit requires this bit to be high when accessing external memory (assuming that you've included U3B in your circuit). If you do clear bit 3 accidentally, you'll crash the system and will have to reboot.

Listing 3-1. Displays the value of each bit in Port 1.

```
10    PORT1 = 0FFH
20    PRINT "PORT 1 Bit Values:"
30    PRINT "Bit 0 = ",(PORT1.AND.1)
40    PRINT "Bit 1 = ",(PORT1.AND.2)/2
50    PRINT "Bit 2 = ",(PORT1.AND.4)/4
60    PRINT "Bit 3 = ",(PORT1.AND.8)/8
70    PRINT "Bit 4 = ",(PORT1.AND.10H)/10H
80    PRINT "Bit 5 = ",(PORT1.AND.20H)/20H
90    PRINT "Bit 6 = ",(PORT1.AND.40H)/40H
100   PRINT "Bit 7 = ",(PORT1.AND.80H)/80H
110   END
```

Listing 3-2. Allows you to set or clear individual bits of Port 1.

```
10   INPUT "Enter a bit to set or clear (0-2, 4-7) :",X
20   IF X=3 THEN  PRINT "Do not change bit 3!" :  GOTO 10
30   INPUT "Enter 1 to set, 0 to clear :",Y
40   IF Y=1 THEN PORT1=PORT1.OR.2**X
50   IF Y=0 THEN PORT1=PORT1.AND.0FFH-2**X
60   END
```

Run the program and follow the on-screen instructions to set or clear a bit. To monitor a port bit as you set and clear it, you can use a logic probe, voltmeter, or oscilloscope. For example, to monitor bit 0, place a logic probe on pin 1 of U1, or connect the + lead of a voltmeter to pin 1 and the - lead to ground.

Accessing Memory

Listing 3-3 allows you to read and write to external RAM. Here is an example of what happens when you run this program:

```
Enter 0 (read), 1 (write), or 2 (quit): 1
Free memory ranges from 397H to 1FFFH
Enter an address to write to : 1000H
Enter data to be written : 55H
55H has been written to address 1000H
Enter 0 (read), 1 (write), or 2 (quit): 0
External RAM ranges from 0 to 1FFFH
Enter an address to read : 1000H
55H is stored in address 1000H
```

If you write to an address outside the range specified as free memory, you will overwrite the RAM currently in use to store your program and run BASIC-52. If you do this accidentally, your system may crash and you'll have to reset the system and re-enter the program.

If you prefer decimal numbers to hex notation, change each PH0 in the program to PRINT. (PH0. includes a period; PRINT does not.)

Real-time Clock

Listing 3-4 demonstrates BASIC-52's real-time clock by displaying an on-screen 60-second timer.

Listing 3-3. Allows user to read and write to external memory.

```
10    DO
20    INPUT "Enter 0 (read), 1 (write), or 2 (quit): ",RW
30    IF RW=0 THEN GOSUB 70
40    IF RW=1 THEN GOSUB 120
50    WHILE RW<>2
60    END
70    PH0."External RAM ranges from 0 to ",MTOP
80    INPUT "Enter an address to read : ",A
90    B=XBY(A)
100   PH0.B," is stored in address ",A
110   RETURN
120   PH0."Free memory ranges from ",LEN+512," to ",MTOP
130   INPUT "Enter an address to write to :",A
140   INPUT "Enter data to be written :",B
150   XBY(A)=B
160   PH0.B," has been written to address ",A
170   RETURN
```

For the timer to be accurate, you must set XTAL to match the timing crystal your system uses.

Further Experiments

Feel free to continue experimenting with BASIC-52 programs, using the programming reference as a guide. You can do quite a bit with just these circuits.

Listing 3-4. Real-time clock.

```
10 CLOCK 1:TIME=0:SEC=0
20 DO
30 ONTIME 1,60
40 WHILE SEC<60
50 END
60 TIME=TIME-1
70 SEC=SEC+1
80 PRINT SEC
90 RETI
```

Listing 3-5. This program uses BASIC-52's GET instruction to detect when the user has pressed a key.

```
10    CLOCK1:TIME=0:SEC=0
20    PRINT "Press any key to quit"
30    DO
40    ONTIME 1,100
50    G=GET
60    UNTIL G<>0
70    END
100   TIME=TIME-1
110   PH0. PORT1
120   RETI
```

Exiting Programs

Some programs, such as Listing 3-3's, continue to run until the user requests to end it. In BASIC-52, there are several ways to detect that the user wants to stop a program.

Set a User Variable

In Listing 3-3, the program displays a menu of choices on the host computer's screen. The program continues to run until the user selects *QUIT* by entering 2, which sets the variable RW to 2 and causes the DO...WHILE loop and the program to end.

Use GET

Sometimes, selecting a menu option isn't convenient or appropriate. Listing 3-5 reads and displays the value of PORT1 once per second until the user presses any key at the host computer. The program uses BASIC-52's GET operator to detect a keypress. GET stores the ASCII code of a keypress at the host computer. Setting a varialble equal to GET (line 50) causes GET to reset to 0. You can detect a keypress by reading GET periodically. If GET

Listing 3-6. This program will end only when the user presses CONTROL+C.

```
10 CLOCK 1:TIME=0:SEC=0
20 DO
30 ONTIME 1,100
40 WHILE 1=1
50 END
100 TIME=TIME-1
110 PH0. PORT1
120 RETI
```

Listing 3-7. This program ends when $\overline{\text{INT1}}$ (pin 13) is brought low and causes an interrupt routine to execute.

```
10     CLOCK 1:TIME=0:SEC=0
20     A=0
30     PRINT "Bring INT1 (pin 13) low to end program."
40     DO
50     ONTIME 1,100
60     ONEX1 200
70     WHILE A=0
80     END
100    TIME=TIME-1
110    PHO. PORT1
120    RETI
200    A=1
210    RETI
```

doesn't equal zero, it means that a key was pressed. In Listing 3-5, when GET no longer equals 0, the program ends.

Wait for CONTROL+C

You can always end a program by pressing CONTROL+C at the host's keyboard. The only exceptions are runaway programs that have crashed the system and force you to reboot. Listing 3-6 is an expanded version of Listing 3-5. It continues to read and display PORT1 in an endless loop (DO...WHILE 1=1), until you press CONTROL+C.

Detect a Switch Press

A final method will end a program without any input from the host's keyboard. You can use this in stand-alone projects that don't connect to a host computer at all. Listing 3-7 ends when the 8052-BASIC's pin 13 ($\overline{\text{INT1}}$) goes low, which causes an interrupt routine to execute. Bring the pin low by jumpering it briefly to GND, or connect a pushbutton switch as described in Chapter 7.

4

Saving Programs

In Chapter 3's experiments, the BASIC-52 programs that you wrote were stored in RAM. This is fine for temporary use, but every time you power down, your program disappears and you have to start over.

This chapter shows you two ways to save BASIC-52 programs more permanently: by adding nonvolatile memory to the BASIC-52 system, and by downloading your programs to your host system's disk. The nonvolatile memory may be battery-backed RAM, EEPROM, or EPROM. You can also use this memory for storing assembly-language programs or data that you want to save when you power down or reset. Disk storage is a convenient way to save programs if you want to edit them off-line, upload them to a different BASIC-52 system, or just save back-up copies.

Nonvolatile Memory Options

One of BASIC-52's handiest features is its programming commands that store programs in nonvolatile (NV) memory: EPROM, EEPROM, or battery-backed RAM. The commands assume that the NV memory is addressed beginning at 8000h in external data memory.

With the addition of NV memory, you have two areas that may contain BASIC-52 programs: the NV memory, addressed beginning at 8000h, and the RAM, addressed beginning at 0. To distinguish between the two areas, you can call the memory beginning at 8000h the EPROM

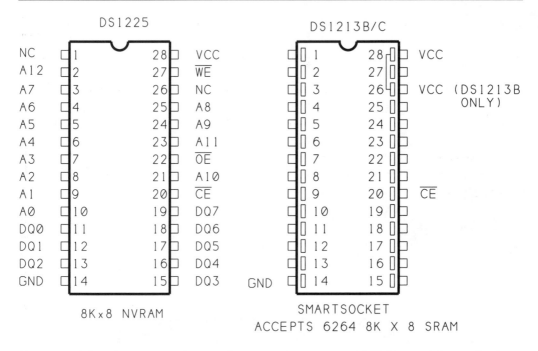

Figure 4-1. Pinouts for Dallas Semiconductor's 8K NVRAM and SmartSocket.

space (even though it may contain NVRAM, EEPROM, or EPROM), and call the memory beginning at 0, up to 7FFFh or the top of RAM, the RAM space.

BASIC-52's programming commands are designed to meet the requirements for EPROMs, using either of two programming algorithms, or procedures. You can use the same commands to store programs in NVRAM or EEPROM. Like EPROMs, these devices provide nonvolatile storage—in other words, their contents don't disappear when power is removed. Plus, they have two advantages over EPROMs: they don't need any special programming voltages, and they don't need ultraviolet exposure to erase. This makes them much more convenient to use.

For these reasons, the first circuit we'll look at offers a choice of NVRAM or EEPROM for nonvolatile storage. Later, we'll add circuits that allow you to program EPROMs, for those who want this option.

NVRAM

Dallas Semiconductor offers NVRAM chips that you can use for nonvolatile storage. These work exactly like static RAM, except that they contain a lithium cell and backup circuits that retain the RAM's contents when the main power supply is removed. The backup is guaranteed for at least ten years. Dallas also makes a product called the SmartSocket, which consists of an IC socket with an embedded lithium cell and backup circuits. To create a NVRAM, you plug your own static RAM chip into the SmartSocket.

Eight kilobytes is a convenient size that will store many short BASIC-52 programs, or fewer longer ones. For an 8K NVRAM, you can use a DS1225 NVRAM, or a DS1213B or DS1213C SmartSocket with a 6264 or similar static RAM. Figure 4-1 shows the pinouts.

The 1213B and 1213C SmartSockets differ only in that the 1213B will also accept a 24-pin 2K SRAM, with pins 1, 2, 27, and 28 unused, and the 1213C will also accept a 32K SRAM, which has address inputs at pins 1 and 26.

The DS1225 offers a choice of two write-protect voltages. On the -AB version, write protection is guaranteed when the power supply is less than 4.5V, and write operations are allowed when the power supply is greater than 4.75V. The SmartSockets use these same voltages. On the -AD and -Y versions of the DS1225, write protection is guaranteed when the supply is less than 4.25V, and write operations are allowed when the supply is greater than 4.5V. Either type should work in a BASIC-52 system with a regulated +5V supply. Access times of 250 nanoseconds or less are fine for the NVRAM.

Don't be confused by the fact that Dallas describes its devices by the number of bits they store, rather than the number of bytes. For example, they call the 8-kilobyte DS1225 a 64K device.

You can order NVRAMs directly from Dallas Semiconductor (no minimum order), and from other vendors.

EEPROM

The other option for program storage is EEPROM. A typical EEPROM is guaranteed for 10,000 to 100,000 write cycles, compared to infinite write cycles for NVRAM. Access times for reading an EEPROM are similar to those for static RAM, but writing to EEPROM takes much longer. Most require 2 to 10 milliseconds after a write operation before you can access the chip again. In spite of the drawbacks, I've included EEPROM as an option because an 8K EEPROM may cost less than a comparable NVRAM.

A typical part number for an 8K EEPROM is 2864 or 28C64. Figure 4-2 shows the pinout for a 28(C)64 EEPROM. Notice that its pinout, too, is very similar to that of a 6264 static RAM.

EEPROMs have two common ways of indicating that they are busy performing a write operation and are unable to be accessed. In one type, when the EPROM is busy, the data pins hold the last-written data, but with one or more bits inverted. BASIC-52's programming

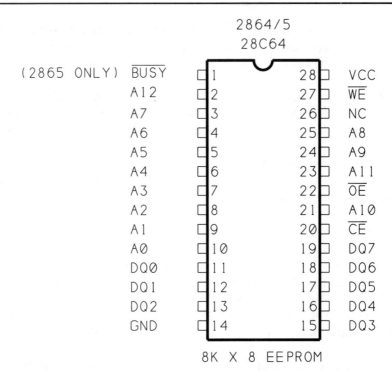

Figure 4-2. Pinout for 8K EEPROM.

commands verify each byte after programming it, so the inverted data automatically keeps BASIC-52 from programming another byte until the EEPROM is ready to receive it.

Other EEPROMs have a busy output, usually at pin 1, which goes low when the EEPROM is busy. For this type, you can tie the busy output to pin 12 of U1. BASIC-52's programming commands wait for a high logic level at this pin after programming each byte. Note that this means that pin 12 of the 8052-BASIC must be high (or not connected) during programming of any device. However, using the BUSY output is optional, since programming won't continue until the programmed byte verifies.

Whether you choose EEPROM or NVRAM, be sure to ask for a data sheet for the device you buy, so you can verify its pinout, capacity, and timing characteristics.

Adding NVRAM or EEPROM

Figure 4-3 shows the added circuits for the NVRAM or EEPROM at U8. Because the circuits are an addition to Figure 3-1's circuits, the parts continue the same numbering sequence, beginning with U8. AND gate U3C is the third gate of Figure 3-1's U3. Table 4-1 is a parts list of the components needed to add Figure 4-3's circuits to Figure 3-1.

The Microcontroller Idea Book

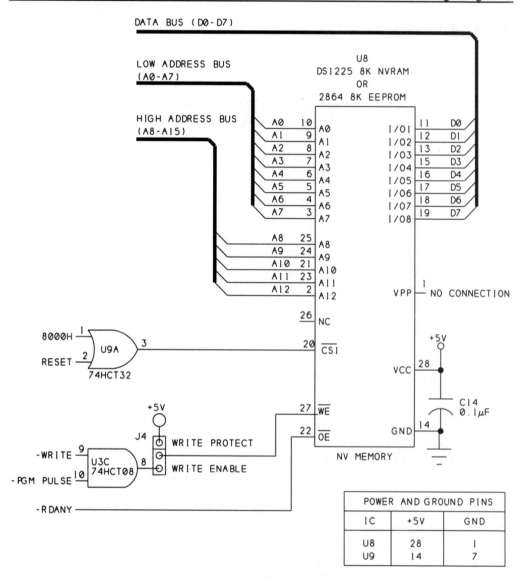

Figure 4-3. Circuits for adding NVRAM or EEPROM.

The pinout and wiring of U8 are similar to that of the RAM at U7. The data and address lines are wired exactly the same as for U7. U8 is accessed from 8000h to 9FFFh. This location is used because BASIC-52's programming commands assume that the nonvolatile memory begins at 8000h.

OR gate U9A prevents the NVRAM or EEPROM from being accidentally overwritten during power-up. When the 8052-BASIC first powers up, its port pins are in an unknown state for a brief period, until the reset algorithm in the chip brings them all high. During this

Table 4-1. Parts list for Figure 4-3.

Semiconductors

U8	8-kilobyte NV memory (DS1225 NVRAM or DS1213 SmartSocket with 6264 SRAM or 2864 EEPROM), access time 250 nanoseconds or less
U9	74HCT32 quad OR gate

Capacitors (16WVDC, 20% tolerance)

C14	0.1-microfarad ceramic disc

Miscellaneous

J4	SIP header, 3-terminal, and shorting block

IC sockets

---

time, there is a small chance that the right combination of outputs will cause a write operation to occur at U8.

Since this could destroy the information stored in the chip, we need a way to prevent U8 from being written to for a brief time after power-up. OR gate U9A prevents accesses to U8 until RESET goes low. The delay caused by the charging of R1 through C1 (in Figure 3-1) ensures that the reset algorithm has enough time to bring the port pins high.

U8's Chip Select (pin 20) goes low only when both of these are true: RESET is low, and the 8052-BASIC is reading or writing to an address from 8000h to 9FFFh.

Output-enable (pin 22) connects to $\overline{\text{RDANY}}$, to allow U8 to be accessed as data or program memory. This enables U8 to store assembly-language routines as well as BASIC-52 programs.

For writing to U8, AND gate U3C allows a choice of two control signals. $\overline{\text{WRITE}}$ is the conventional signal for writing to data memory. In addition, BASIC-52 uses a special $\overline{\text{PGM}}$ $\overline{\text{PULSE}}$ signal to store BASIC-52 programs in NV memory beginning at 8000h. Either of these signals will bring $\overline{\text{WE}}$ on U8 low.

The Microcontroller Idea Book

Jumper J4 is optional. It enables you to write-protect U8 by jumpering $\overline{WE}$ to +5V. You might want to do this if you have critical programs or data stored in U8, and you want to be sure that you don't overwrite them accidentally.

Wiring Tips

When you add the circuits for NV memory, use sockets for U8 and U9. If you previously tied unused pins 9 and 10 of U3 to ground or +5V, be sure to remove these connections before you wire the ones shown in Figure 4-3. Since pins 4, 5, 9, 10, 12, and 13 of U9 are unused CMOS inputs, you should wire these to +5V or ground. You may instead use a 74LS32 for U9. If you do so, leave the unused inputs open.

Using the Programming Commands

When Figure 4-3's circuit is added, you're ready to power up and try the programming commands. Begin by entering any simple BASIC-52 program, such as one of the examples in Chapter 3.

Setting MTOP

If you have a 32K RAM at U7, you have an additional step to perform before you store a program in U8. On bootup, BASIC-52 tests contiguous memory and sets MTOP to the highest value it finds below E000h. But BASIC-52's programming commands won't work unless MTOP is below 8000h. To enable program storage, type the following command:

```
MTOP=7FFFh
```

This ensures that BASIC-52 won't try to store RAM programs, variables, or strings in the area that you've reserved for permanent program storage (although it doesn't prevent you from writing to the area with BASIC-52's XBY operator). If U7 is an 8K device, MTOP is 1FFFh, well below 8000h, so you don't have to worry about changing it.

Saving a Program

To copy the current program from U7 to U8, type

```
FPROG
```

The screen will display the number 1, indicating that this is the first BASIC-52 program to be stored in the device, and after a short delay, the READY prompt should return.

`PROG` is an alternate command that uses a slower programming algorithm, and should also work.

If BASIC-52 is unable to program the chip, you'll see this:

```
ERROR: PROGRAMMING
```

If you get this error message, double-check your wiring. When the programming command executes, pins 20, 22, and 27 should toggle, along with the address and data lines.

Running a Stored Program

When you have a program saved, you can run it from the NV memory. BASIC-52's RAM and ROM commands switch from RAM mode, where BASIC-52 runs the program stored in RAM (U7), to ROM mode, where it looks in U8 for programs to run. When you've programmed successfully, run your program by typing

```
ROM
RUN
```

or

```
RROM
```

You can store multiple programs, space permitting, and run each by specifying its number. For example, to run the second program stored, type

```
RROM2
```

To return to editing programs in RAM, type

```
RAM
```

Another useful command is XFER. In ROM mode, type

```
XFER
```

to copy the current program from ROM into RAM, where you can edit it, and then use FPROG to store the revised version in U8 if you wish.

Adding Bootup Options

The commands FPROG1-FPROG6 enable you to store additional information besides programs. FPROG1 saves the current baud rate and causes BASIC-52 to boot immediately to the READY prompt, without waiting to receive a SPACE character. FPROG2 saves the current baud rate and also tells BASIC-52 to automatically run the first program in NV memory on bootup. This is what allows you to disconnect the system from its host and run it as a stand-alone system.

You can also permanently store a value for MTOP in U8. If you have a 32K RAM at U7, storing MTOP will ensure that you can use FPROG, and that your stored programs will be preserved when you reboot or power down.

If U7 is 32K, type

```
MTOP=7FFFH
FPROG3
```

Now, when your system boots up, MTOP will automatically be set to 7FFFh. FPROG3 also saves the baud rate and boots to the READY prompt without requiring you to press the space bar.

If you want to save MTOP and also run a program on bootup, use FPROG4, which combines the features of FPROG2 and FPROG3. FPROG5 is another useful command. It prevents BASIC-52 from clearing external data memory on bootup. FPROG6 enables you to add your own assembly-language reset routine.

If you use FPROG2-FPROG6, BASIC-52 will no longer auto-detect your host's baud rate. You must use the baud rate and crystal value that were in use when you executed the FPROG command.

Erasing NV Memory

Eventually, your NVRAM or EEPROM will fill with programs, or you may just want to erase what you've stored and start fresh. Listing 4-1 is a program that erases U8 by writing 0FFh to all locations.

To use the program, enter the listing and type RUN. The READY prompt will return when erasing is complete. Line 30 verifies each erasure, and is required only for EEPROM,

Listing 4-1. Erases NVRAM or EEPROM.

```
10    FOR I=8000H TO 9FFFH
20    XBY(I)=0FFH
30    IF XBY(I)<>0FFH THEN GOTO 30
40    NEXT I
50    END
```

because of its longer write times. The program erases all of the stored programs and any options selected with FPROG1-6 in U8.

Adding more NVRAM or EEPROM

If you want to add an additional 8K of NV RAM or EEPROM, wire another circuit exactly like Figure 4-3's, except connect pin 20 of the new NVRAM or EEPROM to A000h (pin 10 of U4) ORed with RESET, so that the chip will be accessed from A000h to BFFFh.

Adding EPROM

Adding EPROM requires more circuitry than NVRAM or EEPROM, because an EPROM must have a programming voltage at its VPP pin during programming. To use the faster FPROG commands, which follow Intel's Intelligent programming algorithm, you should also raise the EPROM's supply voltage (VCC) to +6 volts during programming.

Although EPROMs do require additional components, once you have them in the circuit, you can use the 8052-BASIC system as a general-purpose EPROM programmer, as described in Chapter 13. You can store assembly-language programs or any information that you want to save in EPROM, whether it's for use by the 8052-BASIC system or another project.

EPROM Types

Since EPROMs were first developed in the 1970's, each generation of devices has allowed larger capacities, faster programming, and reduced programming voltages. Although the recommended programming algorithms, or procedures, for EPROMs are alike in many ways, the details often vary, depending on the device and manufacturer.

Programming Algorithms

For critical applications, there is no substitute for consulting the EPROM's data sheet and following its recommendations exactly. But for general use, you can get reliable results with most EPROMs by using one of the two algorithms supported by BASIC-52.

50-millisecond programming. This algorithm is an older, slower procedure. To program a location in the EPROM, you apply a programming voltage to the VPP input, set the address and data lines to the desired values, and apply a 50-millisecond programming pulse at the PGM input to write the data into the EPROM at the selected address. You then increment the address, apply the new data and programming pulse, and continue in this way until all locations are programmed. After programming, you compare the EPROM's contents to the programming data to verify that all locations programmed correctly. (BASIC-52 varies from this standard by verifying each location immediately after programming.)

This is the recommended algorithm for older, smaller-capacity EPROMs like the 2-kilobyte 2716 and 4-kilobyte 2732, and some 8-kilobyte 2764s. These typically require a programming voltage of 21 or 25 volts at the EPROM's VPP input.

Intelligent programming. This algorithm uses much shorter programming pulses, and verifies after each attempt. After each 1-millisecond programming pulse, you read the EPROM location to see if the programming succeeded. If not, you try again, up to 25 times. When the location verifies, you apply a final pulse equal to three times the total amount of programming pulses already applied. For example, if it takes five attempts to verify, you would apply a final 15-millisecond pulse. Finally, when all locations are programmed, you verify each once more.

For Intelligent programming, VPP is typically +12.5 volts, and VCC, the EPROM's main power supply, is also raised from +5 to +6V during programming.

Intelligent programming is the recommended algorithm for many 8K EPROMs. Intel's 2764 EPROM uses 21V, 5—millisecond programming, while the 2764A uses 12.5V, Intelligent programming.

Quick-pulse programming. Some CMOS 8K EPROMs (27C64) can use an even faster programming algorithm called Quick-Pulse. In Quick-Pulse programming, VPP is typically 12.75V, VCC is 6.25, and the programming pulses are 100 microseconds. BASIC-52 doesn't offer Quick-Pulse programming as an option.

Choosing an algorithm. As a rule, you can program an EPROM using a slower algorithm than the recommended one, so you should be able to program any 12.5V EPROM with 50-millisecond programming, with VPP at 12.5V and VCC at +5V. And, any EPROM that can use Quick-Pulse programming should also program with the Intelligent or 50-millisecond programming algorithm and voltages. But whatever you do, don't exceed the recommended programming voltages for the device at VCC and VPP.

EPROM Pinouts

Figure 4-4 shows the pinout for a 2764 8K EPROM. Once again, the pin functions and locations are similar to those in an 8K RAM. During normal operation, the data pins (DQ0-DQ7) are read-only. Pin 27, which is Write Enable ($\overline{WE}$) on RAM, is $\overline{PGM}$, or program pulse, on the EPROM, and pin 1, which has no connection on RAM, is VPP, or programming voltage, on the EPROM.

EPROM-programming Circuits

Figure 4-5 shows additions to Figure 4-3's circuits that enable you to program a 12.5V 8K EPROM instead of NVRAM or EEPROM. Table 4-2 is a parts list for Figure 4-5's circuits.

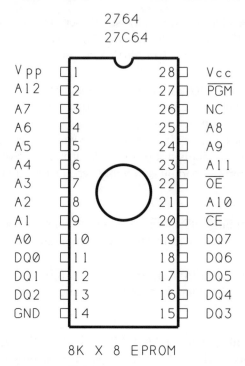

2764
27C64

Vpp	1	28	Vcc
A12	2	27	$\overline{PGM}$
A7	3	26	NC
A6	4	25	A8
A5	5	24	A9
A4	6	23	A11
A3	7	22	$\overline{OE}$
A2	8	21	A10
A1	9	20	$\overline{CE}$
A0	10	19	DQ7
DQ0	11	18	DQ6
DQ1	12	17	DQ5
DQ2	13	16	DQ4
GND	14	15	DQ3

8K X 8 EPROM

Figure 4-4. Pinout for 8K EPROM.

The components continue the numbering sequence begun in Figures 3-1 and 4-4. The additional circuits for the PROG commands are at pin 1 of U8. Jumper J5 allows you to configure the memory site for the type of NV memory you're using.

On NVRAM or EEPROM, pin 1 has no connection (or, on some EEPROMs, it's a BUSY output). On the EPROM, it's VPP, which is +5V during read operations and 12.5V during programming. $\overline{PGM\ EN}$ (pin 6 on the 8052-BASIC) controls the programming voltage by going low during programming operations and otherwise remaining high.

To prevent accidental programming during power up, OR gate U10A's output remains high until RESET goes low. U10 is not an ordinary OR gate—it's a 75453 peripheral driver. Unlike ordinary logic gates, U10's open-collector output can pull up to 30V without damaging the chip. The output also has much greater current-sinking ability than other logic gates (up to 300mA), and can easily provide base current to drive transistor Q1.

When pin 3 of U10A is high, Q1 is off, and VPP connects to +5V through germanium diode D2. The diode's voltage drop is just 0.3V, so VPP is actually at about 4.7V. Intel's data sheets specify that read operations require VPP to be at least 3.8V for the 2764A, or VCC-0.7V for the 27C64, so 4.7V is within the specifications.

CIRCUITS FOR EPROM PROGRAMMING WITH PROG COMMANDS (50-MSEC PROGRAMMING)

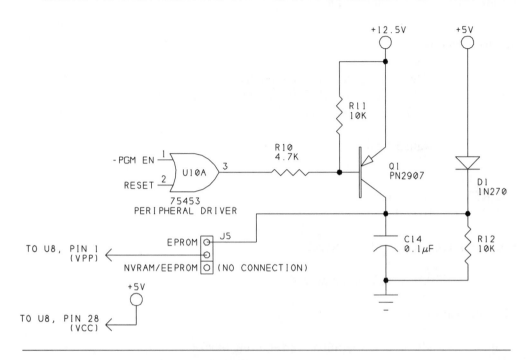

ADDITIONAL CIRCUITS FOR EPROM PROGRAMMING WITH FPROG COMMANDS
(INTELLIGENT PROGRAMMING)

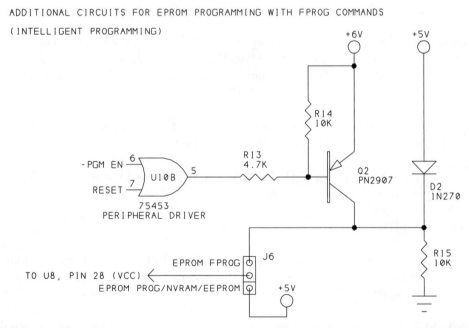

Figure 4-5. Additional circuits for programming EPROMs.

Table 4-2. Parts list for Figure 4-5.

Semiconductors

D2,D3	1N270 or similar germanium diode
Q1,Q2	PN2907 or similar PNP general-purpose transistor
U10	75453 dual peripheral OR driver

Resistors (1/4-watt, 5% tolerance)

R11,R14	4,700-ohm
R12,R13	10,000-ohm
R15,R16	10,000-ohm

Capacitors(16WVDC, 20% tolerance)

C15	0.1-microfarad ceramic disc

Miscellaneous

J5-J6	SIP header, 3-terminal, and shorting block

When BASIC-52 executes a programming command, $\overline{\text{PGM EN}}$ goes low, pin 3 of U10 goes low, and Q1 switches on. This brings VPP to 12.5 volts. Diode D2 prevents current from flowing into the 5V supply. When programming is finished, $\overline{\text{PGM EN}}$ goes high again, and VPP returns to +4.7V.

Resistor R10 limits U10A's output current, and R11 ensures that pin 3 of U10 pulls up to 12.5V. Capacitor C14 provides power-supply decoupling.

If you happen to have an older 21V EPROM, the circuit should also work with a +21V supply in place of +12.5V.

FPROG Circuits

If you want to use the FPROG commands for faster EPROM programming, additional circuits are required. These are identical to the circuits that switch VPP, except that they instead switch VCC to +6V during programming.

With the FPROG circuits shown in Figure 4-5, during normal (non-programming) operation, VCC is actually slightly less than +5V, due to D3's voltage drop. This should cause no problems with EPROMs that have a 10 percent power-supply tolerance; in other words, ones that are guaranteed to operate from supplies of 4.5 to 5.5V. You do want to be sure that your main supply is a solid +5V, or even a little higher.

The data sheets for some EPROMs specify 5-percent tolerance: the supply must be between 4.75 and 5.25V to guarantee operation within the specifications. In this case, you will be operating near or just below the recommended supply voltage, especially if your main supply is slightly under +5V. When you are not programming the EPROM, you can move J6 to connect pin 28 directly to +5V. But overall, 10-percent-tolerance EPROMs are a better choice for this circuit.

If you are using a NVRAM or EEPROM, set J6 to +5V, since VCC must remain at 5V for these devices.

Power Supplies for Programming

You have several options for creating the programming power supplies of +12.5V and, optionally, +6V.

Benchtop Supply

For occasional use, if you have a benchtop supply that can supply the needed outputs, you can add terminals to the appropriate connections in your BASIC-52 system, and connect the supply leads to them when needed.

Adjustable Regulator

Figure 4-6 shows a circuit that regulates a DC supply of 15 to 18V to 12.5V or 6V. For the 15V supply, you can use a benchtop supply, a wall-transformer AC-to-DC adapter, or even two 9-volt transistor batteries connected in series. The supply must have a DC output, but it doesn't have to be regulated. You'll need one LM317 and an R1 and R2 for each output voltage, but you can power both LM317's from the same supply.

Typical current requirements for programming an NMOS 2764A are 50 milliamperes at 12.5V and 75 milliamperes at 6V, or 125 milliamperes total. For a CMOS 27C64, it's 30 milliamperes for each, or 60 milliamperes total.

Each regulating circuit uses an LM317 adjustable regulator. You set the output voltage of the LM317 with R1 and R2, using the formula shown. The LM317 creates a constant 1.25V reference across R1. The current through R1 also flows through R2, and the voltage across the pair of resistors is the regulator's output.

Intel's EPROM data sheets specify this range for the programming voltages:

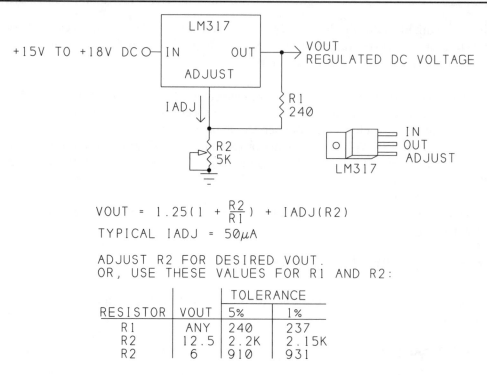

Figure   4-6.   Power supply circuit for EPROM-programming voltages.

VPP: 12V to 13V

VCC: 5.75V to 6.25V

If you use 5%-tolerance resistors for R1 and R2, you may have to vary the value of R2 for the proper output, especially to meet the requirement for Vcc. Or, you can use a 5K potentiometer for R2 and adjust for the desired output, or use 1%-tolerance resistors for a more precise output.

You can wire the LM317 circuits to your 8052-BASIC circuit board, and add terminals or jacks for connecting a 15V supply. Wire the LM317's output to the appropriate connections in Figure 4-5.

Switching Regulators

A third way to generate programming voltages is to use switching regulators like those available from Maxim Semiconductor. These can create the programming voltages from your +5V supply. For example, the MAX633 can create outputs of 6 and 12.5V from a +5V supply. The chip requires an additional inductor and capacitor, plus two resistors to set the output voltage. Maxim's data books have more details about this and similar chips.

Storing Programs on Disk

With BASIC-52's ability to store programs in on-board memory, disk storage isn't necessary. But storing programs on the host system's disk is convenient, since you can save as many programs as you want without worrying about running out of program memory. Since the programs are stored as ASCII text, you can write or edit them with any text editor, and then upload them as needed to the target system.

Most communications software allows you to upload and download files. In *Procomm Plus,* you use the PGUP and PGDN keys. In the Windows Terminal Accessory, use the Transfers menu.

Uploading to the 8052-BASIC System

When you upload a program to the 8052-BASIC system, you have to ensure that BASIC-52 has enough time to process each line before the next one arrives. If there isn't enough time, you'll have missing characters or lines in uploaded programs. There are a couple of ways to ensure that your uploads are complete.

Most software allows you to add delays after each transmitted line or character. You can experiment with different values to find the shortest delays that allow you to upload reliably. If you keep your program lines short, the delays between lines can be shorter.

If these options aren't available, try using a slower baud rate, which gives BASIC-52 a little more time to process each line before the next one arrives.

Downloading to the Host Computer

To download a BASIC-52 program from the target's RAM to the host's disk, type `LIST` to list the current program, but before you press ENTER to execute the command, set up your host's software to download, or receive, an ASCII file. When prompted, specify a filename. When the transfer is ready to go, press ENTER to send your program to the host. When you see the READY prompt, end the transfer by whatever means your software requires. (In *Procomm Plus,* press ESCAPE.) You should now have a file on disk containing the program you just listed.

You can test your download by erasing the program in the 8052-BASIC system's RAM, and then uploading it back into RAM.

Chapter 4

First, type NEW to erase the program. To restore your program by uploading it from disk, set up your host's software to upload, or send, an ASCII file, and enter the name of your previously downloaded file. As the file loads, you'll see each program line on screen. The file will contain a READY prompt after the program listing. This causes BASIC-52 to display an error message, which you can ignore. Type LIST to view the uploaded program, and type RUN to run it.

With BASIC-52 programs on disk, you can use any text editor to view or modify the program. Save the file as pure ASCII text, with no formatting commands added. You can also use your text editor to create a program from scratch, then upload it to BASIC-52, rather than typing the lines using BASIC-52's line editor.

5

Programming

When you have your 8052-BASIC system up and running, you're ready to start writing and running your own programs. This chapter is an introduction to the BASIC-52 programming language. It includes a summary of BASIC-52's abilities, some examples that illustrate what you can do with it, plus tips for writing and debugging programs.

For a complete reference to BASIC-52, see the BASIC-52 programming manual (either version), which includes many more examples and details about the language and how it works. You can learn a lot about BASIC-52 by browsing through the programming manual and experimenting on your own.

Programming Basics

Like other BASIC programs, BASIC-52 programs are built around a set of keywords, or reserved words. Each keyword has a specific meaning to the BASIC-52 interpreter. or example, the program line PRINT XTAL tells BASIC-52 to find the stored value of the XTAL operator and send it to the console input device (the serial port of the host computer), which will then display the value it receives.

If you're familiar with BASIC programming, most of BASIC-52's keywords and conventions will be familiar. If you have little programming experience, or if your experience is with assembly language, C, Pascal, or another language, you'll have more to learn. But on the whole, BASIC-52 makes it easy to quickly write and test your programs.

Writing a short BASIC-52 program involves these steps:

Define what you want to do
Write program lines to accomplish it
Test the results
As necessary, revise and retest

Longer programs involve the same basic steps, except that you can divide the program into a series of smaller tasks, or modules, and program and test each individually. Then, when the modules are working, you can combine them in one big program and test the result.

Modular programming can save a lot of headaches by limiting the amount of untested program code you have to work with at one time. A long, untested program almost certainly contains many errors will be hard to find and fix. It's much easier in the long run to test the pieces first, and BASIC-52 makes this easy to do.

Command and Run Modes

BASIC-52 has two modes of operation: command and run. *Command mode* refers to anything you type without a line number. BASIC-52 executes these lines immediately after you press ENTER. *Run mode* refers to running stored programs with the RUN command. A program consists of a series of program lines, with each line beginning with a line number.

BASIC-52 includes some keywords that you can use only in command mode, but not in programs. PROG is an example. Most of BASIC-52's other keywords are usable in either command or run mode. A few, such as DO...WHILE, are usable in RUN mode only.

Tips for Writing BASIC-52 Programs

The following advice is intended to make your programs easier to write and debug, and to help you avoid some common mistakes:

• **Number program lines by 10s.** Each line in a BASIC-52 program must begin with a line number. BASIC-52 uses the numbers to order the statements. Traditionally, BASIC programs begin at line 10, and count up in multiples of 10: 20, 30, and so on. This way, if you later discover that you need to add a few lines in the middle, you can, using the unused numbers that remain.

• **Divide long programs into modules.** Break up big projects. Use subroutines for independent functions. A subroutine is a block of statements that the main program jumps to with a GOSUB statement. At the end of the subroutine, a RETURN statement causes the program to jump back to the program line following the GOSUB statement.

Subroutines have two advantages. First, they help you to break up your program code into discrete units, with each having a specific purpose. This makes the program code easier to debug and easier to understand in general, especially if you return to it a week, month, or year after writing it when the details are no longer fresh in your mind. Second, subroutines make it easier to reuse your code if you have a similar task in another project. For example, all or most of the code involved with controlling a display module can usually be written as a subroutine, or perhaps a series of subroutines. This way, if you want to use the same display module in more than one project, you can reuse the code without having to pick through your previous programs to find the program lines that you need.

- **Keep program lines short.** Short lines are easier to edit with BASIC-52's line editor, which requires retyping the entire line to make a change. They're also easier to read. If you upload programs from disk, shorter lines can eliminate problems caused by BASIC-52's not having enough time to process each line before the next one arrives. Although BASIC-52 allows you to place multiple statements on one line, with up to 79 characters per line, shorter is better.

There are two situations where you might want to combine a series of short lines into fewer, longer program lines: when the program has to execute as fast as possible, or when you need to store the program in the smallest possible space. Even then, though, you can develop the program with short lines, and combine them only after the program is debugged and ready for permanent storage.

- **Check syntax and spelling carefully.** BASIC-52's syntax consists of the rules of grammar and punctuation that your program lines must follow. For example, a FOR loop must include a variable, limits, and a NEXT instruction. Leave any of these out, and your loop won't work. There's no room for spelling errors either. BASIC-52 doesn't know that you meant LIST when you typed LSIT.

- **Document your programs.** Many of BASIC-52's keywords aren't too hard to decipher. For example, it makes sense that the STOP instruction halts program execution. But your own comments throughout the program can help you remember why you wrote each program line, and what it's supposed to accomplish.

BASIC-52 allows you to add comments, preceded by REM (remark). Try to write comments that do more than just define the keywords in the line. Also explain the purpose behind what you are doing. For example, this comment

```
10 REM read value from external memory
20 A=XBY(0FE00H)
```

does nothing more than define the BASIC-52 instruction that follows. In contrast,

```
10 REM Read the states of switches 1-8
20 A=XBY(0FE00H)
```

tells you why you are executing the instruction.

The problem with adding comments to BASIC-52 programs is that they slow program execution. They also make the program longer, so that it needs more memory. So you might want to keep comments to a minimum in the final version that you store in NV memory.

You can, however, store fully documented copies of your program on disk. If you wish, you can use your personal computer's text editor to add comments on unnumbered lines, like this:

```
REM Read the states of switches 1-8
20 A=XBY(0FE00h)
```

Then, as you upload the program to your 8052-BASIC system, all of the lines will display on the host computer, but BASIC-52 will store only the numbered lines, discarding the unnumbered remarks.

- **Use short variable names for faster execution speed**. BASIC-52 allows variable names of up to eight characters. Programs with shorter variable names will run faster and require less memory to store. Even if you limit yourself to 1- and 2-letter variables, you still have hundreds to choose from. Longer names, such as REVERSE, QUIT, and so on have the advantage of being more meaningful—it's easier to guess their meaning without adding comments. So there are times when you might choose a longer name. But longer names can cause other problems, as the next paragraph explains.

- **Be sure that variable names don't contain keywords.** In BASIC-52 you can't name a variable ON, because ON is already defined by BASIC-52. You also can't name a variable MONTH, ONE, ACTION, or any other word that contains ON. Short variable names are much less likely to contain an embedded keyword. Also be aware that BASIC-52 identifies a variable only by its first and last characters, plus its length, so, for example, it considers MAXIMUM and MINIMUM to be the same variable, while MAX and MIN are different.

- **Avoid variables that begin or end with the letter *F*.** BASIC-52 has a couple of bugs relating to variable names that begin or end in F. Specifically, when *F* is the last character in a variable name followed by a space, BASIC-52 drops the F from the variable name. And, if you should name a variable FP, FPR, or FPRO, and follow the name by a space, BASIC-52 will also drop the F from the name. The easiest way to avoid problems is to avoid any variable name that begins or ends in F.

• **Hexadecimal numbers that begin with A through F must have a leading 0, and all hexadecimal numbers must end in H**. Here are some examples of valid hexadecimal numbers:

Valid Hex Number	Decimal Equivalent
0DH	208
0AH	10
15H	21
0FFFFH	65,535
0CH	12

Here are some invalid hex numbers, and a valid hex number that doesn't have its intended value:

Invalid Hex Number	Problem
FFH	no leading 0
0C	no trailing H
10 (intended as decimal 16)	no trailing H. BASIC-52 will interpret at decimal 10 (0AH)

BASIC-52 Bugs and Things to Watch Out For

This section is a summary of other bugs and other minor problems with BASIC-52 to be aware of as you program. Many of BASIC-52's bugs and limits have been eliminated in newer versions of BASIC-52 developed by other sources, described in Chapter 15.

Assembly-language Issues:

In external code memory, if 2002h contains 5Ah and bit 5 at 2048h is set, BASIC-52 will try to call a user-written token table. If 2001h contains 0AAh, BASIC-52 will try to call a user-written reset routine at 2090h. If the expected table or routine isn't present, the system will crash. (See Chapter 13.) Solution: avoid writing to code memory at 2001h, 2002h, and 2048h. (In Figure 3-1's circuit, the RAM in this area (if any) is accessed as data memory only, so you don't have to worry about this.)

The address following a CALL instruction must be at least 2000h.

Miscellaneous Items:

Floating-point calculations have errors when the numbers are very large or very small.

The value returned for the ASC(*character*) operator is incorrect for these seven characters:

+   - = .   ? /   *

ONTIME and ONEX1 will not cause interrupts during an INPUT statement. User delay in responding to an INPUT may cause the program to miss interrupts.

Finding Program Errors

Writing a program that does what you want isn't always easy. A single missing character or program line can cause a program to stop in its tracks, or continue to execute but with unintended results, or, worst of all, crash the system and require rebooting.

BASIC-52 will detect and warn you of many programming errors. If BASIC-52 detects an error when you try to run a program, it will display the line containing the error, along with an error message, and will stop the program at that point.

If you get an error message, examine the offending line carefully. Many problems are due to syntax errors, where missing or incorrect characters make it impossible for BASIC-52 to interpret the program line correctly.

Other times, a program will run without problems, but it won't do what you intended. For example, it's easy to forget that a hexadecimal number beginning in *A-F* must have a leading zero, or that all hexadecimal numbers must end in *H*. Each of these BASIC-52 statements has a different result, and none will produce an error message:

BASIC-52 Statement	Resulting Action
XBY(1000H)=20H	Writes 20H to 1000H in external data memory
XBY(1000)=20	Writes 14H to 3E8H in external data memory
XBY(1000H)=20	Writes 14H to 1000H in external data memory
XBY(1000)=20H	Writes 20H to 3E8H in external data memory

The Microcontroller Idea Book

It can be hard to find an error that gives no error message. The best way to narrow the search is to write and test your programs in small modules, so that the amount of code to search through remains manageable.

BASIC-52 Keywords by Function

The following is a quick reference to BASIC-52's keywords, grouped by function. After this is a more detailed list, arranged alphabetically, with the syntax and a brief description of what each keyword does. Some of the keywords, like RUN, LIST, and PRINT, are ones that you'll use constantly. A few, like NULL or UIO, have specialized uses that you may never need. Again, for a more complete reference, see the BASIC-52 programming manual.

Running and Listing Programs

CONT
LIST
NEW
RAM
REM
ROM
RROM
RUN
STOP
XFER

Storing Programs in NV Memory

FPROG
FPROG1-FPROG6
PGM
PROG
PROG1-PROG6

Program Control Structures (loops and subroutines)

DO UNTIL
DO WHILE
END
FOR TO [STEP] NEXT]
GOSUB
GOTO
IF THEN [ELSE]
ON GOSUB
ON GOTO
RETURN

Printing and Displaying Information on the Host Computer

PH0.
PH1.
PRINT, P., ?

Additional PRINT Formatting

CR
SPC
TAB
USING, U.

Input/Output

CBY
DBY
GET
INPUT
LIST#
NULL
PORT1
PH0.#
PH1.#
PRINT#, P#, ?#
XBY

System Control Values

BAUD
FREE
LEN
MTOP
STRING

Math Operators

```
=
+
-
*
/
**
>
<
<>
>=
<=
ABS
ATN
COS
EXP
INT
LET
LOG
NOT
PI
RND
SGN
SIN
SQR
TAN
```

Logical Operators

```
.AND.
.OR.
.XOR.
```

Assembly-language Interfacing

```
CALL
LIST@
PH0.@
PH1.@
PRINT@, P@, ?@
UI0
UI1
UO0
UO1
```

Data Storage

```
ASC
CHR
CLEAR
CLEARS
DATA
DIM
LD@
POP
PUSH
READ
RESTORE
ST@
```

Timers and Interrupts

```
CLEARI
CLOCK0
CLOCK1
IDLE
IE
IP
ONERR
ONEX1
ONTIME
PCON
PWM
RCAP2
RETI
T2CON
TCON
TIME
TIMER0
TIMER1
TIMER2
TMOD
```

Quick Reference to BASIC-52

This quick reference to the BASIC-52 programming language lists the keywords alphabetically, along with brief descriptions of function and use.

Conventions

The reference uses the following typographic conventions:

KEYWORDS (boldface uppercase)
BASIC-52 keywords

placeholders (italics)
Variables, expressions, constants, or other information that you must supply

[*optional items*] (enclosed in square brackets)
Items that are not required

repeating elements... (followed by ellipsis (three dots))
You may add more items with the same form as the preceding item.

C = command mode
R = run mode

variable = *expression*   C,R
Assigns a value to a variable

expression = *expression*   C,R
Equivalence test (relational operator)

expression + *expression*   C,R
Add

expression − *expression*   C,R
Subtract

expression * *expression*   C,R
Multiply

expression **/** *expression*   C,R
Divide

expression ****** *expression*   C,R
Raises first expression to value of second expression (exponent)

expression **<>** *expression*   C,R
Inequality test (relational operator)

expression **<** *expression*   C,R
Less than test (relational operator)

expression **>** *expression*   C,R
Greater than test (relational operator)

expression **<=** expression   C,R
Less than or equal test (relational operator)

expression **>=** *expression*   C,R
Greater than or equal test (relational operator)

?
Same as PRINT

ABS (*expression*)   C,R
Returns the absolute value of *expression*

expression **.AND.** *expression*   C,R
Logical AND

ASC(*character*)   C,R
Returns the value of ASCII character

ATN(*expression*)   C,R
Returns the arctangent of *expression*

BAUD *expression*   C,R
Sets the baud rate for LPT (pin 8). For proper operation, XTAL must match the
system's crystal frequency.

CALL *integer*   C,R
Calls an assembly-language routine at the specified address in program memory.

The Microcontroller Idea Book   75

CBY(*expression*)   C,R
Retrieves the value at *expression* in program, or code, memory.

CHR(*expression*)   C,R
Converts *expression* to its ASCII character.

CLEAR   C,R
Sets all variables to 0, resets all stacks and interrupts evoked by BASIC.

CLEARI   C,R
Clears all interrupts evoked by BASIC. Disables ONTIME, ONEX1.

CLEARS   C,R
Resets BASIC-52's stacks. Sets control stack = 0FEh, argument stack = 1FEh, internal stack = value in 3Eh in internal RAM.

CLOCK0   C,R
Disables the real-time clock.

CLOCK1   C,R
Enables the real-time clock.

CONT   C
Continues executing program after STOP or CONTROL+C.

COS(*expression*)   C,R
Returns the cosine of *expression*

CR
PRINT option. Causes a carriage return, but no line feed, on the host display.

DATA *expression* [*,...,expression*]   R
Specifies expressions to be retrieved by a READ statement.

DBY(*expression*)   C,R
Retrieves or assigns a value at *expression* in internal data memory.

DIM *array name* [(*size*)] [*,...array name*(*size*)]   C,R
Reserves storage for an array. Default size is 11 (0-10). Size limits are 0-254.
Example:
   DIM B(100)
   Reserves storage for 100-element array B

DO: [*program statements*]**:** **UNTIL** *relational expression* R
Executes all statements between DO and UNTIL until *relational expression* is true.

DO: [*program statements*]**:** **WHILE** *relational expression* R
Executes all statements between DO and WHILE until *relational expression* is false.

END R
Terminates program execution.

EXP (*expression*) C,R
Raises *e* (2.7182818) to the power of *expression*

FOR *counter variable* **=** *start-count expression* C,R
  TO *end-count expression* [
  STEP *count-increment expression*]**:** [*program statements*]**:**
  NEXT [*counter variable*]
Executes all statements between FOR and NEXT the number of times specified by the counter and step expressions.

FPROG, FPROG1-FPROG6 C
Like PROG, PROG1-PROG6, but using Intelligent programming algorithm.

FREE C,R
Returns the number of bytes of unused external data RAM.

GET R
Contains the ASCII code of a character received from the host computer's keyboard. After a program reads the value of GET (For example, G=GET), GET returns to 0 until a new character arrives.

GOSUB *line number* R
Causes BASIC-52 to transfer program control to a subroutine beginning at *line number.* A RETURN statement returns control to the line number following the GOSUB statement.

GOTO *line number* C,R
Causes BASIC-52 to jump to *line number* in the current program.

IDLE R
Forces BASIC-52 to wait for ONTIME or ONEX1 interrupt.

IE C,R
Retrieves or assigns a value to the 8052's special function register IE.

IF *relational expression* R
  THEN *program statements*
  [**ELSE**] [*program statements*]
If *relational expression* is true, executes program statements following THEN. If *relational expression* is false, executes program statements following ELSE, if used.

INPUT [**"***Prompt message***"**][,] *variable* [,*variable*] [,...*variable*] R
Displays a question mark and optional prompt message on the host computer and waits for keyboard input. Stores input in *variable*(s). A comma before the first variable suppresses the question mark.

INT(*expression*) C,R
Returns integer portion of *expression*.

IP C,R
Retrieves or assigns a value to the 8052's special function register IP.

LD@ *expression* C,R
Retrieves a 6-byte floating-point number and places it on the argument stack. *Expression* points to the most significant byte of the number.

LEN C,R
Returns the number of bytes in the current program

[**LET**] *variable* **=** *expression* C,R
Assigns a variable to the value of *expression*. Use of LET is optional.

LIST[*line number*][*-line number*] C,R
Displays the current program on the host computer.

LIST# [*line number*][*-line number*] C,R
Writes the current program to LPT (pin 8).

LIST@ [*line number*][*-line number*] C,R
Writes the current program to a user-written assembly-language output driver at 40C3h. Setting bit 7 of internal data memory location 27H enables the driver.

LOG(*expression*)   C,R
Returns natural logarithm of *expression*.

MTOP [=*highest address in RAM program space*]   C,R
Assigns or reads the highest address BASIC-52 will use to store variables,
strings, and RAM programs. Usually 7FFFh or lower, since EPROM space begins at 8000h.

NEW   C
Erases current program in RAM; clears all variables.

NOT (*expression*)   C,R
Returns 1's complement (inverse) of *expression*.

NULL [*integer*]   C
Sets the number (0-255) of NULL characters (ASCII 00) that BASIC-52 sends
automatically after a carriage return. Only very slow printers or terminals need
these extra nulls.

ON *expression* **GOSUB** *line number* [,*line number*] [,...,*line number*]   R
Transfers program control to a subroutine beginning at one of the line numbers in
the list. The value of *expression* matches the position of the line number selected,
with the first line number at position 0.

Examples:

```
X=1
ON X GOSUB 100,200,400
```
Transfers program control to a subroutine at line 200 (position 1 in the list)

```
X=0
ON X GOSUB 800,300
```
Transfers program control to a subroutine at line 800 (position 0 in the list)

ON *expression* **GOTO** *line number* [,*line number*] [,...,*line number*]   R
Transfers program control to one of the line numbers in a list of numbers. The
value of *expression* matches the position of the line number selected, with the
first line number at position 0.
Example:

```
X=0
ON X GOTO 800,300
```
Transfers program control to line 800 (position 0 in the list)

ONERR *line number*   R
Passes control to *line number* following an arithmetic error. Arithmetic errors in-
clude ARITH. OVERFLOW, ARITH. UNDERFLOW, DIVIDE BY ZERO, and
BAD ARGUMENT.

ONEX1 *line number*   R
On interrupt 1 (pin 13), BASIC-52 finishes executing the current statement, and
then passes control to an interrupt routine beginning at *line number*. The interrupt
routine must end with RETI.

ONTIME *number of seconds, line number*   R
When TIME = *number of seconds,* BASIC-52 passes control to an interrupt rou-
tine beginning at *line number.* The interrupt routine must end with RETI.
CLOCK1 starts the timer.

expression **.OR.** *expression*   C,R
Logical OR

P.
same as PRINT

PCON   C,R
Retrieves or assigns a value to the 8052's special function register PCON.

PGM   C,R
Programs an EPROM, EEPROM, or NV RAM with data from memory. The following data must be stored in internal data memory in the locations listed:
1Bh,19h   High byte, low byte of first address of data to program
1Ah,18h   High byte, low byte of first address to be programmed - 1
1Fh,1Eh   High byte, low byte indicating number of bytes to program
40h,41h   High byte, low byte indicating width of programming pulse.
             High byte = ((65536 - pulse width in seconds * XTAL/12) / 256.
             Low byte = ((65536 - pulse width in seconds * XTAL/12) .AND. 0FFh.
26h   For Intelligent programming, set bit 3.
             For 50-millisecond programming, clear bit 3.

PH0.   C,R
Same as PRINT, but displays values in hexadecimal format. Uses two digits to
display values less than 0FFh.

PH0.#   C,R
Same as PRINT#, but displays values in PH0. hexadecimal format

PH0.@   C,R
Same as PRINT@, but outputs values in PH0. hexadecimal format.

PH1.   C,R
Same as PRINT, but displays values in hexadecimal format. Always displays
four digits.

PH1.#   C,R
Same as PRINT#, but displays values in PH1. hexadecimal format.

PH1.@   C,R
Same as PRINT@, but outputs values in PH1. hexadecimal format.

PI   C,R
Constant equal to 3.1415926.

POP *variable* [,...*variable*]   C,R
Assigns the value of the top of the argument stack to *variable*.

PORT1   C,R
Retrieves or assigns a value to PORT1 (pins 1-8).

PRINT [*expression*] [,...*expression*] [,]   C,R
Displays the value of *expression*(s) on the host computer. A comma at the end of
the statement suppresses the CARRIAGE RETURN/LINEFEED. Values are separated
by two spaces. Additional PRINT options are CR, SPC, TAB, USING.

PRINT#   C,R
Same as PRINT, but outputs to LPT (pin 8). BAUD and XTAL values affect the
PRINT# rate.

PRINT@   C,R
Same as PRINT, but outputs to a user-defined output driver. Requires an assembly-language output routine at 403Ch in external program memory. Setting bit 7
of internal data memory location 24h enables the output routine.

PROG   C
Stores the current RAM program in the EPROM space.

PROG1   C

Saves the serial-port baud rate. On power-up or reset, BASIC-52 boots without having to receive a space character. The terminal's baud rate must match the stored value.

PROG2   C

Like PROG1, but on power-up or reset, BASIC-52 also begins executing the first program in the EPROM space.

PROG3   C

Like PROG1, but also saves MTOP. On power-up or reset, BASIC-52 clears memory only to MTOP.

PROG4   C

Like PROG2, but also saves MTOP. On power-up or reset, BASIC-52 clears memory only to MTOP.

PROG5   C

Like PROG3, but also reads 5Fh in external data memory on power-up or reset. If 5Fh contains 0A5h, BASIC-52 doesn't clear external data memory. If data memory location 5Eh contains 34h, BASIC-52 will automatically begin executing a program in external data memory.

PROG6   C

Like PROG5, but if external data memory location contains 5Fh, BASIC-52 calls a user-written assembly-language reset routine beginning at program memory 4039h.

PUSH *expression* [,...*expression*]   C,R

Places the values of *expression*(s) sequentially on BASIC-52's argument stack.

PWM *expression1, expression2, expression3*   C,R

Outputs a pulse-width modulated (PWM) sequence of pulses on pin 3. *Expression1* is the width of each high pulse, expressed in clock cycles. *Expression2* is the width of each low pulse, expressed in clock cycles. *Expression3* is the number of PWM cycles output. One clock cycle = 12/XTAL. One PWM cycle = one high pulse plus one low pulse. *Expression1* and *Expression2* must each be at least 25. Maximum for each *Expression* is 65535.

RAM   C

Selects the current program in the RAM space.

RCAP2   C,R
Retrieves or assigns a value to the 8052's special function registers RCAP2H and RCAP2L.

READ *variable* [*,...,variable*]   R
Retrieves the expressions in a DATA statement and assigns each expression to a variable.

REM   C,R
Introduces a comment, or remark. BASIC-52 ignores all text after REM in a program line.

RESTORE   R
Resets READ pointer to the first expression in the DATA statement.

RETI   R
Returns program control to the line number following the most recently executed ONEX1 or ONTIME statement.

RETURN   R
Returns program control to the line number following the most recently executed GOSUB statement.

RND   C,R
Returns a pseudo-random number between 0 and 1 inclusive.

ROM [*program number*]   C
Selects a program in the EPROM space (beginning at 8000h). Default program number is 1.

RROM [*program number*]   C,R
Changes to ROM mode and runs the specified program. Default program number is 1.

RUN   R
Executes the current program. Clears all variables.

SGN (*expression*)   C,R
Returns +1 if *expression* >=0, zero if *expression* = 0, and -1 if *expression* <0.

SIN(*expression*)   C,R
Returns the sine of *expression*

Chapter 5

SPC(*expression*)
PRINT option. Causes the display to place *expression* additional spaces (besides the minimum two) between values in a PRINT statement.

Example:

```
PRINT "hello",SPC(3),"good-by"
hello      good-by
```

SQR(*expression*)   C,R
Returns square root of expression.

ST@ *expression*   C,R
Copies a 6-byte floating-point number from the argument stack to external data memory. *Expression* points to the most significant byte of the number.

STOP
Halts program execution.

STRING *expressions, expression2*   C,R
Allocates memory for strings (variables each consisting of a series of text characters).
Expression1 = (*Expression2* * number of strings) + 1.
Expression2 = maximum number of bytes (characters) per string + 1. Executing STRING clears all variables. Maximum number of strings is 255.
Examples:

```
STRING 91,9
```
reserves space for ten 8-character strings

```
STRING 9,4
```
reserves space for two 3-character strings

T2CON   C,R
Retrieves or assigns a value to the 8052's special function register T2CON.

TAB(*expression*),
PRINT option. Specifies the position (number of spaces) to begin displaying the next value in the PRINT statement.
Example:

```
PRINT TAB(5) "hello"
     hello
```

```
PRINT TAB(2) "hello"
   hello
```

TAN(*expression*)   C,R
Returns the tangent of *expression*.

TCON   C,R
Retrieves or assigns a value to the 8052's special function register TCON.

TIME   C,R
Retrieves or assigns a value, in seconds, to BASIC-52's real-time clock.

TIMER0   C,R
Retrieves or assigns a value to the 8052'S special function registers TH0 and TL0.

TIMER1   C,R
Retrieves or assigns a value to the 8052's special function registers TH1 and TL1.

TIMER2   C,R
Retrieves or assigns a value to the 8052's special function registers TH2 and TL2.

TMOD   C,R
Retrieves or assigns a value to the 8052's special function register TMOD.

U.
PRINT option. Same as USING.

UI0   C,R
Restores BASIC-52's console input driver after using UI1.

UI1   C,R
Allows a user-provided assembly-language console (host computer) input routine
to replace BASIC-52's console input driver. External program memory location
4033h must contain a jump to the user's routine.

UO0   C,R
Restores BASIC-52's console output driver after using UI1.

UO1   C,R
Allows a user-provided assembly-language console (host computer) output routine to replace BASIC-52's console output driver. External program memory location 4030h must contain a jump to the user's routine.

USING (F*N*)
PRINT option. Causes BASIC-52 to output numbers in exponential format with
N significant digits. BASIC-52 always outputs at least 3 significant digits. Maxi-
mum *expression* is 8.

Example:

```
PRINT USING(F3),3,4.1,100
3.00 E 0
4.10 E 0
1.00 E 2
```

USING(0)
PRINT option. Causes BASIC-52 to output numbers from ±.99999999 to ±0.1 as
decimal fractions. Numbers outside this range display in USING(FN) format.
USING(0) is the default format.

USING (#[...#][.]#[...#])
PRINT option. Causes BASIC-52 to output numbers using decimal fractions,
with # representing the number of significant digits before and after the decimal
point. Up to eight # characters are allowed.

Example:
```
PRINT USING(###.##),3,4.1,100
   3.00
   4.10
00.00
```

XBY(*expression*)   C,R
Retrieves or assigns a value in external data memory.

XFER   C
Copies the current program from the EPROM space (beginning at 8010h for program 1) to RAM (beginning at 200h), and selects RAM mode.

expression **.XOR.** *expression*   C,R
Logical exclusive OR

XTAL   C,R
Assigns a value equal to the system's crystal frequency, for use by BASIC-52 in
timing calculations.

6

Inputs and Outputs

So far, our BASIC-52 circuit consists of the 8052-BASIC microcontroller, RAM, nonvolatile memory for permanent program storage, and a serial interface to a host computer. Now it's time to add inputs and output interfaces that enable the system to monitor and control devices outside of these circuits. The options include low-cost buffers and latches, as well as programmable chips with features like individual bit control, automatic generation of control signals, and the ability to configure a port as input, output, or bidirectional.

The Memory Map

But before we start adding components, it's time to draw a memory map for the system. The memory map is a diagram that shows the range of addresses a microcontroller or other computer can access, along with each component that the computer reads or writes to and the addresses where each component resides. The components may be memory chips like RAM or EPROM, or they may be other components that the computer accesses by specifying an address. Drawing a memory map helps to ensure that each component has a unique address or range of addresses.

Figure 6-1 shows the memory map for our design. Each 64K area of external memory consists of eight 8K blocks. Remember that 8 kilobytes equals 8192 in decimal, but 2000 in hexadecimal.

Internal code memory consists of the 8052-BASIC's ROM, which uses the addresses from 0 to 1FFFh.

External data memory beginning at 0 is also required. BASIC-52 reserves the first 512 bytes for its own use, and it stores the current BASIC-52 user program immediately above this area. The memory map allows a choice of using an 8K RAM from 0 to 1FFFh, or a 32K RAM, which uses the entire area from 0 to 7FFFh. (The 8052 also has 256 bytes of internal data memory, which the memory map doesn't show.)

Two 8K blocks of combined code/data memory are reserved beginning at 8000h. As Chapter 4 showed, BASIC-52's programming commands store programs in nonvolatile memory beginning at this location.

For the input and output, or I/O, circuits described in this chapter, the memory map reserves the top block of data memory, from E000h to FFFFh. I/O interfaces include connections to buffers, latches, switches, displays, motors, or just about anything besides the system's main memory. The I/O circuits don't have to use this block, but BASIC-52 encourages it, since it clears external memory only up to E000h on bootup (unless you specify a lower value by saving MTOP with a PROG3 command.)

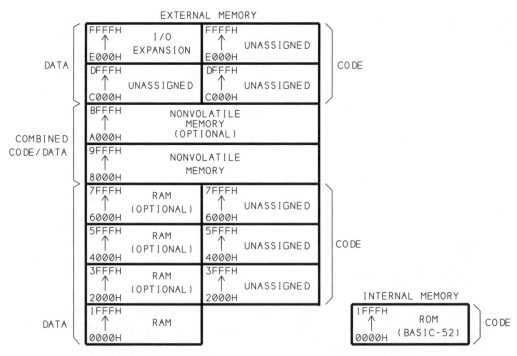

Figure   6-1.   Memory map for the 8052-BASIC system's internal and external data and program memory.

Unassigned space remains in the memory map, but there's nothing wrong with this since it leaves room for additions. Also, this isn't the only way to configure an 8052-BASIC system. For example, if you use a single 8K EPROM at 8000h, you can use the area from A000h to BFFFh for additional I/O.

Not shown are two areas that BASIC-52 reserves for optional enhancements. If you customize BASIC-52 by adding your own instructions, commands, or reset routines, BASIC-52 expects to find parameters relating to these in code memory from 2001h to 2090h. And, if you want to call assembly-language interrupt routines, BASIC-52 expects to find vectors for these in code memory from 4003h to 41FFh. For these, you can use EPROM, EEPROM, or NV RAM, as Chapter 13 shows.

Uses for I/O Ports

Just about all microcontroller circuits need to be able to do more than just read and write to memory. Other uses involve sensing and controlling of conditions, events, or devices external to the basic circuits. For example, a microcontroller-based drilling machine for printed-circuit boards might have these responsibilities:

Detect when a user presses a switch.
Move the pc board so that the hole to be drilled lies under the drill bit.
Set the speed of rotation for the drill bit.
Lower the bit into the board, then raise it after drilling.
Detect problems, such as a bit that doesn't lower or a drilling obstruction.
Display messages to prompt the user for input or show progress.

These functions all involve reading and writing, but instead of reading and writing to memory, the microcontroller reads sensors and switches, and writes to motors and displays. Reading and writing to devices other than memory is often called input/output, or I/O for short.

Adding Ports

The 8052-BASIC has a few pins on Port 1 that you can use for I/O. Chapter 3 included programs for reading and writing to these. But many projects will require more I/O than these few pins can offer.

Figure 6-2 shows a circuit that allows you to add up to eight 8-bit ports to the main circuit. You can design the ports as inputs or outputs, in any combination.

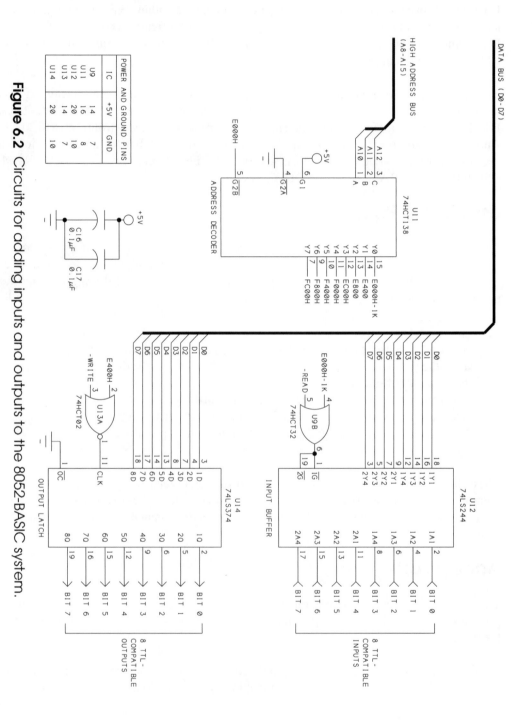

Figure 6.2 Circuits for adding inputs and outputs to the 8052-BASIC system.

The Microcontroller Idea Book

U11 is a 74HCT138 3-to-8-line decoder that generates individual chip-enable signals for eight 1K blocks in the memory area from E000h to FFFFh. It works the same way that U6 generates chip selects for 8K blocks in the main circuit.

U11 is enabled whenever pin 7 of U6 is low, which occurs when the 8052-BASIC reads or writes to addresses from E000h to FFFFh.

Address lines A10, A11, and A12 determine which of U11's outputs goes low when the chip is enabled. As with U6, each output is low for a different memory area. For example, pin 15 is low only when addresses from E000h to E3FFh are being read or written to.

One possible point of confusion is that both pin 7 of U6 (in Figure 3-1) and pin 15 of U11 are chip-selects with a starting address of E000h. One controls memory accesses in the entire 8K block from E000h to FFFFh, while the other controls only the 1K block from E000h to E3FFh. To distinguish the two, I've labeled U11's pin 15 as E000H-1K.

U12 and U14 are examples of input and output ports that U11 can enable.

An Input Port

U12 is a 74LS244 octal buffer that adds eight inputs to the circuit. The buffer's Y outputs connect to the system's data bus (D0-D7). The chip has two groups of four buffers, with each having its own enable input ($\overline{1G}$ and $\overline{2G}$). For this application, the enables are tied together, and all eight buffers are accessed as a group.

I used an LSTTL device for the buffer rather than a CMOS 74HC244 for a couple of reasons. The LSTTL chip has Schmitt-trigger inputs, which are less sensitive to noise. Plus, unlike CMOS, the LSTTL buffer requires no pull-up resistors at unused inputs.

OR gate U9B ensures that U12 is enabled only when U2 (the 8052-BASIC chip) reads an address from E000h to E3FFh. When this occurs, output-enable pins 1 and 19 go low, the buffer's outputs follow its inputs, and U2 reads the data that U12 has placed on D0-D7.

After a read operation, pins 1 and 19 go high and U12's outputs are high-impedance. In other words, the outputs are electrically similar to an open circuit, which ensures that they won't interfere with other operations on the data bus.

In the circuit, U12 is read-only. Write operations to E000h have no effect. To access U12 at a different address, wire pin 4 of U9B to a different output of U11.

Memory decoding options. Note that although U12 holds just one byte of information to read, you can access it at any address from E000h to E3FFh. This may seem like a waste of

1023 (3FEh) addresses. Indeed, if using every byte of memory is critical, you can use other methods in place of U11 to more completely decode, or divide, the memory space.

Programmable logic is one possibility, for those who have access to a logic compiler and device programmer. But for many circuits, complete decoding of memory isn't necessary, and less-than-complete decoding using off-the-shelf parts is more practical.

An Output Port

To complement U12's input byte, U14 provides eight bits of output. U14 is a 74LS374 octal flip-flop, which is very similar to the 74HCT373 octal latch at U4. On the '373, 1Q-8Q follow 1D-8D until pin 11 goes high, after which 1D-8D no longer change. In contrast, on the '374, 1Q-8Q change only on pin 11's rising edge, when 1D-8D are latched to 1Q-8Q.

Here again, I chose LSTTL over CMOS, this time because the LSTTL device can sink 12ma at 0.25V, compared to 6ma at 0.2V for the 74HC374. However, the 74HC374 can also source 6ma at 4.2V, so it's a better choice if you need to draw current from a logic-high output.

U14's eight data inputs connect to the data bus (D0-D7). Its output control (pin 1) is tied low so that the outputs are always enabled. If you want to be able to disable the outputs, you can instead tie pin 1 to an unused bit on Port 1.

NOR gate U13A clocks U14 only when U2 writes to addresses from E400h to E7FFh. When this occurs, the data written is latched to the outputs of U14. The outputs do not change until the next time the chip is written to.

In the circuit, U14 is write-only. Reading address E400h will return the value 0FFh. To access U14 at a different address, wire pin 2 of U13A to a different output of U11.

Since U12 is read-only and U14 is write-only, you could use the same address for both, by having them share the same output of U11. For example, if you wire both pin 2 of U13A and pin 4 of U9B to pin 7 of U11, both will be accessed at FC00h. Write operations will access U12, and reads will access U14. In this way, you can add up to eight input ports and eight output ports, with eight chip-select addresses in all.

Wiring Tips

Add Figure 6-2's circuits to Chapter 3's circuits, including the connections shown to D0-D7, A10-A12, E000h, $\overline{READ}$, and $\overline{WRITE}$ in the main circuit. The schematic continues the component numbering sequence from the earlier schematics. Use sockets for the ICs. Wire U13's unused inputs (pins 5, 6, 8, 9, 11, and 12) to GND or +5V. Also add a couple of 0.1-microfarad ceramic decoupling capacitors from +5V to GND, near the added ICs.

If you wish, you can wire U14's inputs and U12's outputs to headers for easy access when you want to connect clip-on jumpers, probe leads, or ribbon cables to the inputs and outputs.

Basic Tests

What can you do with these new inputs and outputs? First, some simple tests. You read and write to the ports exactly as you read and write to external memory. This BASIC-52 statement will display the value of the byte at U12's inputs:

```
PRINT XBY(0E000h)
```

Or, you may prefer a hexadecimal display:

```
PH0. XBY(0E000h)
```

To verify that you're reading all bits correctly, jumper each input in turn to ground and +5V and read the results. Open inputs are undefined and may read as high or low.

To test U14's outputs, use this BASIC-52 statement:

```
XBY(0E400h) =xx
```

where *xx* is the value you want to write to the chip. To set all bits, write 255 or 0FFh. To clear them, write 0. To verify that all bits are responding, connect a logic probe, voltmeter, or oscilloscope to each of the outputs of U14 in turn and verify that the bits respond correctly to your commands.

Input Examples

Figure 6-3 shows some inputs that you can interface to U12.

(A) TTL or CMOS logic outputs powered at 5 volts can directly drive U12's inputs.

(B) To translate lower voltages to 5-volt logic, use a 74HCT03 or similar open-drain NAND gate with a pullup resistor to 5 volts.

(C) To translate higher voltages to 5-volt logic, use a 74HC4050 buffer or 74HC4049 inverter, powered at 5 volts. These chips can safely accept inputs up to 15 volts.

(D) You can also detect the state (open or closed) of a toggle or slide switch at a port pin.

(E) An optocoupler is another way to interface different voltage levels, and it also electrically isolates the input from the microcontroller circuit.

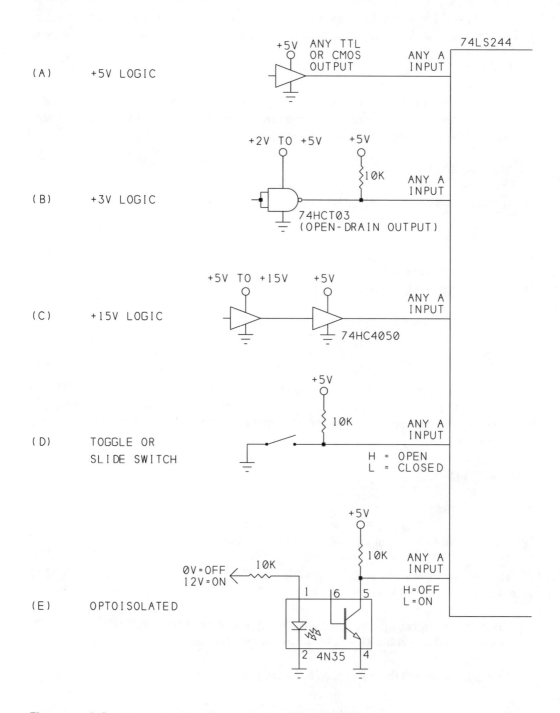

Figure **6-3.** Input interfaces for the 74LS244 buffer.

The Microcontroller Idea Book

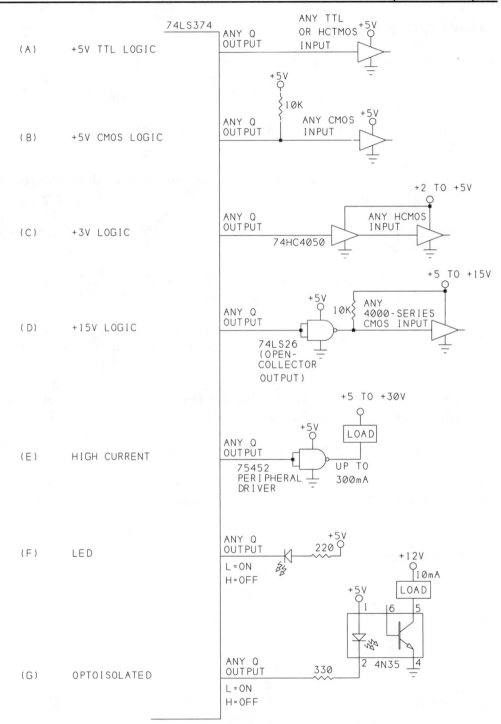

Figure 6-4. Output interfaces to the 73LS374 octal latch.

Output Examples

Figure 6-4 shows some basic outputs that you can connect to U14:

(A) Outputs can directly drive any TTL or HCTMOS logic input powered at 5 volts.

(B) To interface to 5-volt HCMOS or 4000-series CMOS devices, add a pull-up resistor to ensure that high outputs are greater than 3.5 volts.

(C) To translate an output to a lower voltage, use a 74HC4050 buffer or 74HC4049 inverter powered at the lower voltage.

(D) To translate an output to a higher voltage, use a 74LS26 NAND or similar high-voltage, open-collector gate, with a pullup resistor to the higher voltage.

(E) For high-current outputs, you can use Texas Instruments' 7545X series of peripheral drivers. The 75452 NAND gate can sink up to 300 milliamperes at 0.5V.

(F) U14 can directly drive an LED. Since the 74LS374 can sink more current than it can source, connect the LED so that it turns on when the output is low. With a 220-ohm current-limiting resistor, the LED's forward current is around 13 milliamperes.

(G) As with inputs, an optocoupler is another way to interface different voltages, and to electrically isolate an output from the microcontroller circuit.

Reading and Controlling Individual Bits

Unlike assembly language for the 8052, BASIC-52 has no logical operators for setting and clearing individual bits in a byte. But you can use the .AND. and .OR. operators to accomplish the same thing.

Listing   6-1.   Displays the value of each bit at input port E000h.

```
10    A=XBY(0E000H)
20    PRINT "Bit 0 = ",(A.AND.1)
30    PRINT "Bit 1 = ",(A.AND.2)/2
40    PRINT "Bit 2 = ",(A.AND.4)/4
50    PRINT "Bit 3 = ",(A.AND.8)/8
60    PRINT "Bit 4 = ",(A.AND.10H)/10H
70    PRINT "Bit 5 = ",(A.AND.20H)/20H
80    PRINT "Bit 6 = ",(A.AND.40H)/40H
90    PRINT "Bit 7 = ",(A.AND.80H)/80H
100   END
```

Listing 6-2.   Sets or clears a bit at output port E400h.

```
5     REM variable A contains the last data written to 0E400h
10    INPUT "Enter a bit to set or clear (0-7) :",X
20    INPUT "Enter 1 to set, 0 to clear :",Y
30    IF Y=1 THEN A=A.OR.2**X
40    IF Y=0 THEN A=A.AND.0FFH-2**X
50    XBY(0E400H)=A
60    END
```

Listing 6-1 is a program that reads the buffer and displays the value of each bit. The program is similar to Listing 3-1, which displays the bit values at Port 1.

Line 20 finds the logic state of bit 0 by logically ANDing the byte with a *mask byte* that is all 0's except for bit 0: 00000001. The result is 1 if bit 0 is 1, and 0 if bit 0 is 0. Lines 30-90 are similar, except that each time a different bit in the mask byte is 1. In each case, the program divides the result by 2 raised to the power of the bit number. Since (2**0 equals 1, line 20 leaves out this step.) Each PRINT statement shows the logic state of one of the bits.

At the output port, if you want to change just one bit in the byte, you have to know the current value of the byte. The simplest way to accomplish this is to save the last value you wrote. Or, you could wire an input buffer at the same address, with each input bit connecting to the corresponding output bit, and read the input when you need to know the current value.

Listing 6-2 prompts you for a bit to set and clear, then does so. It assumes that you've stored the current value of E400h in variable A.

To set a bit, line 30 logically ORs the current value with a mask byte that is all 0s except for the bit to be set. For example, to set bit 4, the mask byte is 0001 0000, or 10h, which leaves bits 0-3 and 5-7 unchanged, but forces bit 4 to be 1.

To clear a bit, line 40 logically ANDs the byte with a mask byte that is all 1s except for the bit or bits to be cleared. For example, to clear bit 3, the mask byte is 1111 0111, or F7h. The result is that bits 0-2 and 4-7 are unchanged, but bit 3 must be 0.

Line 50 writes the new byte to the port.

Table 6-1. Popular peripheral interface chips.

8253/4Programmable Interval Timer
Three independent 16-bit counters, 6 modes, up to 10 Mhz

8255 Programmable Peripheral Interface
Three 8-bit I/O pins, 3 modes, direct bit set/reset ability

8256 Multifunction Microprocessor Support Controller
Asynchronous serial interface, baud rate generator, five 8-bit timer/counters, two 8-bit I/O ports, 8-level interrupt controller, programmable system clock

8259 Programmable Interrupt Controller
Eight-level priority controller, programmable interrupt modes

8279 Programmable Keyboard/Display Interface
Scanned interfaces to 64-contact key matrix and 16-character display.

The 8255 Programmable Peripheral Interface

In addition to the inputs and outputs provided by U12 and U14, there are specialized peripheral-interface chips that you can add to your system. Table 6-1 lists several examples.

One of the most popular of these is the 8255 programmable peripheral interface, or PPI. Figure 6-5 shows the pinout, and Table 6-2 shows the pin functions. The chip adds 24 bits of I/O, plus the option to use special control and handshaking signals to communicate with peripherals.

Intel originally introduced the 8255 as a peripheral for its 8085 microprocessor, but it remains a popular chip for use with 8052s and other computer chips. Manufacturers of compatible chips include AMD, OKI, Toshiba, and NEC, which calls its chip the μPD71055.

If you use the 8255, you'll want a copy of its data sheet, which more fully explains its abilities and configuration options.

8255 Variants

You have a choice of the original NMOS 8255 or the CMOS 82C55. The CMOS version usually costs a little more, but has some advantages. First, it has lower power consumption, with supply currents of 10 milliamperes (10 microamperes in standby mode with CS=high), compared to 120 milliamperes for the 8255.

The 82C55 also has CMOS-compatible outputs, which means that they can drive either LSTTL or CMOS inputs. When driving CMOS inputs, the NMOS 8255's outputs should have pull-up resistors to ensure that high outputs are at least 3.5 volts.

A third advantage to the 82C55 is greater current-sourcing ability, which can be important if you want to directly drive a transistor or source more than a fraction of a milliampere. Intel's 82C55 can source 2.5 milliamperes at 3 volts, compared to just 0.4 milliamperes at 2.4 volts for the 8255. However, NEC's CMOS 71055 has the same current-sourcing ability as the NMOS 8255, so it depends on the manufacturer. All can sink 2.5 milliamperes at 0.45 volts. The 74LS374 latch (U14) has greater output drive ability than any of the 8255s.

Speed Ratings

The 8255 is also available with different speed ratings, including 3 Mhz and 5 Mhz. The 5-Mhz part is sometimes called the 8255-5. From the ratings, it may seem that the 8255 is too slow to interface to a 12-Mhz 8052-BASIC. But what does the speed rating actually refer to? Since the 8255 was developed for the 8085, I suspect that it refers to the maximum

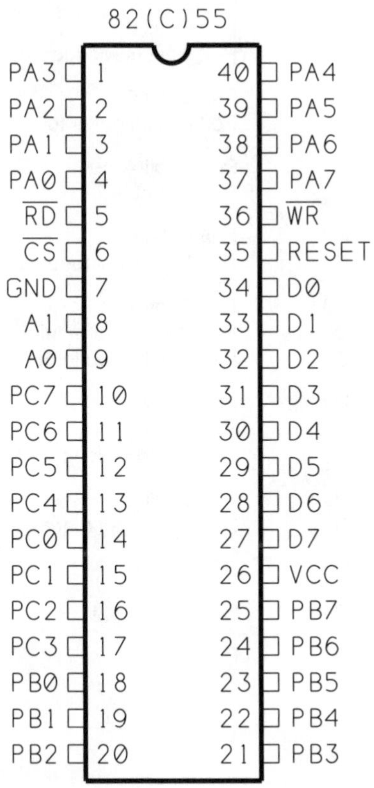

82(C)55

PA3	1	40 PA4
PA2	2	39 PA5
PA1	3	38 PA6
PA0	4	37 PA7
$\overline{RD}$	5	36 $\overline{WR}$
$\overline{CS}$	6	35 RESET
GND	7	34 D0
A1	8	33 D1
A0	9	32 D2
PC7	10	31 D3
PC6	11	30 D4
PC5	12	29 D5
PC4	13	28 D6
PC0	14	27 D7
PC1	15	26 VCC
PC2	16	25 PB7
PC3	17	24 PB6
PB0	18	23 PB5
PB1	19	22 PB4
PB2	20	21 PB3

Figure 6-5. Pinout of the 8255 Programmable Peripheral Interface.

Table 6-2. Pin functions for the 8255 Programmable Peripheral Interface.

Pin	Symbol	Input/Output	Function
1	PA3	I/O	Port A, bit 3
2	PA2	I/O	Port A, bit 2
3	PA1	I/O	Port A, bit 1
4	PA0	I/O	Port A, bit 0
5	$\overline{RD}$	I	Read
6	$\overline{CS}$	I	Chip select
7	GND	I	Signal ground
8	A1	I	Port select 1
9	A0	I	Port select 0
10	PC7 $\overline{OBFA}$	I/O O	Port C, bit 7 Port A output buffer full
11	PC6 $\overline{ACKA}$	I/O I	Port C, bit 6 Port A acknowledge
12	PC5 IBFA	I/O O	Port C, bit 5 Port A input buffer full
13	PC4 $\overline{STBA}$	I/O I	Port C, bit 4 Port A strobe
14	PC0 INTRB	I/O O	Port C, bit 0 Port B interrupt request
15	PC1 IBFB $\overline{OBFB}$	I/O O O	Port C, bit 1 Port B input buffer full Port B output buffer full
16	PC2 $\overline{STBB}$ $\overline{ACKB}$	I/O I I	Port C, bit 2 Port B strobe Port B acknowledge
17	PC3 INTRA	I/O O	Port C, bit 3 Port A interrupt request
18	PB0	I/O	Port B, bit 0
19	PB1	I/O	Port B, bit 1
20	PB2	I/O	Port B, bit 2

Pin	Symbol	Input/Output	Function
21	PB3	I/O	Port B, bit 3
22	PB4	I/O	Port B, bit 4
23	PB5	I/O	Port B, bit 5
24	PB6	I/O	Port B, bit 6
25	PB7	I/O	Port B, bit 7
26	Vcc	I	Power supply (+5V)
27	D7	I/O	Data bit 7
28	D6	I/O	Data bit 6
29	D5	I/O	Data bit 5
30	D4	I/O	Data bit 4
31	D3	I/O	Data bit 3
32	D2	I/O	Data bit 2
33	D1	I/O	Data bit 1
34	D0	I/O	Data bit 0
35	RESET	I	Reset ports to input; clear control register
36	$\overline{\text{WR}}$	I	Write
37	PA7	I/O	Port A, bit 7
38	PA6	I/O	Port A, bit 6
39	PA5	I/O	Port A, bit 5
40	PA4	I/O	Port A, bit 4

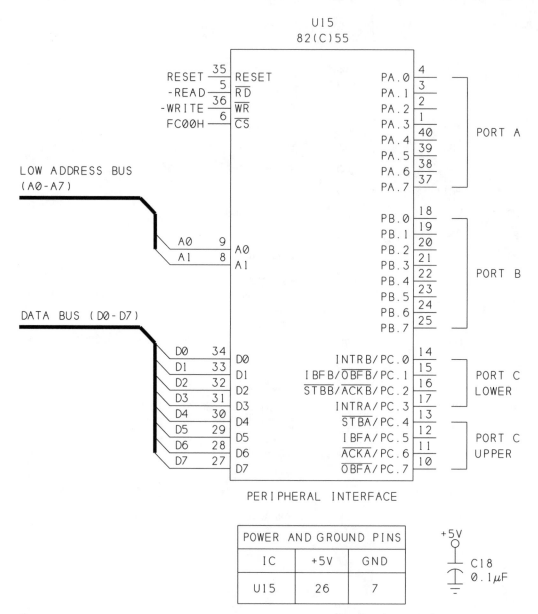

Figure 6-6. Connections for adding an 8255 Programmable Peripheral Interface.

crystal frequency of an 8085 interfaced to the 8255. Because the signal timings for an 8052 are very different, these ratings don't apply and you have to look at the timing diagrams to determine what will work. For use with the 8052-BASIC, use a 5-Mhz or faster 8255 if your crystal is 12 Mhz. Slower crystals can use the 3-Mhz or 5-Mhz versions.

An 8255 Interface

Figure 6-6 shows an 8255 (U15) accessed at FC00h in the 8052-BASIC system. Many of the pins connect directly to matching signals in the system: D0-D7 connect to the system's data bus, A0 and A1 connect to the lowest two address lines, and the $\overline{RD}$ and $\overline{WR}$ inputs connect to U2's matching outputs. $\overline{CS}$ connects to pin 7 of U11 (from Figure 6-2), which selects the chip at addresses from FC00h to FFFFh. U15 actually uses four of these addresses: FC00h through FC03h.

U15's RESET input is controlled by the same RESET signal at pin 9 of the 8052-BASIC. The three new I/O ports are Port A, Port B, and Port C. Address lines A0 and A1 select the port to be accessed, with Port A at FC00h, Port B at FC01h, and Port C at FC02h.

The port pins should connect only to voltages in the range -0.5V to +6.5V. According to Intel's data sheet, the 82C55 has bus-hold circuits that eliminate the need for external pull-ups on its CMOS inputs.

The Control Word

You configure the 8255 by writing a control word to a control register addressed at FC03h. The control word has two functions: selecting modes of operation, and setting and clearing port bits. When bit 7 of a byte written to the control register is 1, the control word selects modes of operation for each port and determines whether a port is input, output, or bidirectional. Many combinations of modes and I/O are available. When bit 7 of a byte written to the control register is 0, the control word sets and clears individual bits of Port C. The control word is write-only; you can't read it.

Mode Setting

Figure 6-7, from Intel's data sheet, describes the mode-set control word. The ports are divided into two groups. Group A consists of Port A plus bits 4-7 of Port C, and Group B consists of Port B plus bits 0-3 of Port C. This grouping enables Ports A and B to each use half of Port C for handshaking, or control, signals.

To set the mode, bit 7 of the control word must be 1. Bit 2 selects mode 0 or 1 for Group B, and bits 5 and 6 select mode 0, 1, or 2 for Group A. Bits 0, 1, 3, and 4 select whether a port is input or output, with each half of Port C selected independently.

The simplest mode is **Mode 0**, *Basic Input/Output*. The ports behave very much like the inputs and outputs at U12 and U14. Outputs are latched, so they change only when written to. The inputs are not latched, so the present, or current, value of the input is always read.

This statement configures all ports as inputs in mode 0:

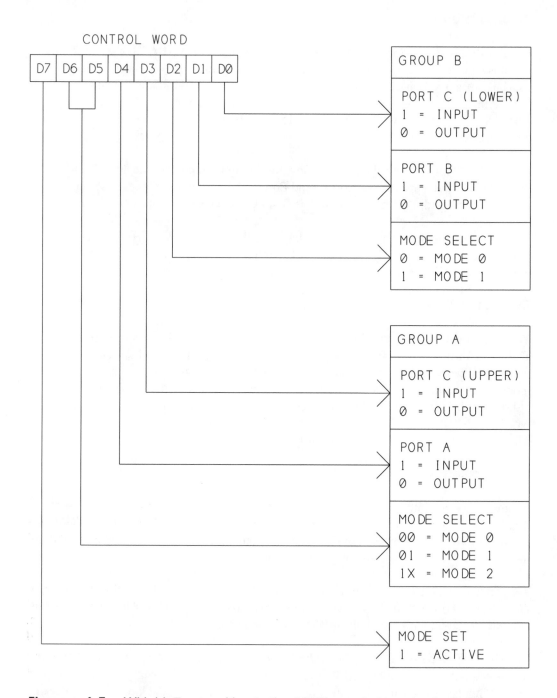

Figure 6-7. With bit 7 set, writing to the 8255's control word selects the modes of operation for each port.

```
XBY(0FC03h)=9BH
```

On reset, the 8255 uses this mode, until you tell it differently.

To read Port A, use

```
PRINT XBY(0FC00H)
```

or

```
PH0. XBY(0FC00H)
```

To read Port B or C, use the same statement, but with `0FC01H` or `0FC02H` to select the port you desire.

To configure all all bits as outputs in mode 0, use this statement:

```
XBY(0FC03h)=80H
```

Then, to write a value to Port A, use

```
XBY(0FC00h)=xx
```

where *xx* is the value to be written.

Use FC01h to write to Port B, and FC02h for Port C.

Combinations of Inputs and Outputs

Fourteen other combinations of inputs and outputs are possible by setting or clearing bits 0, 1, 3, and 4 in the control word as shown in Figure 6-7. To change the mode settings, determine which bits to set and clear for the configuration you want, convert the value to decimal or hexadecimal, and write the value to 0FC03h.

One handy feature of the 8255 is that you can read back the last value written to an output port. With the ports configured as outputs, you can use the same statements you use to read the input ports. At Port B or C, reading an output port gives the value in the output latch, which contains the last value you wrote to the port. Port A works a little differently. Instead of reading the output latch, you read the actual logic states on Port A's pins. This means that at Port A, if a bit is shorted to ground, you will read back a 0 for that bit, even if the last value written to it was a 1.

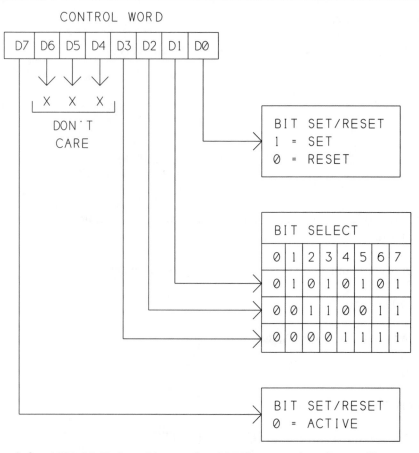

Figure 6-8. With bit 7=0, writing to the 8255's control register will set or clear individual bits in Port C.

Bit Control

Another useful feature of the 8255 is the ability to set and clear individual bits on Port C. You do so again by writing to the control register, as Figure 6-8 shows. Bit 7 must be 0. Bit 0 selects set or reset (clear) for the bit, and bits 1-3 select the bit to set or clear. For example, this BASIC-52 statement sets bit 7 of Port C:

```
XBY(0FC03h)=0Fh
```

To clear bit 7, use this statement:

```
XBY(0FC03h)=0Eh
```

The Microcontroller Idea Book

To set or clear a different bit, determine which bits to set and clear for the result you want, convert the value to decimal or hexadecimal, and write the value to 0FC03h.

Adding Handshaking

For many applications, Mode 0 is all you need. Modes 1 and 2 add handshaking, or control, signals for components that require them.

Mode 1 is *Strobed Input/Output*. It uses Port C for handshaking signals that let the 8052-BASIC and the peripheral tell each other whether or not they're ready to send or receive data, and to confirm that data has been received. Mode 1 also latches the input data, so you can use an external signal to latch data into U15, and save it until the 8052-BASIC has time to read it. In Mode 1, you can configure Ports A and B to be inputs, outputs, or one of each.

Each port has its own set of handshaking signals on Port C, as described in Table 6-2.

Input Control. For input ports, these are the added signals:

$\overline{\text{STB}}$ (strobe input) causes data to load into the 8255's input latch. In Mode 1, the 8052-BASIC can't read the data at U15's ports until $\overline{\text{STB}}$'s rising edge latches the data in. You can use an output of a clock or counter chip to latch data into U15 at timed intervals, or latch data when a user presses a key.

IBF (input buffer full output) goes high to indicate that the 8255 has loaded data in response to $\overline{\text{STB}}$. When the 8052-BASIC reads the data, the rising edge of $\overline{\text{RD}}$ brings IBF low again. You can use IBF to clear or reset the device that generated STB.

INTE (interrupt enable) is an internal signal that you must set to enable INTR, described next. For Group A, you set INTE by writing 1 to Port C, bit 4. For Group B, write 1 to Port C, bit 2. The BASIC-52 statement to set INTE for Port A is this:

```
XBY(0F03h)=9
```

For Port B, it's this:

```
XBY(0F03h)=5
```

Writing to these locations sets internal bits in U12. However, these write operations have no effect on the $\overline{\text{STB}}$ inputs, which share the same bit addresses at Port C.

INTR (interrupt request output) goes high when INTE is set and both $\overline{\text{STB}}$ and IBF are high, to signal that the 8255 has data waiting to be read. INTR can connect to an interrupt input on the 8052-BASIC (pin 13, for example), to cause it to jump to an interrupt routine that reads the newly latched data. The falling edge of $\overline{RD}$ brings INTR low again as the CPU reads the data.

Output Control. For output ports in Mode 1, there is a complementary set of signals:

$\overline{OBF}$ (output buffer full output) goes low to indicate that the CPU has written data to U12. $\overline{OBF}$ can signal a peripheral device (a display, for example) that it's time to read data that the 8255 is holding for it.

$\overline{ACK}$ (acknowledge input) strobes low to tell the 8255 that the peripheral device has read the data. $\overline{ACK}$'s falling edge brings $\overline{OBF}$ high.

INTE (interrupt enable) is set to enable INTR. Its function is similar to its function for Mode 1's inputs, except that Group A uses bit 6 of Port C, and Group B uses bit 2 of Port C.

INTR (interrupt request output) goes high to signal that a peripheral has accepted the data written to U12. The falling edge of $\overline{WR}$ brings INTR low, and INTR goes high again when $\overline{ACK}$ and $\overline{OBF}$ are both high and INTE is set, to signal that the peripheral has read and acknowledged the data.

For both inputs and outputs, connecting INTR is optional.

Mode 1 leaves two bits of Port C unused. If Port A is input, the unused bits are 6 and 7. If Port A is output, the bits are 4 and 5. You can use these as general-purpose inputs or outputs. Bit 3 of the mode-select control word selects an input or output function for both bits.

Mode 2 (*Strobed Bidirectional Bus I/O*) is similar to Mode 1, except that data can flow both ways. Mode 2 can use all of the control signals used by Mode 1's input and output modes, and is available only for Port A. With Port A in Mode 2, Port B can be Mode 0 or 1, input or output. The remaining three bits of Port C (0-2) can also be input or output, selected with the control word.

7

Switches and Keypads

Most microcontroller projects will include switches, a keypad, or some other way of allowing users to control the circuits inside. The control might involve flipping a switch begin an operation, pressing a key to to select an option, or entering a number for the program to use in its operations. For simple tasks, you can use toggle, slide, or pushbutton switches. Other projects might call for a keypad with an array of switches, with each labeled with a number, letter, or other description. This chapter shows how to add each of these to your system.

Simple Switches

Figure 7-1 shows two single-pole, single-throw toggle or slide switches connected to an input port. Each has contacts that connect when the switch is closed, and open when the switch is open.

In (A), when the switch is open, the pull-up resistor brings the input high. When the switch closes, the input connects to ground and reads low. Switch (B) is the reverse: when the switch is open, the pull-down resistor brings the input low. When the switch closes, it connects to +5V and reads high.

You can connect a switch to an unused bit on the 8052-BASIC's Port 1, to an input on an 8255 PPI, or to a input on a 74LS244 buffer. The 8052-BASIC has internal pullups that bring the inputs to +5V when they are not being driven by another source. So, if you connect

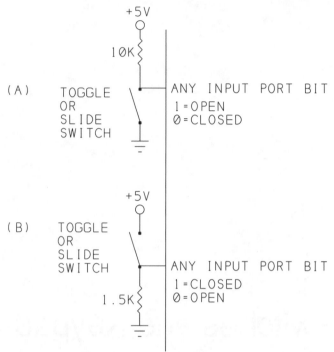

Figure **7-1.** You can detect the state of a toggle or slide switch at an input port.

switch (A) to one of these inputs, the external pull-up is optional. The pulldown resistor for switch (B) is 1.5K to ensure a valid logic low for LSTTL inputs. With an 8052-BASIC or CMOS input, you can use a 10K pulldown resistor.

If you want to offer a choice among several options, a rotary switch can do the job. Figure 7-2 shows an 8-position switch connected to an 8-bit input port.

Reading a Switch

To find the state of a switch, you read the byte at its address and use BASIC-52's logical operators to find the value of the bit of interest, just as you did when reading input ports in Chapter 6. For example, to find the logic state of a switch at bit 7 of an input port at E000h, use this statement:

```
A=(XBY(0E000H).AND.80H)/80H
```

Or, in more general terms, use this format:

```
A=(XBY(address).AND.2**bit)/2**bit
```

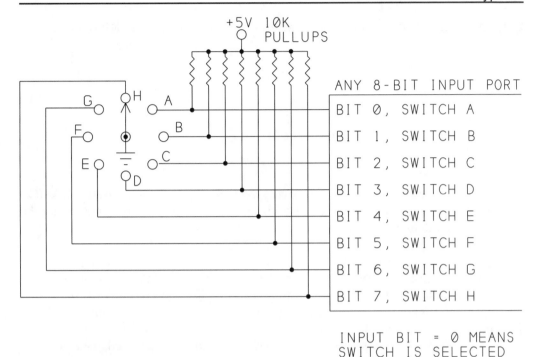

Figure 7-2. Use a rotary switch to allow users to choose from among several options.

where *address* is the location of the byte to be read in memory and *bit* is the bit number of the switch.

Detecting a Switch Press

Momentary switches are useful when you want to get the computer's attention. For example, you might have a program that normally displays the current temperature and time, but switches to a setup routine when you press a switch. On a normally open pushbutton (momentary) switch, the contacts close when you press the switch, then open as you release it. In a normally closed momentary switch, the contacts open when you press, and close on release.

Using Interrupts

An easy way to detect a switch press is with an external interrupt. The 8052-BASIC automatically detects the switch press and branches to an interrupt-handling subroutine.

Listing 7-1. Displays a message when external interrupt 1 is detected.

```
10    ONEX1 100
20    DO
30    WHILE 1=1
40    END
100   PRINT "Interrupt detected"
110   RETI
```

For a pushbutton-triggered interrupt, connect a switch like Figure 7-1's to the 8052-BASIC's $\overline{INT1}$ input at pin 13. Pin 13 will then be normally high. When you press and release the switch, pin 13 will briefly go low.

Listing 7-1 is a simple program that waits for interrupts and jumps to an interrupt-handling routine when it detects one, signified by pin 13 going low. Line 10 enables external interrupt 1 and specifies line 100 as the location to branch to when the 8052-BASIC detects an interrupt request at pin 13. Lines 20-30 are an endless loop that waits for an interrupt. Lines 100 and 110 are the interrupt-service routine. In this example the routine doesn't do very much; it just displays an on-screen message that the interrupt was detected, then returns to the main program loop.

Edge-detecting Interrupts

BASIC-52's TCON operator allows you to write to the 8052's special-function register TCON, which enables you to set up interrupt 1 as edge-detecting or level-detecting. The default after bootup or reset is edge-detecting, where interrupts are triggered by a falling edge at pin 13. If you want a rising edge to trigger an interrupt, you'll have to add an inverter at pin 13.

Edge-triggering is handy for detecting switch presses, because the interrupt routine executes only once, when the switch is first pressed, no matter how long you hold down the switch.

Switch debouncing. Even with edge-triggered interrupts, however, switch bounce can cause multiple interrupts to occur with a single switch press. Switch bounce occurs because manual presses of mechanical switches tend to be sloppy. When you press a switch, the contacts normally bounce open and closed several times before they close positively, and bounce again as you lift your finger and the contacts open.

The computer has to be able to tell the difference between a bounce and a genuine switch press. Otherwise, each time you press a switch, and again when you release it, the computer will detect several rapid switch presses. One way to handle switch bounce is to ignore keypresses that are less than a certain length, usually around 10-20 milliseconds, with the exact value depending on the switch characteristics. Ignoring switch bounce is called switch debouncing.

You can debounce a switch in hardware or software. Because BASIC-52 is slow, it has some debouncing built-in. When the 8052-BASIC detects an interrupt, it will ignore all interrupts that occur before it exits the interrupt-handling routine. So, if an interrupt-handling routine takes 20 milliseconds to execute, you probably don't need to add any debouncing circuits or delays. To add additional software debouncing, you can just add a delay loop like this to the interrupt routine:

```
105  FOR I=1 TO 100:NEXT I
```

Adjust the total count to the minimum value that prevents extra interrupts due to switch bounce.

Figure 7-3 shows a hardware debouncing circuit that uses a 74HC14 inverter with Schmitt-trigger input. The circuit generates a clean pulse when S1 is pressed, in spite of switch bounce that may occur.

Point B, the inverter's input, is normally low, and point C, the inverter's output, is normally high. When S1 is pressed, C1 discharges slowly through R2 and the switch contacts. If switch bounce occurs, the voltage at the inverter's input can't change rapidly enough to affect the logic state of the input. Only when the switch remains closed for around 50 milliseconds does point B go high enough to cause point C to switch low.

In a similar way, when the switch contacts open, C1 charges slowly though R1 and R2, and pin C goes high again only when the contacts have remained closed for around 50 milliseconds. The Schmitt-trigger input ensures that the output pulse is clean even if the input changes slowly.

As with software debouncing, you can experiment to find the minimum values that prevent unwanted interrupts due to switch bounce. The debounce time increases as you increase the values of C1 and R2.

Level-detecting interrupts

If you use a level-detecting interrupt instead of an edge-detecting one, the interrupt routine executes whenever there is a low logic level at pin 13. So, for example, if you press and hold the switch in the above example, the interrupt routine will execute again and again, until you release the switch.

Level-triggered interrupts can be useful if you have multiple interrupt sources. If each source generates an interrupt request by turning on an open-collector output, you can tie all of the

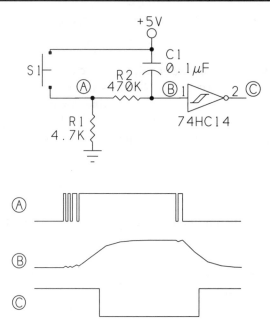

Figure 7-3. A hardware debouncing circuit, using a 74HC14 Schmitt-trigger inverter.

outputs together and the combined output will be low when any interrupt source is active. To enable the 8052-BASIC to identify the interrupt source, each source can also set a port bit. Latching the interrupt requests (with a flip-flop, for example) will ensure that no requests are missed. The 8052-BASIC can clear the latch by writing to another port bit when it identifies the source.

For level-triggered interrupts, use this statement to clear bit 2 of the TCON register:

```
TCON=(TCON=TCON.AND.0FBH)
```

To return to edge-triggered, use this statement to set bit 2 of TCON:

```
TCON=(TCON=TCON.OR.4)
```

Polling

When you don't want to use an interrupt, an alternate way to detect a keypress is by polling, which consists of having the program check periodically to see if the switch has been pressed. In a program that prompts for input and then waits for the user to press a key, you can poll continuously until you see a response. Listing 7-2 is an example that assumes that you have two normally open pushbuttons connected to pins 1 and 2 of the 8052-BASIC, as in Figure 7-4. This program stops reading the switch as soon as it detects a switch press, so debouncing

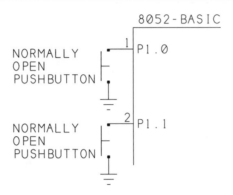

Figure 7-4. Two pushbuttons connected to port pins on the 8052-BASIC.

isn't required. When you use polling, you have to be sure to check the switch often enough so that you won't miss a switch press. For example, if you read the switch once per second, and you press the switch for just 100 milliseconds, you may not detect the switch press.

Latching a Switch Press

Another solution to switch detecting is to latch the switch press, as Figure 7-5 shows. In this circuit, a switch press causes the $\overline{Q}$ output of a 74HC74 flip-flop to go low and remain low until an external signal clears the flip-flop.

The circuit uses two port bits: one input (P1.0) and one output (P1.1). Both should be set high to begin. The flip-flop's $\overline{Q}$ output connects to P1.0, which the program can read at its leisure. If the bit is low, someone has pressed the switch. To reset the bit, the program brings P1.1, low, then high to clear the flip-flop and bring $\overline{Q}$ high again, ready to detect another switch press. You can use any free port bits in place of P1.0 and P1.1.

Listing 7-2. Monitors two switches and displays a message when one is pressed.

```
10    PORT1 = PORT1.OR.3 :REM set bits high to use as inputs
20    PRINT "Please press switch P1.0 or P1.1"
30    DO
40    A=PORT1.AND.3 :REM look at bits 0 and 1 only
50    UNTIL A<3
60    IF A=1 THEN S=1
70    IF A=2 THEN S=0
80    PRINT "switch P1.",S," pressed"
90    END
```

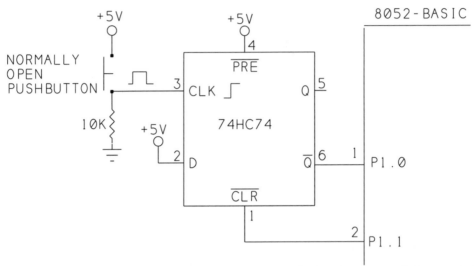

Figure 7-5. You can use a 74HC74 D-type flip-flop to latch a switch press. A second port pin clears the flip-flop.

Adding a Keypad

Keypads offer more options than individual switches or pushbuttons, but at lower cost and smaller size than a full keyboard. Examples of products that may use keypads include electronic locks, EPROM programmers, and many test instruments. On some devices, the keys have custom legends that describe the specific functions of the keys, but generic numbered keypads are also useful.

Keypad Types

Some keypads have attached cables that terminate in a connector. Others have headers to which you can solder wires or connect your own cable.

Different keypads follow different decoding schemes for detecting which key is pressed. Some have a dedicated connector pin for each key and a single common pin to which the pins connect when a key is pressed (Figure 7-6). You can wire and access these like a series of individual switches, with a pull-up or pull-down resistor at each switch.

Other keypads use matrix encoding, where the switch connections are arranged in a rectangular array. Figure 7-7 illustrates a typical hex keypad that uses matrix encoding. There are four rows (Y) and four columns (X) to which the switches connect. Each key corresponds to a hexadecimal digit.

The Microcontroller Idea Book

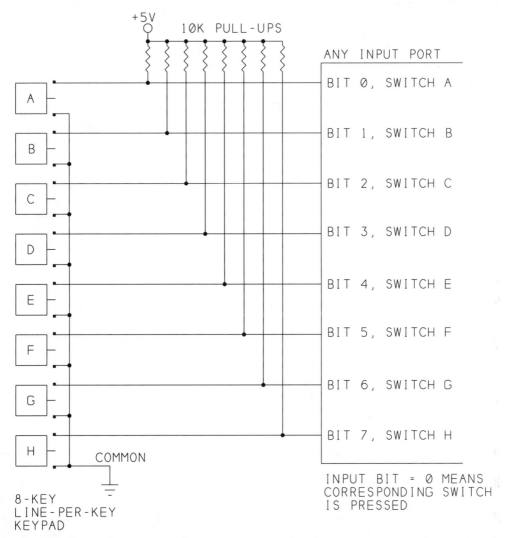

Figure 7-6. A line-per-key keypad is a series of momentary switches, with each switch having a common terminal.

In this keypad, each key acts as a normally open pushbutton whose contacts connect one row and one column when the key is pressed. In Figure 7-7, pressing key #1 connects Y1 and X1, pressing key #2 connects Y1 and X2, and so on down to key #F at Y4, X4. By determining which row and column are connected, you can detect which key has been pressed.

Matrix encoding saves on hardware, since each key doesn't require a dedicated signal line. With Figure 7-7's keypad, you can detect any of 16 key presses with 8 signal lines. Sixteen keys is a popular size for keypads, but larger and smaller sizes are also available. Telephone-

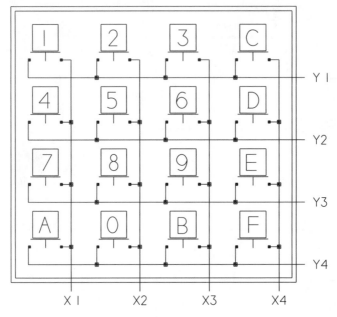

Figure   7-7.   A matrix-encoded keypad.

style keypads are widely available and versatile, since they have all 10 digits plus two keys (* and #) that you can designate for special functions.

Decoding Unfamiliar Keypads

You can find surplus keypads for a dollar or so each. These usually include no explanation of their pin connections, so it's up to you to figure out how to decode them.

To decode an unknown keypad, you need only an ohmmeter and a pencil and paper to record your findings. To determine the key connections one by one, begin by clipping an ohmmeter lead to one of the keypad's connector pins. Set the ohmmeter to a low scale, such as 200 ohms.

Press a key and hold it down while touching the other ohmmeter lead to each of the remaining keypad pins in turn. When the ohmmeter reads a few ohms or less, you've found the pins that correspond to the key in question. If you find no connection, move the first ohmmeter lead to a different pin and repeat the procedure. When you find the two pins that connect, write down their numbers and the key they correspond to.

Follow the same procedure for the other keys. As you progress, you may detect a pattern that makes it easier to guess which pins will correspond to each keypress. Some keypads don't seem to correspond to any obvious layout, however. When you know how the keypad decodes, you can wire the connections and write your programs to match.

The Microcontroller Idea Book

Custom Keypads

It's also possible to create a keypad with legends that match your application. One source for these in single or small quantities is Sil-Walker, which offers a variety of membrane keypads in kit form.

A kit consists of the basic keypad, optional colored pads, a faceplate, and a bezel. To create a custom keypad, you apply an optional colored pad and your own legend to each key. You can apply a legend using silk-screen printing, transfer-lettering, or a felt marker. You then press the faceplate over the keypad, and press the bezel onto the faceplate and its mounting surface to secure the keypad in its final location.

Using a Matrix-encoded Keypad

In a matrix-encoded keypad, the usual way to detect a keypress is with scanning circuits. In Figure 7-7's keypad, rows Y1-Y4 could be tied high through pull-up resistors. Columns X1-X4 could then be scanned, or brought low in sequence. As each column goes low, the logic level at each row is checked, repeating until a row goes low, indicating that a key is pressed.

The column and row that are low identify the key that is pressed. For example, if X3 and Y2 are low at the same time, key #6 has been pressed.

A Keypad Encoder

An easy way to interface a matrix-encoded keypad to the 8052-BASIC is to use National Semiconductor's 74C922 16-key encoder chip (or the 74C923, which handles up to 20 keys). Figure 7-8 shows the pinout, truth table, and waveforms of the 74C922. The chip is a member of the 74C family, which uses CMOS technology but TTL-type part designations (like the HCMOS family, but not high-speed). The chip is available from many parts sources.

The 74C922 has several useful features:

- It automatically translates each keypress into a 4-bit number (0000 to 1111). The chip has four inputs (Y1-Y4) and four outputs (X1-X4) that connect to the X and Y lines on a keypad, and 4 data outputs (A, B, C, D) that identify the key that was pressed. The 74C922 contains its own scanning circuits, including internal row pullups. All you need to add is a capacitor at the OSC input to set the scanning frequency, or you can use an external clock to control the scanning.

- Keypresses are signaled automatically by a Data Available (DA) output, which goes high when a key is pressed. You can tie DA to an interrupt or port pin on the 8052-BASIC.

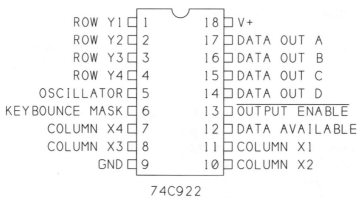

```
        ROW Y1 ▢ 1       18 ▢ V+
        ROW Y2 ▢ 2       17 ▢ DATA OUT A
        ROW Y3 ▢ 3       16 ▢ DATA OUT B
        ROW Y4 ▢ 4       15 ▢ DATA OUT C
     OSCILLATOR ▢ 5      14 ▢ DATA OUT D
 KEYBOUNCE MASK ▢ 6      13 ▢ OUTPUT ENABLE
      COLUMN X4 ▢ 7      12 ▢ DATA AVAILABLE
      COLUMN X3 ▢ 8      11 ▢ COLUMN X1
            GND ▢ 9      10 ▢ COLUMN X2
```

74C922
16-KEY ENCODER

	DATA OUTPUTS			
SWITCH	D	C	B	A
Y1, X1	0	0	0	0
Y1, X2	0	0	0	1
Y1, X3	0	0	1	0
Y1, X4	0	0	1	1
Y2, X1	0	1	0	0
Y2, X2	0	1	0	1
Y2, X3	0	1	1	0
Y2, X4	0	1	1	1
Y3, X1	1	0	0	0
Y3, X2	1	0	0	1
Y3, X3	1	0	1	0
Y3, X4	1	0	1	1
Y4, X1	1	1	0	0
Y4, X2	1	1	0	1
Y4, X3	1	1	1	0
Y4, X4	1	1	1	1

Figure 7-8. Pinout, truth table, and waveforms for the 74C922 16-key encoder for matrix-encoded keypads.

- Latches store the last keypress. When you lift your finger from a key, the keypad's X and Y lines no longer connect, and there is no way to know that a key was pressed. If the computer is busy doing something else while the key is pressed, it may not see the keypress at all. The 74C922 takes care of this by latching the data that corresponds to the last key pressed.

• A single capacitor adds debouncing. A capacitor connected at KBM (keybounce mask) sets the debounce period. With a 1-microfarad capacitor, the 74C922 ignores keypresses shorter than 10 milliseconds. Only when a keypress lasts longer than this does the chip latch the data and bring DA high. In a similar way, after the key opens, the debouncing must time out before a new key press is detected. The debounce period varies directly with capacitor size, with larger values increasing the time. By experimenting with different values, you can adjust the timing until all key bounces are ignored, yet no noticeable delay is required between key presses.

Adding a Keypad

Figure 7-9 shows the 74C922 connected to the 8052-BASIC system. The 74C922 interfaces the keypad to a 72LS244 buffer, as described in Chapter 6. The 74C922 is shown addressed at E000h, but you can use any available chip-select. Pin 13 of the 74C922 is tied low to permanently enable the data outputs. Keypresses are read by reading the buffer at E000h.

The keypad's X and Y lines connect to their corresponding pins on the 74C922. Data outputs A-D connect to D0-D3 on the 8052's data bus. DA, which signals when a key has been pressed, connects to $\overline{INT1}$ on the 8052-BASIC. If you want to use polling to detect keypresses, you can use any input port pin instead of $\overline{INT1}$.

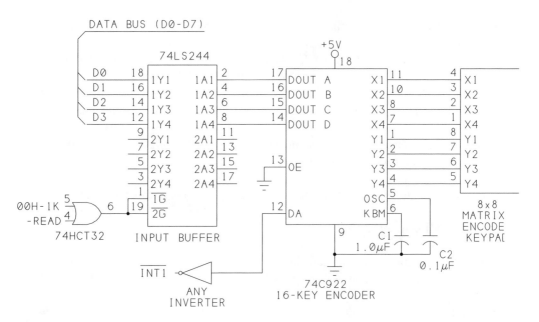

Figure 7-9. Circuits for adding a matrix-encoded keypad to an 8052-BASIC system.

A 1-microfarad capacitor at KBM and 0.1-microfarad capacitor at OSC give a keyboard debounce of 10 milliseconds and a scan rate of around 600 hertz. Larger values will increase the debounce time and decrease the scan rate. The 74C922's data sheet recommends choosing KBM's capacitor to be ten times the values of OSC's capacitor, so be sure to change both if you change either.

Testing the Keypad

Listing 7-3 tests Figure 4's circuit. The program waits for a key press and when one occurs, displays the value of the key on the host computer.

The following paragraphs explain the program in greater detail.

Lines 10-25 are a lookup table that translates the 74C922's A-D outputs into an ASCII code corresponding to the key pressed. The table is stored at locations 1FF0h-1FFFh in external RAM. The lookup table is arranged with the values of the 74C922's data outputs (0-Fh) in ascending order. Notice that the key legends (0-F) do not follow in order in the table, because the legends on the keypad correspond to the data outputs only at keys 4-6 and F.

Lines 30-50 are the main program loop. This does nothing except wait for an interrupt. When you press a key, the 74C922's DA output goes high. The falling edge at $\overline{INT1}$ then causes the program to jump to line 100.

Lines 100-110 read the value of the keypress at AD0-AD3 and, use the lookup table to translate the key press into an ASCII code. For example, if the key labeled "7" is pressed, Y3 goes low when X1 is scanned, and the 74C922's AD outputs identify the keypress as 1000 in binary, or 8 decimal, which the 8052 reads at E000h. Line 100 ANDs AD0-AD7 with 0Fh to clear bits 4-7, leaving 8, the value of the keypress. In line 110, 8 + 1FF0h = 1FF8h, and the value stored at 1FF8h in external memory is 55, which is the ASCII code for the numeral 7.

Line 120 causes the character matching the keypress to display on-screen. The program then returns to the main loop to wait for another key press.

If you have a keypad with different encoding, change the lookup table to match its layout.

Customizing the Interface

Listing 7-3 does little more than test the interface, but you can use the general idea in a specific project. You can also assign special functions to individual keys. In an EPROM programmer, these might be *Select device, Program, Verify,* and so on. If the functions aren't labeled on the keys, you can describe them in an on-screen menu: *Press 1 to select device; press 2 to program;* and so on. Then, when a keypress is detected, instead of just displaying the value of the key, your program would branch to a subroutine that corresponds to the

Listing 7-3. Test program for Figure 7-9's circuits.

```
10   XBY(1F00H)=49  :   REM 1
11   XBY(1F01H)=50  :   REM 2
12   XBY(1F02H)=51  :   REM 3
13   XBY(1F03H)=67  :   REM C
14   XBY(1F04H)=52  :   REM 4
15   XBY(1F05H)=53  :   REM 5
16   XBY(1F06H)=54  :   REM 6
17   XBY(1F07H)=68  :   REM D
18   XBY(1F08H)=55  :   REM 7
19   XBY(1F09H)=56  :   REM 8
20   XBY(1F0AH)=57  :   REM 9
21   XBY(1F0BH)=69  :   REM E
22   XBY(1F0CH)=65  :   REM A
23   XBY(1F0DH)=48  :   REM 0
24   XBY(1F0EH)=66  :   REM B
25   XBY(1F0FH)=70  :   REM F
30   DO
40   ONEX1 100
50   WHILE 1=1
60   END
100  KEY=XBY(0E000H).AND.0FH
110  DAT=XBY(1F00H+KEY)
120  PRINT CHR(DAT)
130  RETI
```

requested function. Chapter 8 describes how to add a small display to a system, so you don't have to use the host computer's display for the menu.

For some projects, you may want to use the numeric values of the keys directly, rather than interpreting them as ASCII codes. In this case, you'll need to revise the lookup table, or create a second table that matches the numeric values of the key legends with their data outputs. For example, a data output of 0 would correspond to 1, instead of 49 (the ASCII code for 1). Again, you usually can't use the keypad encoder's data outputs directly because they don't correspond to the values printed on the keys.

If an application requires that users enter multi-digit numbers on the keypad, your program will have to translate the individual digits into a single value. Listing 7-4 is a program that waits for the user to enter a 4-digit hex address, then displays the data stored at that address in external RAM.

Listing 7-4. Reads the data stored a a 4-digit address entered by the user on a keypad.

```
1     REM lookup table stores the numeric value of each key
10    XBY(1F00H)=1 :   REM 1
11    XBY(1F01H)=2 :   REM 2
12    XBY(1F02H)=3 :   REM 3
13    XBY(1F03H)=0CH :REM C
14    XBY(1F04H)=4 :   REM 4
15    XBY(1F05H)=5 :   REM 5
16    XBY(1F06H)=6 :   REM 6
17    XBY(1F07H)=0DH :REM D
18    XBY(1F08H)=7 :   REM 7
19    XBY(1F09H)=8 :   REM 8
20    XBY(1F0AH)=9 :   REM 9
21    XBY(1F0BH)=0EH :REM E
22    XBY(1F0CH)=0AH :REM A
23    XBY(1F0DH)=0 :   REM 0
24    XBY(1F0EH)=0BH :REM B
25    XBY(1F0FH)=0FH :REM F
30    A=0
40    COUNT=3
50    PRINT "Please enter a 4-digit hex address to read: "
60    DO
70    ONEX1 100
80    WHILE 1=1
90    END
100   KEY=XBY(0E000H).AND.0FH: REM read the key
110   DAT=XBY(1F00H+KEY): REM find its value
120   A=A+(DAT*(16**COUNT)): REM add to the total
130   COUNT=COUNT-1: REM keep track of # of digits read
140   PH0. DAT,
150   IF COUNT=-1 THEN  GOSUB 200: wait for 4 digits
160   RETI
200   PRINT  :  PH0. XBY(A)," is stored at address ",A
210   PRINT "Please enter another 4-digit address to read: "
220   COUNT=3
230   A=0
240   RETI
```

8

Displays

In addition to switches and keypads for user input, most projects also include a display to let users know what's going on inside. The type of display depends on the kinds of information you want to show. For simple status indicators, discrete LEDs will do the job. For numbers, you can use 7-segment displays. And if you need to display text or other symbols in addition to numbers, character-based LCD modules are a good solution. This chapter will show how to use each of these in an 8052-BASIC system.

Using LEDs

Discrete, or individual LEDs (light-emitting diodes) are an easy way to indicate status, such as *On, Ready, Mode selected,* and so on. They are colorful, eye-catching, and easy to interface to 5-volt logic. Available colors now include blue as well as red, green, and yellow. Some individual LED packages can emit red, green, or amber light, depending on the voltages applied.

Like other diodes, current passes through an LED in one direction only. When a positive voltage is applied to the anode, current flows and electrons migrate across an energy gap in the LED, causing it to emit light. The size of the energy gap determines the voltage drop across the LED, as well as the color of light emitted. A tinted case can also vary the color.

Table 8-1. The forward voltage drop across an LED varies with the color.

LED color	typical forward voltage (volts)
Red	1.6
Green	2.0
Yellow	2.0
Blue	3.2

Table 8-1 shows typical forward voltages for different colors of LEDs. Typical LED operating currents are between 10 and 20 milliamperes. For a bright display with low power consumption, look for types labeled high efficiency.

One disadvantage to LEDs is that the light from most is hard to detect in bright light, especially outdoors. A tinted, transparent sheet of plastic mounted over the display can make it more visible in bright light. For red LEDs, transparent red or purple works well.

For best visibility over a wide area, look for LEDs with a wide viewing angle. This means that the LED emits light in a wide cone, so you don't need to view it straight-on.

LED Interfaces

Figure 8-1 shows examples of LED interfaces to output ports in an 8052-BASIC system. The outputs of the 80(C)52 and 82(C)55 can't provide enough current to drive an LED directly. But you can drive an LED with a 74LS374 or 74HC374 latch (A, B), or with a buffer or inverter driven by any output port (C, D).

With LSTTL drivers, you should design your circuit so that a low output turns on the LED, since LSTTL outputs can sink more current than they can source. With HCMOS or HCTMOS outputs, either a high or low output can turn on the LED.

Use a series resistor to limit the current through the LED. For a brighter display, decrease the value of the resistor. Most LEDs can handle 20 milliamperes of continuous current. You can measure the current directly by connecting an ammeter in series with the LED and resistor. Or, you can calculate the current by measuring the the voltage across the series resistor and dividing it by the resistor's value. For example, 2.25V/150 ohms = 0.015 amperes, or 15 milliamperes.

Both LSTTL and HCMOS devices are capable of 20-milliampere output currents. At these higher currents, the output voltage isn't specified, but should be enough to light an LED.

To turn on an LED at a port, write a 1 or 0, as appropriate, to the bit that controls it, as described in Chapter 6. Listing 8-1 assumes that you have eight LEDs connected to the

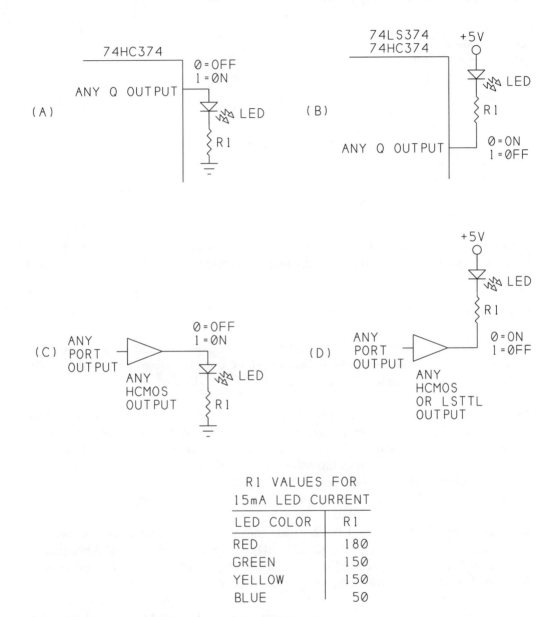

Figure 8-1. LED interfaces to output ports. Use an HCMOS output if you want a high output to turn on the LED. Use either HCMOS or LSTTL if you want a low output to turn on the LED.

Listing   8-1.   Controls eight LEDs at an output port.

```
10    A=0E000H: REM address of LEDs
20    L=0FFH: REM initial control value for LEDs
20    XBY(A)=L: REM turn off all LEDs
30    DO
40    INPUT "Select an LED (0-7): ",B
50    INPUT "Turn on or off (0=off, 1=on)? ",C
60    IF C=0 THEN L=L.AND.(0FFH-2**B)
70    IF C=1 THEN L=L.OR.2**B
90    XBY(A)=L
80    WHILE 1=1
90    END
```

outputs of a 74LS374 addressed at E000h. The LEDs are connected as in Figure 8-1B , with logic-low outputs turning on the LEDs. Listing 8-1 tests the circuit by allowing you to turn individual LEDs on and off.

Bi-color LEDs

Bi-color LEDs have both a red and a green LED inside a single package. By turning on one, both, or neither, you can use a single indicator to show as many as four states. Some bicolor LEDs have two leads, while others have three. Figure 8-2 illustrates.

In the 3-lead, or common-cathode type, the cathodes of both LEDs connect internally (A). To turn on an LED, you ground the cathodes through a current-limiting resistor and apply power to the anode of the desired LED. When both LEDs are powered, you get an amber light. Removing power from both turns the LED off, giving a total of four states that the device can display. Instead of the one current-limiting resistor shown, you can connect a resistor to each anode, to set the current through each LED individually.

In a 2-lead, or parallel-connected, bicolor LED, the anode of each LED connects internally to the other's cathode (B). To turn on the red LED, you apply +5V to terminal A and ground terminal B. To turn on the green LED, you do the reverse: terminal A is ground, and terminal B is +5V. With this type, you can't turn on both LEDs at once.

With either type, by adding an inverter, you can use a single output to control both LEDs (C, D).

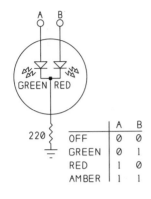

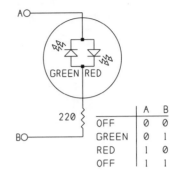

(A) COMMON-CATHODE TYPE, 2-LINE CONTROL

(B) PARALLEL CONNECT TYPE, 2-LINE CONTROL

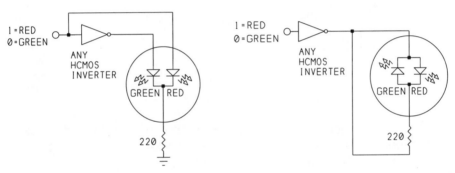

(C) COMMON-CATHODE TYPE, 1-LINE CONTROL

(D) PARALLEL CONNECT TYPE, 1-LINE CONTROL

Figure 8-2. Ways to connect bicolor LEDs .

7-segment Displays

If you want to display numbers, 7-segment displays will do the job. Each digit on the display contains seven segments. Numerals are displayed by turning on different combinations of segments, as Figure 8-3 shows. Decoder chips make it easy to operate one or more displays with a minimum of programming and added components. Seven-segment displays are available as LEDs, where each segment is a light-emitting diode, and as LCDs, where each segment is a liquid-crystal display. We'll look at the LED type first.

7-segment LEDs

A 7-segment LED contains seven individual LEDs arranged in the pattern shown in Figure 8-3. Sometimes there is also a decimal point (or two, one on each side). There are also special leading-digit modules that display only a 1 and a plus-or-minus symbol.

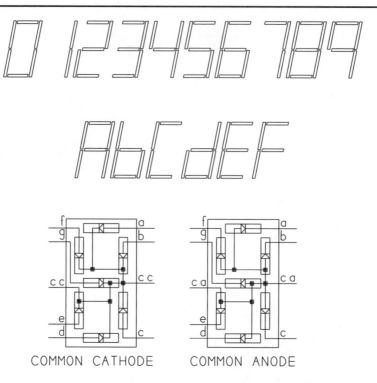

Figure 8-3. A 7-segment display can show numbers from 0 to 9, plus hex digits A-F. In a common-cathode LED display, all of the cathodes connect together, while in a common-anode display, all of the anodes connect.

The displays come in two types: common-anode or common-cathode. In a common-anode display, the anodes of each segment connect internally. To use the display, you connect the anodes to a voltage source and turn on individual segments by grounding them through a current-limiting resistor. A common-cathode display is the opposite: the cathodes connect internally, so you ground the cathodes and apply voltages through current-limiting resistors at the segments you want to light.

Deciphering pinouts

Unfortunately, there isn't much standardization for pinouts of 7-segment displays. If you don't know the pinout for a display, you can find it by experimenting. You'll need a 330-ohm resistor and a 5-volt supply.

Sometimes you'll find *CC* or *CA* stamped on the package to indicate common cathode or common anode. If even this information is lacking, begin by connecting one lead of the

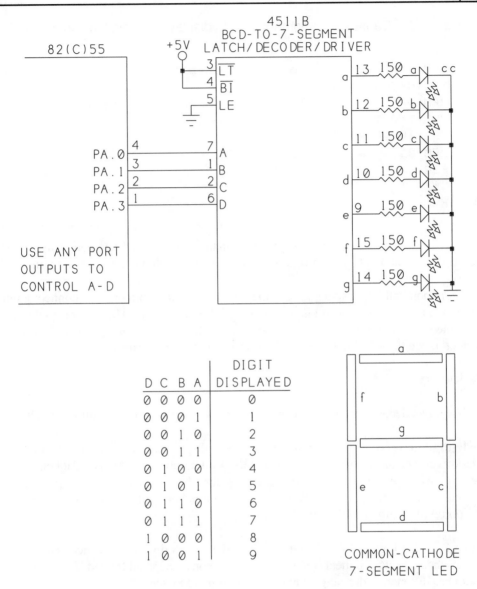

Figure 8-4. Four output port pins can control a 7-segment LED.

resistor to ground on your power supply. Clip the resistor's other end to one of the LED's pins. Use a test lead to touch the power supply's +5V output to each of the other pins in turn.

If only one or two connections cause a segment to light, you have a common-anode display, and the common anode is the pin or pins that connect to +5V when the segment lights. (There

Listing   8-2.   Causes a 7-segment LED to display each digit in sequence.

```
10    REM configure all ports as outputs
20    XBY(0FC03H)=80H
30    REM write each value to the display in sequence
40    FOR I=0 TO 9
50    XBY (0FC00H)=I
60    REM delay after each write
70    FOR J=1 TO 500:NEXT J
80    NEXT I
90    END
```

may be two common-anode pins.) To find the pin that controls each segment, leave the +5V lead on a common-anode pin, and connect the resistor to each pin in turn, noting the results.

For a common-cathode display, to find the common-cathode pin or pins, connect a pin to +5V, and touch the others to ground through the 330-ohm resistor. The pin or pins that cause the segment to light are the common-cathode connections. To find the pin that controls each segment, move the +5V lead to each pin in turn, and note the results.

Interfacing

For 7-segment decoder/drivers, you can choose from single-digit and multi-digit chips.

Single-digit driver. Figure 8-4 shows a 7-segment display controlled by a 4511B latch/decoder/driver. The display shows the value of the 4-bit number at the 4511's data inputs A-D. The 4511 will drive common-cathode displays directly. Common-anode displays require inverters at the segment outputs. You can use any output port bits to control the display. An 8-bit port will control a 2-digit display.

Listing 8-2 tests Figure 8-4's circuits by displaying each digit in sequence. The program assumes that a display connects to bits 0-3 of Port A on an 8255 addressed at FC00h. If your system has different addressing, change the program to match.

Multi-digit driver. If you want to display more than a couple of digits, there are specialized chips that will drive and control multiple-digit displays. One example from Intersil (now part of Harris Semiconductor) is the ICM7218D multiplexed display driver, which can control up to 8 common-cathode digits. Figure 8-5 illustrates. For common-anode displays, use the ICM7218C.

The segments of all eight displays connect to the 7218D's segment-driver outputs (*a-g, dp*). Each display's common cathode connects to one of eight DIGIT outputs. An internal oscillator

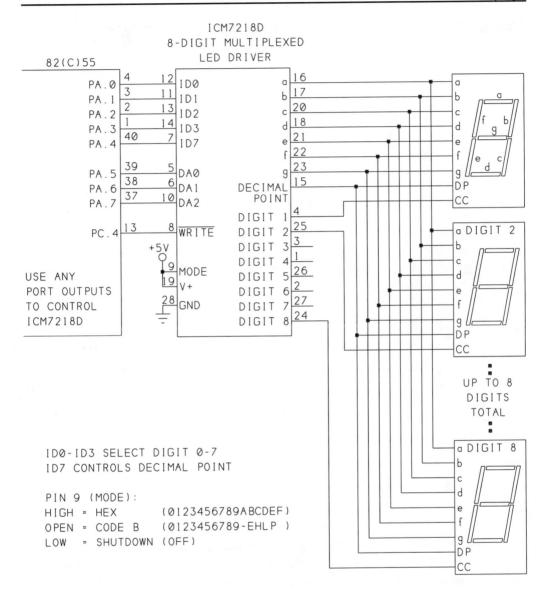

Figure 8-5. The ICM7218D can control up to eight 7-segment LEDs.

turns on each of the digits in sequence. This means that each of the displays is on just 1/8 of the time.

The 7218D drives each segment at 20 milliamperes peak current, for an average current of just 2.5 milliamperes. The chip takes advantage of the fact that LEDs can withstand relatively high pulsed currents, and that a pulsed LED actually appears brighter than a constantly-driven LED with the same average current. Twenty milliamperes is well within the allowed

Listing 8-3. Controls eight 7-segment LEDs with ICM7218 driver.

```
10    REM address of 8255 Port A
20    A=0FC00H
30    REM address of 8255 control word
40    X=A+3
50    REM set 8255 for all outputs
60    XBY(X)=80H
70    REM set WR
80    XBY(X)=9
90    REM write to each digit
100   FOR M=0 TO 7
110   REM step through all numbers at each digit
120   FOR I=0 TO 8
130   REM add 10h to turn off decimal point
140   D=I+10H+M*20H
150   GOSUB 500
160   REM delay to display each digit
170   K=500
180   FOR J=1 TO K :  NEXT J
190   NEXT I
200   NEXT M
210   END

490   REM write data to port A and toggle W (PC.4)
500   XBY(A)=D
510   XBY(X)=8H
520   XBY(X)=9
530   RETURN
```

range for peak current for most LEDs, and the 2.5-milliampere average current causes the displays to appear brighter than you might expect. With all digits displaying 8's, this circuit draws 140 milliamperes, so be sure your power supply can handle it.

To write a value to the display, you select the digit with data-address inputs DA0-DA2, write the data to inputs ID0-ID7, and strobe $\overline{\text{WRITE}}$ low. The $\overline{\text{WRITE}}$ pulse must be at least 400 nanoseconds wide, and ID0-ID7 must remain valid for at least 125 nanoseconds after $\overline{\text{WRITE}}$ goes high. BASIC-52 is slow enough to meet these requirements, using XBY statements to write to the port that controls the 7218C.

Pin 9 allows you to select one of three modes, which determine what digits the displays show. In Code B mode, you can display the message *HELP*.

In Figure 8-5's circuit, an 82(C)55 controls the 7218C. For complete control, the circuit requires 10 outputs. Bits 0-4 of Port A determine the data to be written, including a decimal point controlled by ID7. If you don't need the decimal point, tie pin 7 of the 7218C low. Bits 5-7 of Port A select the digit to write to. If you have four or fewer displays, you can tie one or more of these lines low and free up another port bit.

Port C, bit 4 controls $\overline{\text{WRITE}}$. The display-mode input is tied high to select hexadecimal mode. If you instead tie pin 9 to a port bit, you can turn off the display by bringing the bit low. To allow selecting different modes, connect an additional output bit to the 7218D's MODE input.

Listing 8-3 uses the 7218D to display data, using Figure 8-5's circuit.

7-segment LCDs

An alternative to LEDs is liquid-crystal displays (LCDs). Unlike LEDs, which consume several milliamperes per segment, LCDs are voltage-controlled and require very little operating current.

Compared to LEDs, LCDs are easy to read in bright light. However, because LCDs don't emit light as LEDs do, but merely absorb or transmit it, you need additional lighting to see them in the dark. LCDs also tend to have narrower viewing angles than LEDs. So, whether to use LEDs or LCDs may depend on where and how you will use the display.

Most 7-segment LCD modules contain two or more digits. Like the LEDs, a 7-segment LCD creates a numeral by turning on selected segments.

Each LCD segment contains a thin layer of liquid crystal between two layers of glass. Liquid crystals are organic compounds that act as electrically controlled light polarizers. In a positive-image display (the most common type), applying a voltage across a segment causes the segment to appear dark, or opaque, while removing the voltage causes the segment to appear light-colored, or transparent. Negative-image displays are opaque when not powered, and transparent when powered. By applying and removing voltages across individual segments, you can display numeric, alphabetic, and other characters.

Applying a constant voltage to an LCD segment will eventually destroy it. Instead, you must drive the segment with an alternating voltage, typically a square wave that alternately applies +5 and -5V across the segment.

Single-digit driver. Figure 8-6 shows an LCD module driven by a 4543B LCD latch/decoder/driver. The 4543 is a lot like the 4511 LED driver, with the addition of a phase input that accepts a square wave for driving the segments. A typical drive frequency is around 100 Hertz. A 555 timer provides the phase input, or you can use any oscillator output.

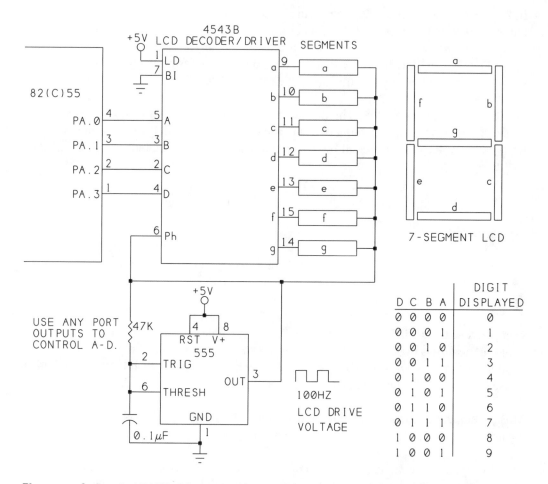

Figure 8-6. A 4543B driver can control a 7-segment LCD. A 555 timer controls the drive voltage.

As in Figure 8-4, you control the display by writing to inputs A-D. If the display contains other types of segments, such as ± or a leading *1*, you can control these as well. For example, for a leading 1, connect digit 1's two segments to pins 10 and 11 on the 4543. When you write 1 to the data inputs, the appropriate segments will light.

Multi-digit driver. As with the LEDs, there are driver chips for multi-digit LCD modules. Figure 8-7 shows Telcom Semiconductor's (formerly Teldyne) TC7211A, which will drive four 7-segment LCDs, and includes an on-chip oscillator and backplane driver.

To display a number using Figure 8-7's circuit, follow these steps:

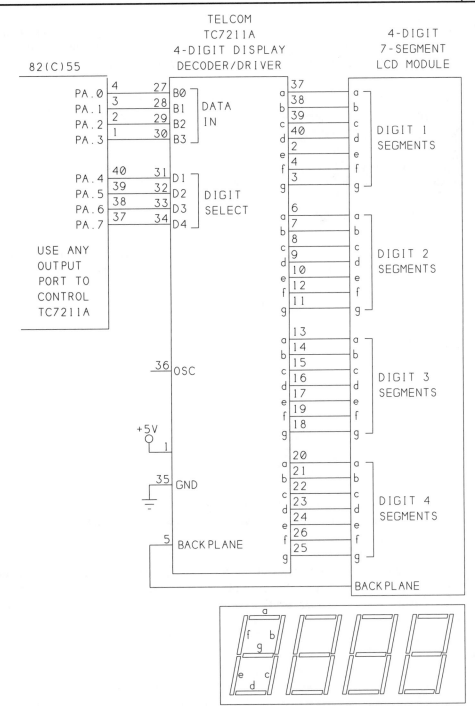

Figure 8-7. With the TC7211A decoder/driver, you can control a 4-digit display with 8 port bits.

(1) Write the number you want to display to data inputs B0-B3, and bring a digit-select input (D1-D4) high to select the digit to write to. You can use the same XBY statement to do both. For example, to write 7 to digit 2, use this statement: XBY (*port address*) =27H.

(2) With the data still on B0-B3, bring the digit-select input low. The data must remain on B0-B3 for at least 200 nanoseconds after the digit-select input goes low. For step 1's example, you would write XBY (*port address*) =07H.

Follow the same procedure for each digit, and the TC7211 will continue to drive the appropriate segments on all four digits. To change the value of a digit, repeat steps 1 and 2.

Displaying Messages

Sometimes a device has to display more complex messages than simple LEDs and 7-segment displays can handle. For example, you might want to display messages like these:

```
Please enter your access code.

Select function:
        Read
        Program
        Verify
        Exit

Wind is from the west at 12 mph

Total cost = $5.82
```

With BASIC-52, you can use the host computer's display, but this is no help if you want to create a stand-alone project that doesn't require a personal computer. In these situations, a character-based dot-matrix LCD module is a solution.

These modules can display messages made up of numbers, characters of the alphabet, and other symbols (for math functions, for example, or even symbols you design yourself). Figure 8-8 illustrates. Devices that use this type of display include laser printers and test equipment.

The Controller Chip

A special controller chip makes it easier to use LCD modules than you might think. Hitachi's HD44780 LCD controller is an 80-lead surface-mount chip that takes care of the details of controlling the individual dots, or segments, on the display. For as low as $10, you can find complete modules that contain an LCD panel and small circuit board containing the

Figure 8-8. With a character-based dot-matrix LCD module, you can display messages as well as numbers.

controller chip. Applying power, reading, and writing to the module require just 14 connections, or fewer, depending on your configuration. The HD44780 can control displays of up to 80 characters.

Learning to program the HD44780 does take some time and experimenting, but the result is a useful and flexible display. Once you've had some practice, future projects using the displays are simpler, and you can reuse or adapt portions of your programs in other projects.

Many LCD modules use the HD44780 or a compatible controller (the OKI M6222 is an example). If a module uses the same 14-line interface discussed below, chances are it's compatible with the HD44780.

About the Modules

The character-based LCD modules are available from many companies, including Philips, Optrex, and Densitron. The surplus market often has good deals. Complete technical information on the controller and displays is available from Hitachi and the display manufacturers, and from some distributors and catalogs.

The display of one of these modules contains one or more rows of character positions. Each character position consists of a matrix that is typically five segments, or dots, wide and eight segments tall. (The HD44780 can also control matrices that are 11 segments tall, for better display of characters with descenders, like *g, p,* and *q.*)

The module forms characters by turning on the appropriate segments in a character position. For example, to display an *L*, the module turns on one vertical column and one horizontal row of segments. For most characters, the bottom row is reserved for displaying a cursor, which leaves 35 segments to form the character.

Displays are available in several sizes. Popular sizes are 1 x 16 (1 line of 16 characters), 2 x 16, and 2 x 20. Displays larger than 80 characters require supplemental driver chips along with the HD44780, but the displays can use the same interface.

Table 8-1 summarizes the signals in the 14-line interface.

Power Supplies and Backlights

The power supply (pin 2) is a simple +5V DC. The modules contain their own oscillators to drive the LCD segments. Typical power consumption for an entire module is just a couple of milliamperes. A contrast input (pin 3) allows you to adjust for best viewing under varying light conditions, viewing angles, and temperatures.

Some LCD modules use backlighting to allow viewing in dim light. A module may be reflective (which does not use backlighting), transmissive (which must use backlighting), or transflective (which may use backlighting or not). With a transflective display, you can add a switch to enable users to turn the backlighting on or off as desired.

One popular type of backlight is an electroluminescence (EL) panel behind the LCD segments. An EL panel emits a diffuse light that provides a bright background for the LCDs. Electroluminescent backlighting requires first of all, a module that contains an EL panel, and second, an inverter module to provide the high-voltage alternating signal required to power the panel. The inverters typically convert +5 volts to around 100 volts RMS at 400 Hertz. Inverters are usually offered along with the modules that use them, so you shouldn't have to construct your own. The backlighting requires several milliamperes.

Incandescent and LED backlights are other options for illuminating LCDs.

Inside the Display Controller

The HD44780 LCD controller is actually a small, specialized microcontroller in itself. It contains its own RAM and ROM, and executes the 11 instructions shown in Table 8-2. The instructions perform tasks like clearing the display, writing a character to the display, selecting a position on the display, and reading information from the display. To use the controller, you need to be familiar with what it contains and the instructions that control it.

Table 8-1. LCD modules containing the HD44780 controller often use this 14-line interface.

Pin	Symbol	Input/Output	Function
1	VSS	Input	Signal Ground
2	VDD	Input	Supply Voltage (+5V)
3	V0	Input	Contrast adjust
4	RS	Input	Register select (1=data; 0=instruction register, busy flag/address counter)
5	R/$\overline{W}$	Input	Read (1)/write (0) select
6	E	Input	Enable
7	D0	I/O	Data bit 0
8	D1	I/O	Data bit 1
9	D2	I/O	Data bit 2
10	D3	I/O	Data bit 3
11	D4	I/O	Data bit 4
12	D5	I/O	Data bit 5
13	D6	I/O	Data bit 6
14	D7	I/O	Data bit 7

Memory Areas

The HD44780's on-chip memory includes a CG (character-generator) ROM, CG RAM, DD (display data) RAM, an instruction register, and a data register.

The **CG ROM** stores the segment patterns for generating 192 different characters, including the Roman (English) alphabet in upper and lower case, numbers, some math and other special symbols, and Japanese kana characters. These are fixed in ROM and can't be altered.

The **CG RAM** stores segment patterns for up to 16 user-designed characters such as logos, special symbols, or other simple graphics characters that you design on the 5 X 8 matrix. To create a custom character, you write a series of 5-bit words to the CG RAM. Each word represents the segment pattern for one row in the desired character. The patterns stored in CG RAM disappear on powering down, so you must reload them on each time you power up.

Table 8-2. Instruction summary for the HD 44780 LCD controller.

Instruction	RS	R/W	D7	D6	D5	D4	D3	D2	D1	D0	Function	Execution time (max)
Display clear	0	0	0	0	0	0	0	0	0	1	Clear display. Reset display from shift. Set DD RAM=0	1.64 msec
Display/cursor home	0	0	0	0	0	0	0	0	1	X	Shift=0. DD RAM=0	1.64 msec
Entry mode set	0	0	0	0	0	0	0	1	I/$\overline{D}$	S	I/$\overline{D}$: increment (1), decrement (0) cursor or display shift after data transfer. S: shift on (1), off (0).	40 μsec
Display on/off	0	0	0	0	0	0	1	D	C	B	D: display on (1), off (0). C: cursor on (1), off (0). B: cursor blink on (1), off(0).	40 μsec
Display/cursor shift	0	0	0	0	0	1	S/$\overline{C}$	R/$\overline{L}$	X	X	S/$\overline{C}$: shift display (1), cursor (0). R/$\overline{L}$: shift right (1), left (0).	40 μsec
Function set	0	0	0	0	1	DL	N	0	X	X	DL: 8-bit (1), 4-bit (0) interface. N: dual (1), single (1) line display.	40 μsec
CG RAM address set	0	0	0	1	CG5	CG4	CG3	CG2	CG1	CG0	Load address counter with CG0-CG5. Subsequent data goes to CG RAM.	40 μsec
DD RAM address set	0	0	1	DD6	DD5	DD4	DD3	DD2	DD1	DD0	Load address counter with DD0-DD6. Subsequent data goes to DD RAM.	40 μsec
Busy flag/address counter read	0	1	BF	AC6	AC5	AC4	AC3	AC2	AC1	AC0	Read busy flag (BF) and address counter (AC0-AC6)	0
CG/DD RAM data write	1	0	D7	D6	D5	D4	D3	D2	D1	D0	Write data (D0-D7) to CG RAM or DD RAM.	40 μsec
CG/DD RAM data read	1	1	D7	D6	D5	D4	D3	D2	D1	D0	Place data from CG RAM or DD RAM on D0-D7.	40 μsec

X=don't care

Each character in the CG ROM and CG RAM has an 8-bit address, or character code. Conveniently, the codes for the upper and lower-case Roman alphabet and common punctuation are same as the ASCII codes for those characters (21h through 7Dh). For example, the pattern for *A* is stored at address 41h, *B* is stored at at 42h, and so on.

An 8-bit **instruction register** (IR) stores instruction codes and addresses, and an 8-bit **data register** (DR) stores character codes. When you read or write to the chip, you must select the appropriate register.

The **DD RAM** stores up to eighty 8-bit character codes. Each character position on the display corresponds to an address in the DD RAM, and the character codes stored in the DD RAM determine what is displayed at each position.

On power up, on a 2-line display, the leftmost position on the top line has an address of 0, with the rest of the positions in the line addressed in sequence. The second line begins at 40h, even if the top line has fewer than 40h positions.

The instructions allow you to configure a module so that the DD RAM's address increments each time a character is written to the display. This way, the characters automatically appear in sequence on the display without your having to specify an address each time.

Because the second line begins at 40h, however, the display will not wrap around automatically to this line. For example, on a 2-line, 16-position display, line 1 ends at 0Fh and line 2 begins at 40h. To move from the rightmost position of line 1 to the leftmost position of line 2, you have to change the address counter to 40h. In addition, some displays with a single physical line of characters have two logical lines. In a 16-character display of this type, the first 8 characters are addressed from 0 to 7, and the second 8 are addressed from 40h to 47h. With this type of display, you must set the address counter to 40h before you write to the second half of the line.

On a small display where all 80 bytes of DD RAM aren't needed, you can use the spare DD RAM as general-purpose RAM.

Reading and Writing

Writing to the LCD module involves the following steps:

Bring RS high to write data, or low to write an instruction.
Bring R/W̄ low.
Bring D0-D7 to their desired states.
Wait at least 140 nanoseconds.
Bring E high for at least 450 nanoseconds.
Bring E low.

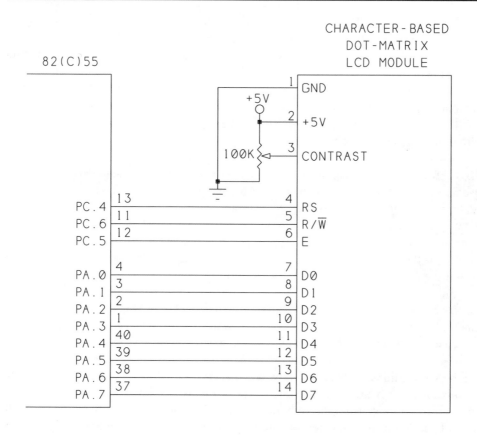

FOR MAXIMUM DISPLAY CONTRAST, TIE PIN 3 OF LCD MODULE TO GND.
FOR WRITE-ONLY INTERFACE, TIE PIN 5 OF LCD MODULE TO GND.

Figure   8-9.   Using an 8255 to control a character-based LCD module.

Read operations are similar to writes, with R/$\overline{\text{W}}$ high instead of low. The data appears on D0-D7 in 320 nanoseconds or less after E goes high.

The HD44780 cannot accept a new instruction until it has finished executing its previous instruction. Table 8-2 shows the maximum time each instruction requires.

BASIC-52 is slow enough that you don't have to worry about the required delays. If you're using an assembly-language routine, your program must include delays after each instruction, or you can use the instruction that reads the HD44780's busy flag at D7 to determine when the module is ready to accept a new instruction.

Interfacing

Full control of an LCD module requires 8 bidirectional lines for reading and writing data and 3 outputs for the control signals. To save four lines, you can use the 4-bit data interface described later. Also, the ability to read the display and the busy flag at D7 are optional. If you give these up, you can use outputs (such as the 74HC374's) instead of bidirectional port bits for D0-D7, and eliminate one of the control lines by tying R/$\overline{\text{W}}$ low.

Figure 8-9 shows an LCD module connected to an 82(C)55, using an 8-bit bidirectional interface. The interface uses Port A and three bits of Port C on an 8255. You can use any of the 8255's port bits, if you write your program to match.

On the LCD module, pins 1-3 connect to ground, +5V, and a contrast potentiometer. For maximum contrast, connect pin 3 directly to ground. Pins 4-6 are the control signals for the LCD module. These connect to three outputs on Port C. The eight data bits, pins 7-14 on the LCD module, connect to Port A.

Listing 8-4 is a BASIC-52 program that initializes a 2-line display and writes *LINE 1* and *LINE 2* to the matching lines.

Initializing the module. On power up, the LCD module must initialize properly. If power-up is clean, with the supply voltage rising from 0.2V to 4.5V in 10 milliseconds or less, the module initializes automatically. But, if power-up doesn't meet this requirement, your program has to provide the initialization routine. It's a good idea to always include an initialization routine in your program, since it does no harm, and if the module doesn't initialize properly, it won't respond correctly or at all.

Table 8-3 summarizes the initialization procedure. In short, the module must first receive three identical commands selecting an 8-bit interface. BASIC-52 easily provides the necessary delays between the commands. To begin the initializing, you must send the instruction to select an 8-bit interface, even if your interface is four bits.

Once this is done, the instructions for Function Set, Display On, Display Clear, and Entry Mode Set tell the controller the configuration you desire. The automatic power-on initialization routine turns the display off, so if you use it, you have to turn the display on by writing 0Ch to the instruction register. When initializing is complete, you can control the display as you wish, though you can't change the number of display lines unless you reinitialize from the beginning.

Listing 8-4 has two subroutines, one for writing characters to the display and one for writing instructions. To write a character, set D equal to the character's code, and call subroutine 800, which sets RS, writes the character to the display, and toggles E. To write an instruction,

Listing   8-4 (page 1 of 2).   Initializes a 2-line LCD module and displays a message on each line.

```
10    REM address of 8255, Port A
20    A=0FC00H
30    REM address of 8255, Port C
40    C=A+2
50    REM address of 8255, Control port
60    X=A+3
70    REM Control word for Enable (PC.5)
80    E=0AH
90    REM Control word for RW (PC.6)
100   RW=0CH
110   REM Control word for RS (PC.4)
120   RS=8

130   REM Initialize LCD module
140   REM initial values
150   XBY(X)=80H: REM Ports A,B,&C are outputs
160   XBY(X)=E  : REM E=1
170   XBY(X)=RW : REM RW=1
180   XBY(X)=RS : REM RS=1

190   REM function set: 8-bit interface, 3 times
200   REM toggle E after each instruction
210   XBY(A)=30H
220   XBY(X)=E+1:XBY(X)=E
230   XBY(A)=30H
240   XBY(X)=E+1:XBY(X)=E
250   XBY(A)=30H
260   XBY(X)=E+1:XBY(X)=E
270   REM function set to match module
280   XBY(A)=38H
290   XBY(X)=E+1:XBY(X)=E
300   REM display on
310   XBY(A)=0CH
320   XBY(X)=E+1:XBY(X)=E
330   REM clear display
340   XBY(A)=01H
350   XBY(X)=E+1:XBY(X)=E
360   REM entry mode set
370   XBY(A)=06H
380   XBY(X)=E+1:XBY(X)=E
```

Listing   8-4 (page 2 0f 2).

```
390   REM display "LINE 1", "LINE 2"
400   D=ASC(L):GOSUB 800
410   D=ASC(I):GOSUB 800
420   D=ASC(N):GOSUB 800
430   D=ASC(E):GOSUB 800
440   D=20H:GOSUB 800
450   D=ASC(1):GOSUB 800
460   I=0C0H
470   GOSUB 900
480   D=ASC(L):GOSUB 800
490   D=ASC(I):GOSUB 800
500   D=ASC(N):GOSUB 800
510   D=ASC(E):GOSUB 800
520   D=20H:GOSUB 800
530   D=ASC(2):GOSUB 800
600   END

790   REM write data to the display
800   XBY(X)=RS+1
810   XBY(X)=RW
820   XBY(A)=D
830   XBY(X)=E+1:XBY(X)=E
840   RETURN

890   REM write an instruction to the display
900   XBY(X)=RS
910   XBY(A)=I
920   XBY(X)=E+1:XBY(X)=E
930   RETURN
```

Table   8-3.   Initialization procedure for LCD modules using HD44780 controller.

Power on
Wait 15 milliseconds after V+ = 4.5V
Function set = 30h
Wait 4.1 milliseconds
Function set = 30h
Wait 100 microseconds
Function set = 30h
Function set to match display module
Display on
Display clear
Entry mode set

---

set I equal to the instruction and call subroutine 900, which clears RS, writes the instruction to the display, and toggles E.

Using the example program as a model, you can experiment with your own messages by adapting the code in lines 400-530.

Listing 8-5 is another test program that displays a prompt on the host's screen and then displays the character you type at the keyboard both on the host's screen and on the LCD module. To use this program, you must add lines 10 through 380 of Listing 8-4 to initialize the module and variables.

The 4-bit Interface

The HD44780's 4-bit data interface can be convenient if you don't have a lot of port bits to spare. The minimum interface requires just 6 outputs, to D4-D7, RS, and E. The drawback is that the 4-bit interface is slower in operation and more complicated to program.

To send an instruction using a 4-bit interface, you send half at a time over D4-D7, along with the appropriate RS and R/$\overline{\text{W}}$ signals. D0-D3 are unused. For example, with an 8-bit interface, writing Z (5Ah) to the display requires the following operations:

clear R/$\overline{\text{W}}$
set RS
write 5Ah to D0-D7
bring E high, then low

Listing 8-5. Displays key presses on the host computer's screen and on an LCD module.

```
1     REM reserve space for 1 string variable,
2     REM 1 character in length
3     STRING 3,1
4     REM You must add lines 10 through 380 of listing 8-4
5     REM to this program

400   Z=0
410   DO
420   INPUT "Press a key: ",$(0)
430   PRINT $(0)
440   REM reset display after 8 characters
450   IF Z=8 THEN Z=0:RW=0:I=1:GOSUB 900
460   REM keep track of how many characters are displayed
470   Z=Z+1
480   REM display the character matching the key press
490   D=ASC($(0),1):GOSUB 800
500   WHILE 1=1
600   END

790   REM write data to the display
800   XBY(X)=RS+1
810   XBY(X)=RW
820   XBY(A)=D
830   XBY(X)=E+1:XBY(X)=E
840   RETURN

890   REM write an instruction to the display
900   XBY(X)=RS
910   XBY(A)=I
920   XBY(X)=E+1:XBY(X)=E
930   RETURN
```

Listing 8-6 (page 1 of 2). Creates and displays a custom character (upside-down question mark) on an LCD module.

```
1    REM You must add lines 5-380 from Listing 8-4 to this
2    REM program.
400 REM R1-R8 store row patterns for custom character
401 R1=4
402 R2=0
403 R3=4
404 R4=8
405 R5=10H
406 R6=11H
407 R7=0BH
408 R8=0

410    REM custom character number
420    CC=0
430    XBY(X)=RS
440    XBY(X)=RW
450    REM display clear
460    XBY(A)=1
470    XBY(X)=E+1:XBY(X)=E
480    REM set CG RAM address to 0
490    XBY(A)=40H
500    XBY(X)=E+1:XBY(X)=E

510    REM store R1-R8 in CG RAM
520    D=(CC)+R1
530    GOSUB 800
540    D=(CC)+R2
550    GOSUB 800
560    D=(CC)+R3
570    GOSUB 800
580    D=(CC)+R4
590    GOSUB 800
600    D=(CC)+R5
610    GOSUB 800
620    D=(CC)+R6
630    GOSUB 800
640    D=(CC)+R7
650    GOSUB 800
660    D=(CC)+R8
670    GOSUB 800
```

The Microcontroller Idea Book

Listing   8-6 (page 2 of 2).

```
680    XBY(X)=RS
690    XBY(X)=RW

700    REM set DD RAM address to 0
710    XBY(A)=80H
720    XBY(X)=E+1:XBY(X)=E
730    XBY(X)=RS+1
740    REM write custom character 0 to display
750    XBY(A)=0
760    XBY(X)=E+1:XBY(X)=E
770    END

790    REM write data to display
800    XBY(X)=RS+1
805    XBY(X)=RW
810    XBY(A)=D
820    XBY(X)=E+1:XBY(X)=E
840    RETURN

890    REM write an instruction to the display
900    XBY(X)=RS
910    XBY(A)=I
920    XBY(X)=E+1:XBY(X)=E
930    RETURN
```

With a 4-bit interface, you have two extra steps:

> clear R/$\overline{\text{W}}$
> set RS
> write 5h to D4-D7
> bring E high, then low
> write 0Ah to D4-D7
> bring E high, then low

Custom Characters

If the 192 characters provided in the CG ROM aren't enough, you can create your own. To design a character, draw a 5 x 7 matrix and fill it with 1s where you want dots, and 0s where you want nothing. Figure 8-10 illustrates, with an example of an upside-down question mark for Spanish-language messages. Listing 8-6 creates the character and stores and displays it.

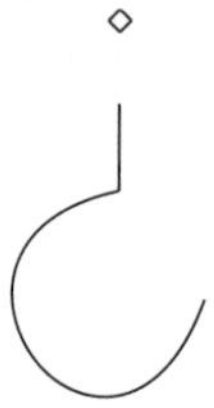

CUSTOM CHARACTER	DOT PATTERN	BIT VALUES	HEX VALUES	ROW #
◇	⬜⬜⬛⬜⬜	0 0 1 0 0	04	0
	⬜⬜⬜⬜⬜	0 0 0 0 0	00	1
	⬜⬜⬛⬜⬜	0 0 1 0 0	04	2
	⬜⬛⬜⬜⬜	0 1 0 0 0	08	3
	⬛⬜⬜⬜⬜	1 0 0 0 0	10	4
	⬛⬜⬜⬜⬛	1 0 0 0 1	11	5
	⬜⬛⬛⬛⬜	0 1 1 1 0	0E	6
	⬜⬜⬜⬜⬜	0 0 0 0 0	00	7

Figure 8-10. You can create custom characters with the HD44780 controller. The CG RAM stores the bit values for each row in the character.

For your own designs, change the values of R1-R8 in lines 401-408 to match the symbol you want.

Mounting Displays in an Enclosure

Mounting a display in an enclosure for a finished project usually involves cutting or drilling the enclosure and wiring the display to the control circuits.

For individual LEDs, you can buy inexpensive mounting rings, and drill matching holes in the enclosure's front panel.

Seven-segment modules often mount on separate circuit boards that fit over an opening cut into the enclosure. For a more finished appearance, you can buy bezels with matching sheets of clear or tinted plastic to cover the displays and mounting hole.

Most character-based LCD modules have a mounting hole in each corner of the circuit board. You'll need to drill matching holes in the enclosure, and cut a hole for the display to show through. Some displays have a ribbon cable attached; others have 14 holes on 0.1" centers, to which you can solder a ribbon cable or a header into which a cable plugs.

Be sure to mount your displays so they will be visible from the expected viewing angle. If necessary, tilt the display slightly in its mounting.

9

Using Sensors to Detect and Measure

With your 8052-BASIC system and some sensors, you can detect and measure properties such as temperature, light, chemical composition, motion, and more. This chapter focuses on how to use sensors in an 8052-BASIC or other microcontroller system.

Sensor Basics

A sensor is a device that responds to a physical property or condition. Other terms for sensor are *detector* and *transducer*. Sensors enable a circuit to learn about the world outside of itself, much as humans use the senses of sight, hearing, touch, smell, and taste.

A sensor may respond in any of a number of ways. For example, litmus paper is a sensor that responds to acidity by changing color. For interfacing to the 8052-BASIC, we're interested in sensors that respond electrically, by varying in voltage, current, or resistance, since these are easily interfaced to electronic circuits.

One obvious use for sensors is in environmental monitoring, including detecting and measuring temperature, light, wind speed and direction, humidity, and so on. But all kinds of electronic devices use sensors, even when sensing isn't the primary purpose. For example, computer printers have sensors that detect when the printer is out of paper. Many cameras can sense light level and distance. And modern automobiles contain all kinds of sensors, including ones to measure engine temperature, composition of exhaust emissions, oil pressure, engine speed, and whether or not the seatbelts are fastened.

You can find a sensor to detect and measure just about any property. Some sensors are readily available from suppliers of other electronic components. These include photodiodes and solar cells, which respond to light, and semiconductors that respond to changes in temperature.

Surplus catalogs sometimes have good deals on sensors from failed or obsolete products— for example, dollar-bill sensors from vending machines and motion detectors from security systems.

Sometimes you can make your own sensors from everyday materials. The conductive foam commonly used to hold CMOS components can double as a simple pressure sensor, since its top-to-bottom resistance decreases as the foam is pressed. A popular homemade moisture detector is a printed-circuit board with two interleaved but untouching copper traces. When the board is wet, water shorts the traces together and changes the resistance between them from very high to a few hundred ohms.

Some projects call for a specialized sensor that you just won't find in the usual sources. A good resource is the *Sensors Buyer's Guide*, published annually by *Sensors* magazine. The guide lists over 1200 companies involved with sensors, and indexes them according to property sensed, technology used, manufacturer, and related products and services. From the list of properties sensed, you can select the category that interests you and consult a list of companies that offer products in that area. Most companies are happy to provide product information and applications hints.

Choosing Sensors

To pick the right sensor for a job, you first need to specify what you want the sensor to do. Below are some of the questions to ask about your desired sensor. The example answers describe a temperature sensor intended for use in a controller used in processing photographic film:

- What property do I want to measure? (temperature)
- What range of inputs do I need to measure? (60-110 degrees Fahrenheit)
- What resolution and accuracy do I need? (accurate to within 0.5 degree Fahrenheit)
- How fast must it respond to input changes? (quick response not critical for this application)
- What kind of output do I need (analog, digital, voltage, current,...)? (8-bit digital output would be ideal, but analog voltage or current output is OK)

• What power supplies are available to power the sensor? (+12V, +5V)

The answers to these questions will help you narrow your choices as you research what's available.

On/off Sensors

Sometimes, all you need to detect is the presence or absence of the sensed property. Some simple sensors act like switches, with a low resistance in the presence of the sensed property, and a high resistance in its absence.

There are many types of sensors that you can use in this way. A magnetic proximity sensor responds to the physical separation of the items connected to each of the switch elements. A vibration sensor responds to rapid motion. Both of these are often marketed as home-security devices for use on doors or windows, but you might come up with other uses for them. Another example is a mercury tilt switch, which uses a ball of liquid mercury as a conductor. The switch contacts open or close when the switch tilts and the mercury rolls to the opposite end of the switch. Figure 9-1 illustrates.

Figure 9-2 shows two ways to detect the state of on/off sensors like these.

Figure 9-2A is an unlatched input. When the resistance across the sensor is high, the pull-up resistor brings the input voltage high. When the sensor's resistance is low, the input goes low.

You can connect this circuit to any unused pin on an input port. If you use the 8052-BASIC's INT1 input, you can use an ONEX1 statement to trigger a subroutine whenever the sensor detects the property in question. If you use an ordinary port input, reading the port bit will tell you the current state of the sensor.

In Figure 9-2B, when the sensor switches from high to low resistance, a 74LS73 JK flip-flop stores the information as a high Q output, which your program can read at its leisure. After reading the input, strobing the CLR input low brings Q low again, until the next sensing event. The flip-flop "remembers" past events, so you don't have to detect or respond to events as they happen.

MERCURY
TILT
SWITCH

Figure 9-1. The tilt, or physical angle, of the mercury switch determines which of its three terminals connect.

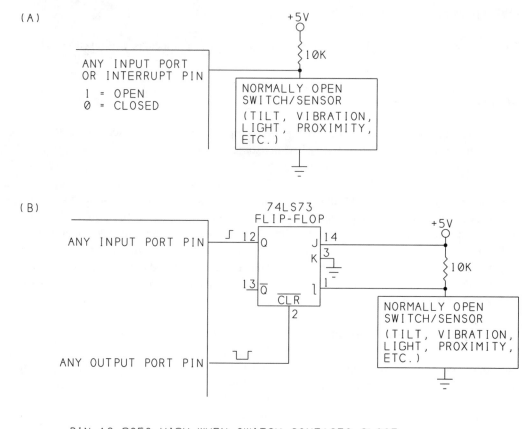

PIN 12 GOES HIGH WHEN SWITCH CONTACTS CLOSE.
STROBE PIN 2 LOW TO CLEAR FLIP-FLOP
AND WAIT FOR NEXT SWITCH CLOSURE.

Figure   9-2.   Two ways to read the state of a normally open switch/sensor: (A) basic input, (B) latched input.

Listing 9-1 assumes that in Figure 9-1B, the Q output connects to bit 0 of an input port at E000h, and the $\overline{CLR}$ input connects to bit 0 of an output port at E400h. The program clears the flip-flop, then reads the input port continuously until the bit in question goes high. It then displays a message, clears the flip-flop, and returns to the main program.

Analog Sensors

The above sensors have just two states: on and off, or open and closed. This makes them easy to use in digital circuits, which recognize only two logic states.

Listing   9-1.   Reads and clears a flip-flop output connected to an input port pin.

```
10    REM clear flip-flop
20    XBY(0E400H)=0
30    XBY(0E400H)=1
40    DO
50    REM read port
60    A=XBY(0E000H)
70    REM see if bit 0 is set
80    IF A.AND.1=1 THEN GOSUB 200
90    WHILE 1=1
100   END
200   PRINT "vibration alarm"
210   REM clear flip-flop
220   XBY(0E400H)=0
230   XBY(0E400H)=1
240   RETI
```

Many sensors have analog outputs, however. They vary continuously in response to changes in the properties they sense. For example, the resistance of a Cadmium-sulfide (CdS) photocell varies with the intensity of light hitting it. If you want to use an analog sensor like this in an 8052-BASIC system, you need to add some components to convert the analog signal to digital.

A comparator provides a way to detect a specific analog voltage. Figure 9-3 shows how to use a comparator to detect a specific light level on a photocell.

A comparator is a special form of op amp with analog inputs, but a digital output. In Figure 9-3, pin 4 is a reference voltage, and pin 5 is the input being sensed. When the sensed input is lower than the reference, the comparator's output is low. When the sensed input is higher than the reference, the comparator's output is high.

R1 and the photocell form a voltage divider. As the light intensity hitting the photocell increases, its resistance decreases and pin 5's voltage rises. To detect a specific light level, adjust R2 so that VOUT switches from low to high when the light reaches the desired intensity. You can read the logic state of VOUT at any input port pin.

R4 is a pull-up resistor for the LM339's open-collector output. R3 adds a small amount of hysteresis, which keeps the output from oscillating when the input is near the switching voltage.

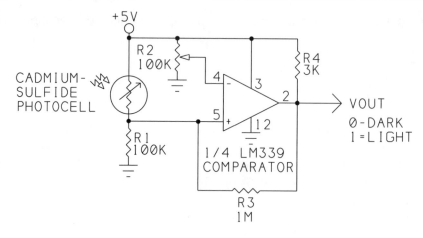

ADJUST R2 SO VOUT SWITCHES AT DESIRED
LIGHT LEVEL.

Figure 9-3. The comparator's output switches at the light level determined

You can use the same basic circuit with other sensors that vary in resistance. Replace the photocell with your sensor, and adjust R2 for the switching level you want. Connect VOUT to any input port pins.

Measuring Analog Signals

Sometimes you need something more sophisticated than a simple level detector. An analog-to-digital converter (ADC) enables you to measure the precise value of an analog voltage.

Some versions of the 8052 microcontroller, including Philips' 80C562, include an on-chip ADC, but the 8052-BASIC doesn't have this feature, so you have to add it externally. There are dozens of converters available, with varying resolution, accuracy, speed, method of conversion, number of analog inputs, and so on. Another option is to use an integrated sensor that contains its own ADC and has a digital output.

National Semiconductor's ADC0848 is an easy-to-use, low-cost, general-purpose, eight-channel ADC. In many ways, the ADC0848 is similar to National's long-popular ADC0808/9 A/D converters, but with some advantages. The ADC0848 does not require an external clock; its control signals interface directly to many microcontrollers; and it is faster, with a typical conversion time of 30 microseconds.

National's data sheet for the ADC0848 has complete specifications, applications information, and example circuits. You'll want a copy of the data sheet if you plan to use the chip.

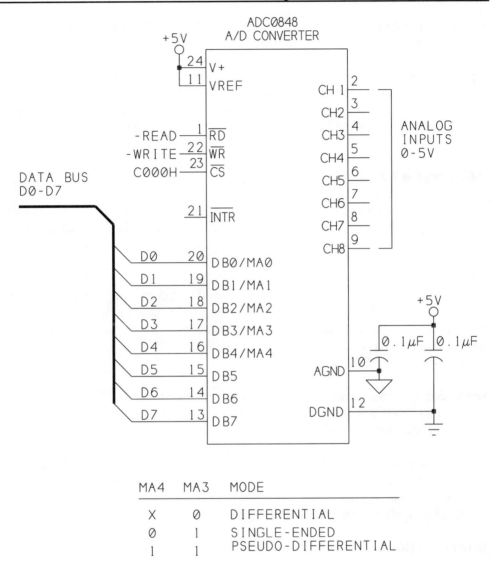

Figure 9-4. The ADC0848 interfaces easily to an 8052-BASIC system, and can measure up to eight analog inputs.

Figure 9-4 shows an ADC0848 interfaced to Chapter 3's 8052-BASIC system. The connections are similar to those used for RAM. $\overline{\text{WRITE}}$ and $\overline{\text{READ}}$ drive the converter's $\overline{\text{WR}}$ and $\overline{\text{RD}}$ inputs. The converter is shown addressed at C000h, but you can use any unused chip-select line. Digital outputs DB0-DB7 connect to the data bus (D0-D7). DB0-DB4 also function as control inputs MA0-MA4.

Up to eight analog inputs can connect to pins 2-9 on the ADC0848. The voltage at VREF determines the converter's full-scale voltage, which is the input that results in an output of 11111111, or FFh. For maximum range, connect VREF to the +5V supply or to a more precise 5-volt reference like an LM336-5.0 reference diode. The analog inputs can then range from 0 to +5 volts.

Adjusting the Range

If your sensor's output is much less than 5 volts, you can increase the resolution of the converter by connecting VREF to a voltage slightly larger than the highest voltage you expect to measure.

To illustrate, consider a sensor whose output ranges from 0 to 0.5 volt. The 8-bit digital output of the converter represents a number from 0 to 255. If VREF is 5 volts, each count equals 5/255, or 19.6 millivolts. A 0.2-volt analog input results in a count of 10, while a 0.5-volt input results in a count of 26. If your input goes no higher than 0.5 volt, your count will never go higher than 26, and the measured values will be accurate only to within 20 millivolts, or 1/255 of full-scale.

But if you adjust VREF down to 0.5 volts, each count now equals 0.5/255, or 2 millivolts. A 0.2-volt input gives a count of 102, a 0.5-volt input gives a count of 255, and the measured values can be accurate to within 2 millivolts.

However, if you decrease VREF as described above, you also increase the converter's sensitivity to noise. With VREF at 5 volts, a 20-millivolt noise spike will cause at most a 1-bit error in the output. If you decrease VREF to 0.5 volt, the same spike can cause an error of 10 bits, since each bit now represents 2 millivolts, not 20.

Minimizing Noise

The rapid switching of digital circuits can cause voltage spikes in the ground lines, and these can cause errors in analog measurements. Good routing of ground wires or pc-board traces can minimize noise in circuits that mix analog and digital circuits.

To minimize noise, provide separate ground paths for analog and digital signals. In Figure 9-4, this means that AGND and any ground connections related to the analog inputs or VREF should be wired together, but kept separate from the ground connections for the digital circuits, including logic chips, the 8052-BASIC, and memory chips. The two grounds are tied together at one place only, as near to the power supply as possible. The schematic uses different ground symbols for the two ground paths. Also be sure to include decoupling capacitors at pins 10 and 12.

Measuring Modes

To allow for different circuit requirements, the ADC0848 offers a choice of three software-selectable modes of operation: single-ended, differential, and pseudo-differential. Figure 9-5 illustrates.

In *single-ended mode,* each analog input is referenced to AGND. This is the simplest mode and will work fine for many applications.

Listing 9-2 causes the ADC to convert each of the eight channels in turn and displays the results on the host computer. For testing the circuits, you can connect a the wiper of a potentiometer to each channel, with the other two leads connecting to AGND and VREF. Verify that the readings for each channel vary from 0 to 255 as you vary the input voltage.

The other modes are useful for more critical measurements where you need to reject background noise or offset voltages.

In *differential mode,* each channel is paired with an adjacent one, with the voltage on one channel referenced to the voltage on the other.

For example, you could connect an output from a sensor to channel 2 and a ground or other reference from that sensor to channel 1. With differential mode selected, channel 1 will read the difference between channel 1's and channel 2's voltage. This mode cancels out errors due to noise that is common to both channels in the pair, such as 60-cycle power-line interference. However,because each channel uses two analog inputs, this mode limits you to four channels.

The third mode of operation is *pseudo-differential.* In this mode, channels 1-7 are all referenced to channel 8. This allows you to make 7 measurements, all with the same reference. This mode is useful if you are have multiple sensors in the same location. Also, if you connect channel 8 to a voltage greater than AGND, the converter's range will shift to match, with a 0 output occurring when an input equals channel 8's voltage.

Reading the ADC

To begin a conversion on the ADC0848, the 8052-BASIC writes to the converter indicating the desired channel and mode. Bits 0-2 specify the channel (000=1, 001=2, 010=3, etc.), and bits 3-4 specify the mode of operation (00=differential, 01=single-ended, 11=pseudo differential). So, for example, in Figure 9-4's circuit, to begin a single-ended conversion at channel 5, you would write 0000 1101, or 0Dh, to the converter's address.

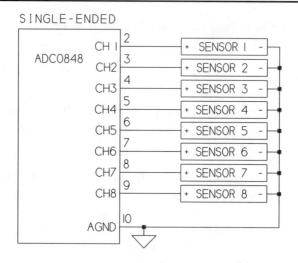

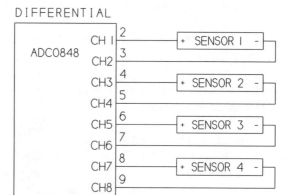

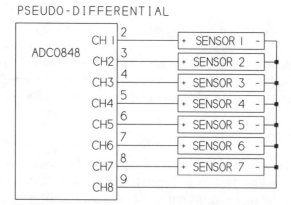

Figure 9-5. Measurement modes available with the ADC0848 are single-ended (A), differential (B), and pseudodifferential (C).

Listing 9-2. Displays measurements of channels 1 through 8 on the ADC0848.

```
10    REM use single-ended mode
20    REM set A to address of ADC
30    A=0C000H
40    FOR I=1 TO 8
50    XBY(A)=8+I-1
60    PRINT "Channel ",I," = ", :  PH0. XBY(A)
70    NEXT I
80    END
```

Writing to the converter causes the conversion to begin automatically. When the conversion is complete, a read operation to the converter's address causes the the converted value to appear at DB0-DB7, where the 8052-BASIC reads it.

The $\overline{\text{INTR}}$ pin indicates when a conversion is complete, and can be used to trigger a read operation. $\overline{\text{INTR}}$ is low when a conversion has occurred that has not yet been read. It goes high after a read and remains high until the next conversion is completed. BASIC-52 is slow enough that you don't have to worry about waiting the maximum 60 microseconds between requesting a conversion and reading the result, so you can ignore $\overline{\text{INTR}}$ and read the result any time after a write.

Packaging Options

The ADC0848 comes in a 24-pin "skinny" DIP, with the pin rows spaced 0.3" apart as on a 14-pin DIP. Sockets of this size, especially wire-wrap, can be hard to find, but in a pinch you can place a 16-pin and 8-pin socket end to end. If you need only four analog inputs, use the ADC0844, in a 20-pin skinny DIP.

Sensor Examples

Now let's look a couple of examples of sensors that you can connect to the ADC0848.

Temperature

The first is an LM34 temperature sensor. Unlike many other temperature sensors, the LM34 requires no calibration. Its output is a simple 10 millivolts per degree Fahrenheit. As Figure 9-6 shows, it's available in several versions. The ones with a narrower range or lower resolution are cheaper. If you prefer Celsius readings, use the LM35.

Figure 9-7 shows how to use an LM385-2.5 voltage reference to set the ADC's VREF to 2.5V. The converter then can measure temperatures from 0 to 250 degrees, and each bit in the ADC0848's output represents a 9.8 millivolt change in the sensor's output.

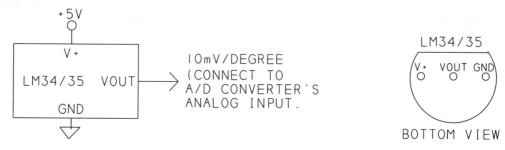

| | LM34/35 TEMPERATURE SENSORS | | | |
DEVICE	ACCURACY	RANGE		SCALE
LM34	±1.6	-50	+300	°F
LM34A	±0.8	-50	+300	°F
LM34C	±1.6	-40	+230	°F
LM34D	±1.6	+32	+212	°F
LM35	±0.4	-55	+150	°C
LM35A	±0.8	-55	+150	°C
LM35C	±0.8	-40	+110	°C
LM35D	±0.8	0	+100	°C

Figure 9-6. The LM34 and LM35 temperature sensors have outputs of 10 millivolts per degree, and need no calibration.

Listing 9-3. Measures and displays temperature reading at ADC0848's Channel 2.

```
10     REM set A to address of ADC
20     A=0C000H
30     REM use single-ended mode
40     REM set C to channel to read (1-8)
50     C=2
60     XBY(A)=8+C-1
70     VREF=2.5
80     B=XBY(A)
90     T=INT(VREF*B*100/255+.5)
100    PRINT "Temperature = ",T
110    PRINT "Press any key to take another measurement"
120    D=GET :  IF D=0 THEN  GOTO 120
130    GOTO 60
140    END
```

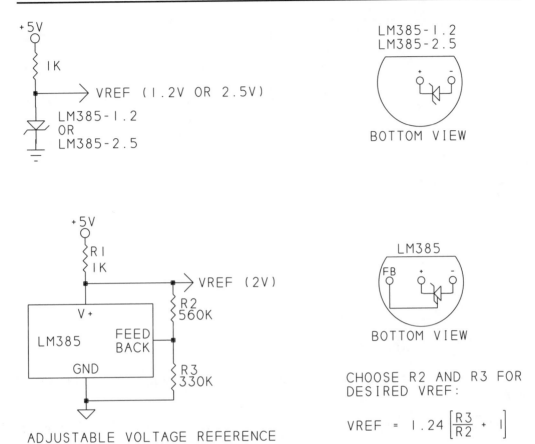

Figure 9-7. The LM385 series of voltage references includes 1.2V, 2.5V, and an adjustable version.

Listing 9-3 assumes that an LM34 connects to CH2 on the ADC0848, and that VREF is 2.5V. On request, it displays the current temperature.

For a smaller range, create a 1.2V reference with an LM385-1.2 and change line 70 in the program to match. Another option is the LM385 adjustable reference, which contains a reference diode and feedback amplifier. With the addition of a voltage source and resistors in a voltage divider, you can set the LM385's output to the reference voltage you need. Use the formula shown to vary the resistors for different outputs.

Solar Energy

Figure 9-8 shows another sensor application, a solar cell that generates a current proportional to the intensity of the light hitting the cell. The output of the solar cell in the example varies

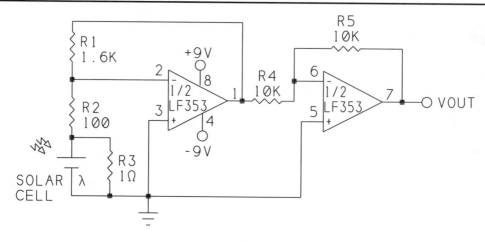

```
SOLAR CELL OUTPUT = 300mA IN FULL SUN.
VOUT VARIES WITH LIGHT INTENSITY

LIGHT LEVEL  | VOUT
DARK         | 0
FULL SUN     | 4.75V
```

Figure **9-8.** VOUT varies with the light intensity, and output current, of the solar cell.

from 0 in darkness to 300 milliamperes in full sun. The voltage across the cell is about 0.5 volt.

An LF353 dual op amp converts the solar cell's current into a voltage that the ADC0848 can measure. Most of the solar cell's current flows through the 1-ohm resistor to ground. Since the solar cell's voltage is only about 0.5 volt, the power dissipated by the 1-ohm resistor is only about 0.15 watt in full sun.

About one percent of the solar cell's output flows through the 100-ohm resistor. This same current flows through the 1.6K resistor, with the result that the voltage at pin 1 of the LF353 varies from 0 to about -4.75V. This voltage is proportional to the intensity of the light hitting the solar cell. The second op amp is an inverter that converts the voltage to positive levels that the ADC0848 can measure.

Listing 9-4 assumes that pin 7 of the LF353 connects to Channel 8 of the ADC0848. On request, the program converts the analog input and displays the result.

The Microcontroller Idea Book

Listing 9-4. Measures and displays solar energy detected by solar-cell circuits at Channel 8 of ADC0848.

```
10    REM set A to address of ADC
20    A=0C000H
30    REM set C to channel to read (1-8)
40    C=8
50    REM use single-ended mode, select channel, start convert
60    XBY(A)=8+C-1
70    REM FS=full-scale voltage (5V)/full-sun output (4.75V)
80    FS=1.05
90    B=XBY(A)
100   T=INT(FS*B*100/255+.5)
110   PRINT "Solar energy = ",T," percent of full sun"
120   PRINT "press any key to take another measurement"
130   D=GET :  IF D=0 THEN  GOTO 130
140   GOTO 60
150   END
```

Level Translating

As you can see, not every sensor has an output that can connect directly to the ADC0848's inputs. A sensor's output may vary from -2 to -1V, from -0.5 to +0.5V, or from -12 to +12V. In all of these cases, you need to shift the signal levels and sometimes adjust the signal range to be compatible with a converter that requires inputs between 0 and 5 volts.

Figure 9-9 shows a general-purpose circuit that can amplify or reduce input levels, and can also raise or lower the entire signal by adding or subtracting a voltage. Separate, independent adjustments control the gain and offset. The circuit is a series of three op amps: a buffer, a level shifter, and an amplifier. The example circuit uses three of the devices in an LF347 quad JFET-input op amp. The LF347 has fast response and high input impedance. You may use a different op amp if you prefer.

The first op amp is a noninverting amplifier whose output at pin 1 equals VIN. The op amp presents a high-impedance input to VIN, to minimize loading effects.

The second op amp is an inverting summing amplifier that shifts pin 1's voltage up or down as R5 is adjusted. Adjusting R5 raises and lowers the voltage at pin 7, but the signal's shape and peak-to-peak amplitude remain constant.

The third op amp is an inverting amplifier whose gain is adjusted by R4. This amplifier increases or decreases the peak-to-peak amplitude of its input.

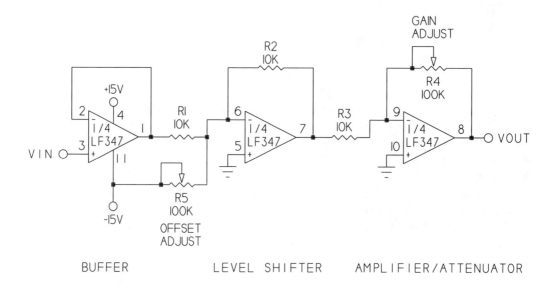

BUFFER   LEVEL SHIFTER   AMPLIFIER/ATTENUATOR

EXAMPLE USE:

Figure   9-9.   With this circuit, you can adjust the level and amplitude of an analog signal so that it varies from 0 to +5V.

As an example of how to use the circuit, if VIN varies from +12V to -12V, adjust R4 for a ±2.5-volt swing at VOUT, then adjust R5 to raise VOUT to achieve the desired 0-to-+5V swing.

Resistor R4 can increase the gain as well as decrease it. If you need to shift the signal level down instead of up, connect R5 to +15V instead of -15V. If you don't need level shifting, you can remove R5 and connect pin 6 only to R1 and R2.

Choosing a Converter

The ADC0848 is a good, general-purpose chip, but you may want to look at other converters, depending on your application. Below are some things to consider when choosing an A/D converter. Example answers describe the ADC0848, using information from its data sheet:

- What is the analog input range? (0V to V+)
- How many analog channels are there? (8)
- What is the converter's resolution? (8 bits)
- How fast is the conversion? (30 microseconds typical, 60 microseceonds maximum)
- How accurate is the conversion? (±.1 LSB (least significant bit), 1/2 LSB version available)
- What are the power-supply requirements and power consumption? (+4.5 to +6V, 15 milliwatts)
- What input modes are available? (single-ended, differential, pseudo-differential)
- How is the converter controlled and interfaced? (control signals are $\overline{WE}$, $\overline{OE}$, $\overline{CS}$
- Are there any special features on-chip (sample-and-hold, voltage reference, etc.)? (an internal clock times the conversions)
- What package types are available? (24-pin 0.3" DIP, 28-lead chip carrier)

Sample and Hold Circuits

An additional component that you may need for rapidly changing analog inputs is a sample-and-hold circuit. To ensure correct conversions, the analog input must not change in value while the conversion is taking place.

A sample-and-hold circuit ensures that the analog signal is stable by sampling the signal at the desired measurement time and storing it, usually as a charge on a capacitor. The converter uses this stored signal as the input to be converted.

When do you need a sample-and-hold? The ADC0848 requires 60 microseconds or less to convert, so you should get good results with inputs that do not vary more than 1 bit in this amount of time. When a rapidly changing input does require one, sample-and-hold ICs like the LF398 are available, or you can use a converter like the ADC0820, which has the sample-and-hold on-chip.

The Microcontroller Idea Book

10

Clocks and Calendars

Many 8052-BASIC systems can make use of a real-time clock that keeps track of seconds, minutes, hours, and even days, months, and years. You can use the clock to trigger operations at specified intervals, such as every five minutes, hourly, daily, on the first of the month, or whatever. Or, a data logger might record the time and date of each measurement it takes, or the times when it detects selected events.

BASIC-52 includes its own real-time clock that counts in 5-millisecond increments. For many timing tasks, this is all you'll need. Another approach is to add a timekeeping chip that automatically keeps track of time and calendar information. Many clocks perform functions beyond simple timekeeping, such as generating periodic interrupts or acting as a *watchdog* that resets the microprocessor in case of program crashes. Plus, using a separate timekeeping chip means that you don't have to devote any of the 8052-BASIC's resources to the task.

This chapter describes how to use both BASIC-52's real-time clock and Dallas Semiconductor's DS1286 Watchdog Timekeeper chip.

BASIC-52's Real-time Clock

The 8052-BASIC, like other computers, has a timing crystal or another frequency source connected to its XTAL pins. In fact, the chip will do nothing at all without this input, since it is what clocks instructions into the chip's CPU for execution. While this clock provides

The Microcontroller Idea Book

an essential timing reference, by itself it doesn't keep track of real-world time measured in seconds, minutes, and hours. But if you know the crystal's frequency, you can measure seconds by counting the oscillations of the crystal. This is what BASIC-52's real-time clock does.

A CLOCK1 statement starts the real-time clock, which causes the TIME operator to increment every 5 milliseconds. Reading the TIME operator tells you the number of seconds that have passed since the clock was enabled. CLOCK0 stops the clock and freezes TIME at its current value. TIME resets to 0 when the count reaches 65536 seconds (18 hours, 12.3 minutes), or when the statement TIME=0 executes. If you stop the clock and then then restart it, TIME will continue counting from where it left off, unless you first reset it to 0.

The ONTIME instruction jumps to a subroutine whenever TIME reaches the value you specify. Because the ONTIME subroutine is an interrupt routine, you use RETI, not RETURN, to end it.

Listing 10-1 is a program that counts seconds, minutes, and hours, and displays the current reading once per second. For accurate timekeeping, the XTAL operator must match the value of your timing crystal.

You can also use ONTIME to trigger periodic operations. Listing 10-2 is a program that toggles bit 7 of Port 1 once per second and displays the logic state of the bit after each toggle.

Clock Accuracy

The more accurate your timing reference, the more accurate your clock will be. You can tune the frequency of a crystal slightly by varying the value of one of the capacitors that connects from the crystal to ground.

Temperature variations will cause a crystal's frequency to drift. Crystal accuracy is rated in parts per million per degree Celsius (often shortened to ppm). Over time, a crystal rated at ±10 ppm should vary no more than 0.001 percent per degree Celsius, or 0.86 seconds per day, if the temperature varies no more than ±1 degree Celsius. If your clock must be super-accurate, choose the most stable crystal you can find and and avoid temperature fluctuations.

You might think that you can get a more accurate real-time clock by adjusting XTAL to match your crystal's actual frequency, rather than its rated value. You could measure the crystal's frequency with a frequency counter, or experiment by varying the value of XTAL and monitoring the real-time clock to find the best match. For example, if your 12Mhz crystal actually oscillates at 11.97 Mhz, you could set XTAL equal to 11970000.

Listing 10-1. Uses BASIC-52's real-time clock to count seconds, minutes, and hours.

```
10    REM set XTAL to match your crystal's frequency
20    XTAL=12000000
30    REM set and initialize clock
40    GOSUB 200
50    REM increment clock variables once per minute
60    DO
70    ONTIME 60,500
80    WHILE 1=1
90    END
200   PRINT "Please enter the current time:"
210   INPUT "AM (0) or PM (1)? ",AP
220   INPUT "Hour (1-12)? ",H
230   INPUT "Minutes (0-59)? ",M
240   INPUT "Seconds (0-59)? ",S
250   REM initialize clock to current seconds
260   TIME=S
270   REM start clock
280   CLOCK 1
290   RETURN
500   REM increment and display time once per minute
510   REM reset seconds
520   TIME=0
530   REM increment minutes
540   M=M+1
550   IF M=60 THEN  GOSUB 700
560   REM display current time
570   PRINT "the time is :"
580   PRINT H,"hours"
590   PRINT M,"minutes"
600   IF AP=0 THEN  PRINT " AM" ELSE  PRINT " PM"
610   RETI
700   REM once/hour timekeeping
710   REM reset minutes
720   M=0
730   REM increment hours
740   H=H+1
750   REM at 12:00, toggle am/pm
760   IF H=12 THEN AP=A
770   REM at 1:00, reset hours
780   IF H=13 THEN H=1
790   RETURN
```

Listing 10-2. Toggles a port bit and displays the result.

```
10    REM toggles P1.7 once per second
20    TIME=0
30    CLOCK 1
40    DO
50    ONTIME 1,100
60    WHILE 1=1
70    END
100   REM reset time
110   TIME=0
120   REM toggle Port 1, bit 7
130   PORT1=PORT1.XOR.80H
140   PRINT "Port 1, bit 7 = ",(PORT1.AND.80H)/80H
150   RETI
```

But in reality, because of the way that BASIC-52 calculates time, small variations in XTAL usually do not effect the real-time clock. Although BASIC-52 will store a XTAL value as precise as 12000001, it uses the same time base for all XTAL values from 11963191 to 12039877. If your crystal frequency is within this range, small adjustments to XTAL won't make the real-time clock more accurate. The value that controls the time base is stored at 4Ah in internal data memory. At 12 Mhz, it's 64h. If you want to experiment, change the value of XTAL, then type PH0. DBY(4AH) to find out if the time base has changed.

A Watchdog Timekeeper

Dallas Semiconductor's DS1286 Watchdog Timekeeper, shown in Figure 10-1, is another way to keep track of time. The chip is easy to use because it contains its own quartz-crystal timing reference, plus a lithium cell for backup power. Once you initialize the clock and calendar and start the oscillator, the clock keeps time for ten years or more, whether or not an external power source is present. You don't have to reset the clock every time you power up.

The DS1286 can be especially useful in battery-powered systems. Since it continues to keep time when the main power supply is off, you can use its interrupt output to power circuitry at programmed times or intervals. For example, by adding circuits to control a power supply, the DS1286's interrupt could trigger a data logger or other instrument to power up at a programmed time. After taking data or performing other operations, the instrument could power itself down until the next interrupt from the DS1286. The longer the time between readings, the greater the power savings.

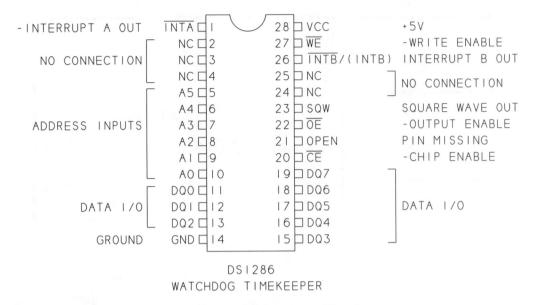

Figure 10-1. Pinout of the DS1286 Watchdog Timekeeper.

The DS1286 contains a series of registers that store time, date, alarm, and configuration information. You can read the current time and date from the DS1286 in hundredths of seconds, seconds, minutes, hours, day of the week, date of the month, and year. Months of different lengths and even leap years are handled automatically. Clock accuracy is better than ±1 minute per month at 25 degrees Celsius.

Figure 10-2 shows the pin connections for a DS1286 in a BASIC-52 system. To accommodate its crystal and power source, the DS1286 a 28-pin encapsulated DIP, just like the one used by Dallas' NVRAMs.

The pinout and wiring are similar to that for static RAM. The chip's access time is 150 nanoseconds, which is well within the 8052-BASIC's timing requirements. The eight data lines (DQ0-DQ7) connect to the data bus. The chip has just six address inputs (A0-A5), which are all it needs to access its 64 bytes. The clock/calendar uses 14 bytes, and 50 bytes of nonvolatile RAM are available for any use. The chip is shown addressed at A000h, but you can use any unused chip-enable. The chip's $\overline{WE}$ and $\overline{OE}$ inputs are driven by $\overline{RDANY}$ and $\overline{WRITE}$.

The DS1286 has two interrupt outputs, $\overline{INTA}$ and INTB. You can program one of these to toggle or pulse whenever the time and/or day match stored values. The other can generate an interrupt if the DS1286's watchdog register isn't accessed periodically. You can use this feature to automatically reset a system if a program crash causes the program to stop

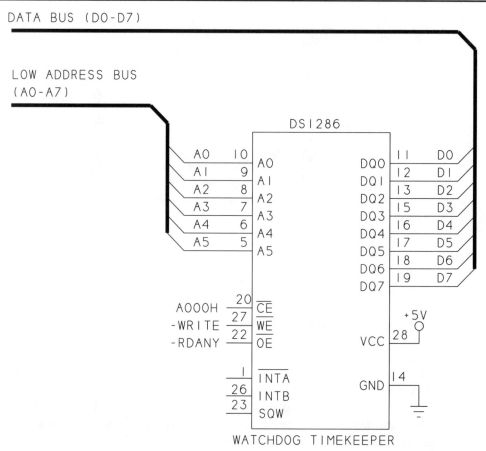

Figure 10-2. Wiring diagram for the DS1286 Watchdog Timekeeper in an 8052-BASIC system.

accessing the watchdog register. When $\overline{\text{IPSW}}$ (register B, bit 6) is 1, the time-of-day interrupt is on $\overline{\text{INTA}}$, and the watchdog interrupt is on INTB. When $\overline{\text{IPSW}}$ is 0, these are reversed, with the watchog on $\overline{\text{INTA}}$ and the time-of-day on INTB. The chip also has a 1024-Hz square-wave output.

Table 10-1 details the functions of the DS1286's registers, which store time, date, configuration, and status information. To initialize the clock/calendar, you write the current time and date into registers 0-2, 4, 6, and 8 through A, then start the clock by clearing $\overline{\text{EOSC}}$ (bit 7 of register 9).

Time and date values are stored in binary-coded decimal (BCD) format. In BCD, a 4-bit nibble represents one decade, and nibbles greater than 9 (1001) are not allowed. Table 10-2 shows numbers expressed in decimal, BCD, and binary. Some values in the DS1286 don't require a full 8 bits. For example, since the month can go no higher than 12, you need only 5 bits to store its value.

Table 10-1. Register functions for the DS1286 Watchdog Timekeeper

Register	Function	Bit 7	Bit 6	Bit 5	Bit 4	Bit 3	Bit 2	Bit 1	Bit 0
0	Clock	0.1 seconds				0.01 seconds			
1		0	10 seconds			seconds			
2		0	10 minutes			minutes			
3	Alarm	MASK	10 minutes alarm			minutes alarm			
4	Clock	0	12/$\overline{24}$	10hr or $\overline{AM}$/PM	10hr	hours			
5	Alarm	MASK	12/$\overline{24}$	10hr or $\overline{AM}$/PM	10hr	hour alarm			
6	Calendar	0	0	0	0	0	days		
7	Alarm	MASK	0	0	0	0	day alarm		
8	Calendar,	0	0	10 date		date			
9	Oscillator	$\overline{EOSC}$	$\overline{ESQW}$	0	10 mo	months			
A		10 years				years			
B	Command	$\overline{TE}$	$\overline{IPSW}$	IBH/$\overline{LO}$	PU/$\overline{LVL}$	WAM	TDM	WAF	TDF
C	Watchdog	0.1 seconds				0.01 seconds			
D		10 seconds				seconds			
E-3F	User	free for any use							

Time of Day Alarm Mask Bits			
Minutes	Hours	Day	Alarm Frequency
1	1	1	Once per minute
0	1	1	When minutes match
0	0	1	When hours and minutes match
0	0	0	When hours, minutes, and days match

Symbol	Function	Symbol	Function
$\overline{EOSC}$	Enable Oscillator	PU/$\overline{LVL}$	Pulse/Level Triggered Interrupts
$\overline{ESQW}$	Enable Square Wave Out	WAM	Watchdog Alarm Mask
$\overline{TE}$	Transfer Enable	TDM	Time-of-day Mask
$\overline{IPSW}$	Interrupt Switch	WAF	Watchdog Alarm Flag
IBH/$\overline{LO}$	Interrupt B High/Low Trigger	TDF	Time-of-day Flag

To generate an interrupt at a specific time, you select an alarm frequency by setting or clearing three mask bits (bit 7 of registers 3, 5, and 7), and storing the desired alarm data in bits 0-6 of the same registers. Clearing a register's mask bit means that the DS1286 will use values in that register to determine the alarm frequency. Setting a mask bit means that the DS1286 will ignore the information in the register. For example, to generate an interrupt at 3:15 daily, you would store the following values:

Register	Mask Byte	Alarm Data
3	0001 0101	15 minutes
5	0000 0011	3 hours
7	1XXX XXXX	days (X=don't care)

Table   10-3.   Decimal numbers and their equivalents in binary and binary-coded decimal. The values 0-9 are identical in BCD and binary.

Decimal	Binary-coded Decimal (BCD)	Binary
0	0000 0000	0000 0000
1	0000 0001	0000 0001
2	0000 0010	0000 0010
3	0000 0011	0000 0011
4	0000 0100	0000 0100
5	0000 0101	0000 0101
6	0000 0110	0000 0110
7	0000 0111	0000 0111
8	0000 1000	0000 1000
9	0000 1001	0000 1001
10	0001 0000	0000 1010
11	0001 0001	0000 1011
19	0001 1001	0001 0011
20	0010 0000	0001 0100
29	0010 1001	0001 1101
30	0011 0000	0001 1110
99	1001 1001	0110 0011

The Microcontroller Idea Book

If you want an alarm frequency other than daily, hourly, or on the minute, there are a couple of ways to achieve it. For an alarm every 10 minutes, you could generate an interrupt once per minute and ignore 9 out of 10 interrupts.

If this seems wasteful, you can update the alarm minutes to the next desired value after each interrupt. Using the example of an interrupt every 10 minutes, you would set the mask bits for when minutes match (0-1-1), and start out by storing 0 in register 3, which will cause an interrupt to occur on the hour. When the interrupt occurs, you would add 10 to register 3 to schedule the next interrupt for 10 minutes after the hour. By continuing to add 10 to register 3 after each interrupt, and returning to 0 on a count of 60, you end up with an interrupt every 10 minutes.

As Table 10-1 shows, many of the DS1286's registers have multiple functions. In register 9, bits 0-4 store the current month, bit 6 enables the square-wave output, bit 7 enables the clock, and bit 5 is always 0. For situations like this, you can create mask bytes and use BASIC-52's logical operators to read and write to selected bits while ignoring other bits in a register. For example, assume that you want to store a month in bits 0-4 of the 1286's register 9, without affecting the settings of bits 5-7.

To do so, follow these steps:

(1) Read the current value of the byte. In our example, with a current month of December, the clock enabled, and the square wave disabled, register 9 will hold these values:

0101 0010

(2) Create a mask byte by setting all bits to be masked, or unchanged, to 1, and clearing the other bits. To alter only the month's value, bits 5-7 are masked:

1110 0000

(3) Logically AND the current value with the mask byte, with this result:

0100 0000

(4) Place the new month's value in bits 0-4 of the byte. To change the month to June (6th month), logically OR the above byte with this:

0000 0110

which results in:

0100 0110

(5) Save the result in the original location (register 9). Bits 5-7 are unchanged from the original, while bits 0-4 have been changed from 12 (December) to 6 (June).

Listing 10-3 shows how to use the DS1286 in a BASIC-52 system. It's a long program, but accomplishes a lot. If you don't need the alarm or another function, you can shorten the program by editing out the code for it.

The program begins with a menu that asks you select the desired function: set-up and initialize, display the time and date, or set the alarm. To initialize the clock/calendar, follow the prompts in the subroutine beginning at line 200, and enter the information requested. The program then uses the subroutine at line 3000 to convert the information to BCD, and stores the result in the appropriate register of the DS1286. When all of the information has been entered, line 470 starts the clock by bringing bit 7 of register 9 low.

Line 1000 begins the subroutine to display the current time and date. Before reading from the DS1286, the program clears $\overline{TE}$ (transfer enable, register B, bit 7). This freezes the registers at their current values, and allows you to read the complete time and date information without errors.

If you don't freeze the registers, if one of them updates in the middle of a series of read operations, you could end up with an invalid time or date. For example, if you read the hour just before 10:00, and read the minutes just after 11:00, you will think that it is 10:00 when it is really 11:00. Freezing the registers ensures that you will read the value of all of the registers as they were when TE went low. Freezing the registers does not stop the clock, however. The DS1286 continues to keep track of the time, and when you bring TE high again, the chip updates the registers to the current time and date.

After the program freezes the registers, it reads the values from the DS1286, uses a subroutine at line 3100 to convert them from BCD to decimal, and displays the results. Finally, the program sets TE to update the registers.

A subroutine at line 2000 handles the third function of the program, setting the alarm. To use this routine, you must wire pin 1 of the DS1286 ($\overline{INTA}$) to pin 13 of the 8052-BASIC ($\overline{INT1}$). A menu asks you what type of alarm you would like, prompts you for additional information, and stores the appropriate values in the DS1286's registers 3, 5, and 7.

Line 2240 configures $\overline{INTA}$ as a low-going pulse. An endless loop at lines 2250-2270 then waits for an interrupt. On interrupt, the program displays the word *ALARM* and the current time and date. You could place any program code in the interrupt routine. For example, you could read sensor data, or write to a port to cause a stepping motor to increment.

Listing   10-3 (page 1 of 4).   Clock and alarm routines for DS1286 Watchdog Timer.

```
10    REM set WT to match address of DS1286 watchdog timer
20    WT=0A000H
30    DO
40    PRINT
50    PRINT "Select function:"
60    PRINT "Initialize and start clock 1"
70    PRINT "Display time and day        2"
80    PRINT "Set alarm                   3"
90    INPUT A
100   IF A=1 THEN   GOSUB 200
110   IF A=2 THEN   GOSUB 1000
120   IF A=3 THEN   GOSUB 2000
130   WHILE 1=1
140   END

200   REM initialize and start clock
210   REM stop clock while initializing
220   XBY(WT+9)=XBY(WT+9).OR.80H
230   REM get time and date, convert each value to BCD and
      store
240   INPUT "year (0-99)? ",X
250   GOSUB 3000
260   XBY(WT+0AH)=X
270   INPUT "month (1-12)? ",X
280   GOSUB 3000
290   XBY(WT+9)=(XBY(WT+9).AND.0E0H)+X
300   INPUT "day of month (1-31)? ",X
310   GOSUB 3000
320   XBY(WT+8)=X
330   INPUT "day of week (1-7)? ",X
340   GOSUB 3000
350   XBY(WT+6)=X
360   INPUT "24-hr (0) or 12-hr (1) clock? ",TT
370   IF TT=0 THEN   GOSUB 3000 ELSE   GOSUB 600
380   INPUT "minutes (0-59)? ",X
390   GOSUB 3000
400   XBY(WT+2)=X
410   INPUT "seconds (0-59)? ",X
420   GOSUB 3000
430   XBY(WT+1)=X
440   XBY(WT)=0
```

The Microcontroller Idea Book   181

Listing 10-3 (page 2 of 4).

```
450  PRINT "Press any key when ready to start the clock"
460  A=GET :   IF A=0 THEN   GOTO 460
470  XBY(WT+9)=(XBY(WT+9)).AND.7FH
480  RETURN

500  INPUT "hour (0-23)? ",X
510  GOSUB 3000
520  XBY(WT+4)=X
530  RETURN

590  REM set up 12-hour clock
600  INPUT "hour (1-12)? ",X
610  INPUT "AM (0) or PM (1)? ",AP
620  GOSUB 3000
630  XBY(WT+4)=X+AP*20H+TT*40H
640  RETURN

1000 REM display current time and date
1010 REM clear TE for error-free reads
1020 XBY(WT+0BH)=XBY(WT+0BH).OR.80H
1030 REM get hours
1040 X=XBY(WT+4).AND.1FH
1050 GOSUB 3100
1060 PRINT "Time = ",X,":",
1070 REM get minutes
1080 X=XBY(WT+2)
1090 GOSUB 3100
1100 PRINT X,":",
1110 REM get seconds
1120 X=XBY(WT+1)
1130 GOSUB 3100
1140 PRINT X,
1150 IF TT=0 THEN 1220
1160 IF AP=1 THEN 1190
1170 PRINT "am"
1180 GOTO 1220
1190 PRINT "pm"
1200 PRINT
```

Listing 10-3 (page 3 of 4).

```
1210 REM get month
1220 X=XBY(WT+9).AND.3FH
1230 GOSUB 3100
1240 PRINT "Date = ",X,"/",
1250 REM get day of month
1260 X=XBY(WT+8)
1270 GOSUB 3100
1280 PRINT X,"/",
1290 REM get year
1300 X=XBY(WT+0AH)
1310 GOSUB 3100
1320 PRINT X
1330 REM get day of week
1340 X=XBY(WT+6)
1350 GOSUB 3100
1360 PRINT "Day of week = ",X
1370 REM set TE when reads are done
1380 XBY(WT+0BH)=XBY(WT+0BH.OR.80H)
1390 RETURN

2000 REM set alarm
2010 PRINT "Select alarm type:"
2020 PRINT "Once per minute (1)"
2030 PRINT "When minutes match (2)"
2040 PRINT "When hours and minutes match (3)"
2050 PRINT "When hours, minutes, and days match (4)"
2060 INPUT AF
2070 REM clear all 3 alarm mask bits
2080 XBY(WT+3)=XBY(WT+3).AND.7FH
2090 XBY(WT+5)=XBY(WT+5).AND.7FH
2100 XBY(WT+7)=XBY(WT+7).AND.7FH
2110 REM set alarm mask bits as needed
2120 IF AF<4 THEN XBY(WT+7)=XBY(WT+7).OR.80H
2130 IF AF<3 THEN XBY(WT+5)=XBY(WT+5).OR.80H
2140 IF AF=1 THEN XBY(WT+3)=XBY(WT+3).OR.80H
2150 IF AF>1 THEN  INPUT "Minute? ",M
2160 IF AF>2 THEN  INPUT "Hour? ",H
2170 IF AF=4 THEN  INPUT "Day? ",D
```

Listing 10-3 (page 4 of 4).

```
2180 REM store alarm settings
2190 IF AF1 THEN X=M :  GOSUB 3000 : XBY(WT+3)=80H+X
2200 IF AF2 THEN X=H :  GOSUB 3000 : XBY(WT+5)=80H+X
2210 IF AF=4 THEN X=D :  GOSUB 3000 : XBY(WT+7)=80H+X
2220 REM turn on alarm
2230 REM time-of-day alarm is edge-triggered, low-going, INTA
2240 XBY(WT+0BH)=0D8H
2250 DO
2260 ONEX1 3200
2270 WHILE 1=1
2280 RETURN

3000 REM convert decimal to BCD
3010 X=INT(X/10)*16+X-INT(X/10)*10
3020 RETURN

3100 REM convert BCD to decimal
3110 X=INT(X/16)*10+(X/16-INT(X/16))*16
3120 RETURN

3200 REM alarm interrupt routine
3210 PRINT "ALARM"
3220 GOSUB 1000
3230 RETI
```

11

Control Circuits

This chapter presents a variety of ways to use an 8052-BASIC system for computer control. The applications include switching power to a load, controlling a matrix of switches, selecting the gain of an op amp, and controlling speed and direction of stepping and dc motors.

Switching Power to a Load

You can use your 8052-BASIC system's port bits to control power to all kinds of devices, including those powered by alternating current (AC), or direct current (DC) at voltages other than 5 volts. Figure 11-1 shows two port bits that control solid-state relays that switch power to AC and DC loads.

A solid-state relay is a simple, safe way to switch power to devices that require high voltages or currents. A logic voltage at the relay's control inputs determines whether or not power is applied to the load.

In a typical solid-state relay, the control voltage is electrically isolated from the switching circuits, which contain an optoisolated triac or a similar device. Many AC solid-state relays include zero-switching circuits, which reduce noise by switching power only when the AC signal is near zero volts.

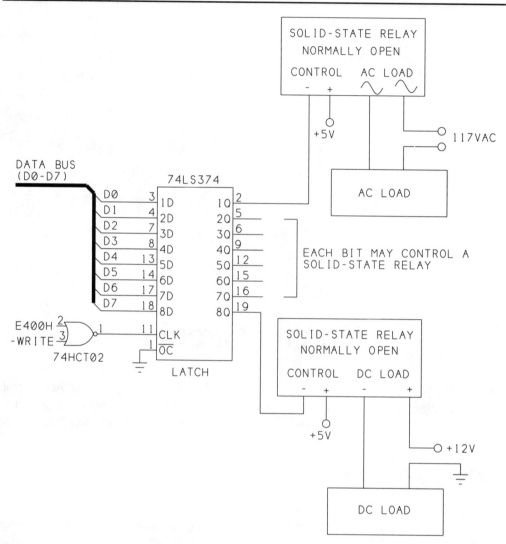

Figure 11-1. Solid-state relays provide an easy way to switch power to AC or DC loads..

Using a solid-state relay saves you the trouble of building a similar circuit from discrete components. Surplus relays are inexpensive, as low as $1.50 each, from vendors such as All Electronics, Marlin Jones, and Hosfelt. If you don't have a data sheet for your relay, look for a pair of control pins, usually labeled + and -. The other two pins connect to the load.

In Figure 11-1, the control bits are outputs of a 74LS374 latch addressed at E400h, as described in Chapter 6. On a normally open relay, the load switches on when its control bit is low. If you want a logic high to turn on the load, wire an inverter between the '374's output and the relay, or use a normally closed relay. Or you can use a 74HCT374 latch in place of

The Microcontroller Idea Book

the LSTTL part, and wire the desired bit to the relay's + input, with the relay's - input connected to GND.

Look for a relay with a control voltage of 5 volts or less, and input control current of 15 milliamperes or less. The relay's rated output voltages and currents should be greater than those of the load you intend to switch.

Take care to work safely when you're wiring, testing, and using circuits that control high-current or high-voltage loads. For circuits that connect to 117V line voltage and have a metal chassis, you can ground the chassis by connecting it to the safety-ground wire in a 3-wire power cord. Insulate any exposed wires and terminals with heat-shrinkable tubing. If in doubt about how to wire the power connections, get qualified help before you continue.

You can control a relay from any output port bit. Just write a 1 or 0 to the corresponding bit to switch the load on or off. If you control a solid-state relay with a port bit on an 8255 or the 8052-BASIC, you may have to add an LSTTL or HCMOS buffer (such as a 74LS244) to supply enough current to the relay's control inputs.

Controlling a Switch Matrix

Figure 11-2 shows how you can use 9 output bits to control an 8 x 8 array of electronic switches. You can connect any of eight X inputs to any of eight Y inputs, in any combination. Possible applications include switching audio or video signals to different monitors or recording instruments, selecting inputs for test equipment, or any situation that requires flexible, changeable routing of analog or digital signals.

A Mitel MT8808 8 x 8 analog switch array simplifies the circuit design and programming. The chip contains an array of crosspoint switches, plus a decoder that translates a 6-bit address into a switch selection, and latches that control the opening and closing of the switches. Maxim is another source for switch arrays like this.

Connecting an X and Y input requires the following steps: Write the X and Y addresses to AX0-AX2 and AY0-AY2. Bring STB high. Bring DATA high to close the switch. Bring STB low to latch the data. To open a connection between an X and Y input, you do the same but bring DATA low to open the switch.

You can make and break as many connections as you want by writing the appropriate values to the chip. All previous switch settings remain until you change them by writing to the specific switch.

You can connect the switches in any combination. For example, you can connect one X input to each of the eight Y inputs, to create eight distinct signal paths. Or, you can connect all eight Y inputs to a single X input, to route one signal along eight different paths.

The MT8808 is shown powered at +5V, but VDD may be anywhere from 4.5V to 13.2V. VEE is an optional negative supply that enables you to switch negative signals.

The switches do have some resistance, which varies with the supply voltage. At 5V, typical switch resistance is 120 ohms; at 12V, it drops to 45 ohms. This should cause no problems in switching standard LSTTL or CMOS signals. If you are routing an analog voltage to a low-impedance input, the switch resistance may attenuate the signal. Maximum switching frequency of the chip is 20 Megahertz.

In Figure 11-2, the switch array is controlled by Port A and bit 7 of Port C (PC.7) on an 82C55 PPI. Bringing PC.7 high opens all of the switches. If you don't need this ability, you can tie RESET low and use PC.7 for something else.

You can use any output port bits to control the MT8808. Logic high inputs at the MT8808 must be at least 3.5V, though, so if you use NMOS or TTL outputs, add a 10K pull-up resistor from each output to +5V.

For a simple test of the switches, you can connect a series of equal resistors as shown to the X inputs. Each X input will then be at a different voltage. To verify a switch closure, measure the voltages at the selected X and Y inputs; they should match.

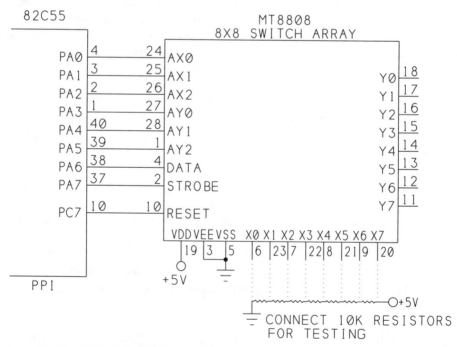

Figure   11-2.   With the MT8808 switch array, an 8-bit output port can connect eight X inputs to eight Y inputs, in any combination.

Listing 11-1. Controls an MT8808 switch matrix.

```
10    REM A=base address of 82C55
20    A=0FC00H
30    REM configure 8255 for all outputs
40    XBY(A+3)=80H
50    REM bring MT8808's Reset low (off)
60    XBY(A+3)=0EH
70    XBY(A)=0
80    DO
90    INPUT "Open (0), close (1), or reset all (2)? ",Z
100   IF Z=2 THEN GOSUB 300
110   IF Z THEN GOSUB 400
120   WHILE 1=1
130   END
290   REM reset all switches by toggling Reset
300   XBY(A+3)=0FH
310   XBY(A+3)=0EH
320   RETURN
400   PRINT "Enter inputs to connect or open: "
410   INPUT "X (0-7)? ",X
420   INPUT "Y (0-7)? ",Y
430   REM write to MT8808 to open or close selected switch
440   B=X+Y*8+Z*40H
450   XBY(A)=B
460   XBY(A)=B+80H
470   XBY(A)=B
480   RETURN
```

Listing 11-1 demonstrates switch operation by asking you whether to open or close a switch or reset them all, then performing the requested action.

Op Amp with Programmable Gain

Figure 11-3 shows a way to set the gain of an operational amplifier by writing to three output port bits. Controlling the gain is National Semiconductor's LF13006 or LF13007 digital-gain-set IC. Each contains a resistor ladder, switches, and decoding logic that enable you to select any of eight gains for an amplifier, attenuator, current source, or other circuit that requires precise, variable outputs.

Each of the gain-set ICs has two outputs, each with a different series of gains, as Figure 11-3 shows. The gain error is guaranteed to be 0.5 percent or less over the full range of operating temperatures.

The Microcontroller Idea Book

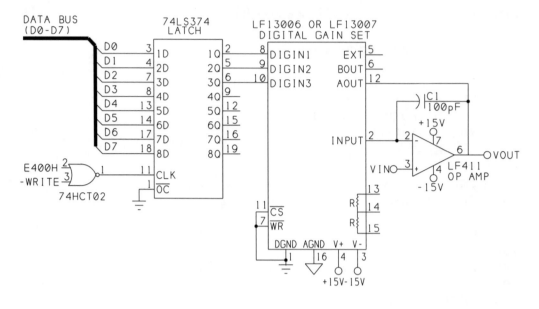

Figure 11-3. An LF13006/7 controls the gain of an LF411 op amp.

The bits that select the gain are outputs of a 74LS374 latch addressed at E400h. The LF13006/7's Chip-Select and Write pins are tied low, which causes the gains at pins 12 and 6 to immediately match the settings at DIGIN1-DIGIN3.

If you want to control up to four gain-set chips and op amps, you can use the five remaining outputs of the 74LS374 to select the desired chip. Tie all of the $\overline{WR}$ inputs to one bit, and tie each $\overline{CS}$ input to one of the remaining bits. Then, to set the gain of an op amp, bring its $\overline{CS}$ input low, then bring $\overline{WR}$ low, then high to latch the data to the desired chip.

You can use just about any op amp with this circuit. Shown is an LF411, which has a wide bandwidth and low input offset and drift. A 10-picofarad capacitor from the op amp's input

Listing 11-2. Demonstrates gain control of op amp.

```
10    REM A=address of output port
20    A=0E400H
30    DO
40    FOR I=0 TO 7
50    XBY(A)=I
60    PRINT "Gain = ",I
70    PRINT "Press any key to continue..."
80    G=GET
90    DO  : G=GET :  UNTIL G<>0
100   NEXT I
110   WHILE 1=1
120   END
```

to output adds stability, as recommended by the LF13006/7's data sheet. I found that the capacitor did keep the op amp's output from oscillating at certain gain settings.

The LF13006/7 also has two matched, uncommitted resistors of about 15K each, which you can use as you wish.

Listing 11-2 steps through the available gains. You can verify circuit operation by connecting a signal such as a sine-wave output of a signal generator to VIN, and monitoring VOUT with an oscilloscope. To use the full range of gains, the signal at pin 3 must be quite small. For example, if your input is 100 millivolts peak-to-peak, at a gain of 128 the output is 12.8 volts.

Controlling a Stepper Motor

Figure 11-4 shows an 8-bit output port controlling a four-phase unipolar stepper motor. Applying power to the motor's four phases, or coils, in sequence causes the motor to turn. The port uses a 74HCT374 latch addressed at 0E400h. If you use a 74LS374, add 10K pullups to the outputs, to ensure that logic-high inputs to U3 and U5 meet the specified minimum of 3.5V.

You can choose from several modes of operation for the motor, with each using a different sequence of pulses. The frequency and sequence of the pulses determine the speed of the motor.

In the circuit shown, after you write values to the port to set the speed and operating mode, the motor continues to run automatically, using the selected parameters. This frees the

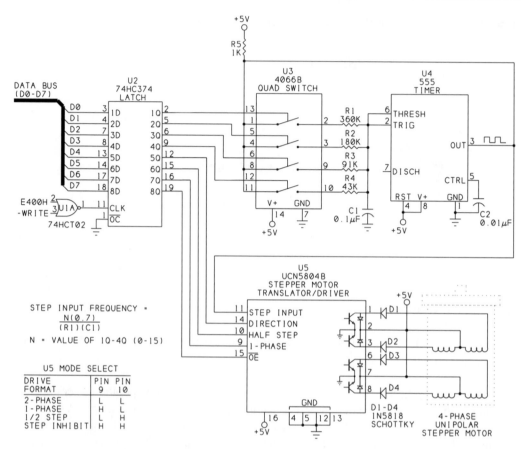

Figure 11-4. The UCN5804B makes it easy to control the speed, direction, and operating mode of a stepper motor.

8052-BASIC to do other things, without having to worry about generating the signals to control each step of the rotation.

The circuit uses a UCN5804B stepper-motor translator/driver (U5) from Allegro Microsystems (formerly Sprague). The chip automatically creates the drive signals for operation in any of three modes.

U3 is a 4066B CMOS quad switch that enables you to select any of 15 speeds. U4 is a 555 timer that outputs a square wave in proportion to the selected speed. U5 uses the square wave to time the steps.

U5 has four outputs that can sink up to 1.5 ampere each, and can sustain up to 35 volts. The chip includes diodes that protect against inductive transients, and thermal protection that disables the outputs if the chip begins to overheat. For high output currents, use a slide-on DIP heat sink to prevent overheating.

The motor is a 4-phase, unipolar type. This type of motor has six leads that connect to two sets of coils, with two coils in each set.

Surplus motors often don't include complete documentation, but you can sort out the leads with an ohmmeter and some experimenting. Begin by looking for a lead that measures an equal resistance (typically 5 to 50 ohms) to two of the other leads. Wire this lead to +5V and pin 2 of U5. Wire the two leads that connect to this lead to pins 1 and 3 of U5 through diodes D1 and D2. Swaping the leads at pins 1 and 3 will reverse the direction of the motor. Identify and wire the remaining three leads in the same way, but using pins 6, 7, and 8 of U5.

The 5V motor is powered directly by a +5V supply. This simple drive circuit is fine for many applications, especially at lower speeds. You can find examples of other drive circuits in the documentation from Airpax or other motor manufacturers.

The data sheet for the '5804B recommends adding D1-D4 to prevent problems in the logic circuits due to mutual coupling in the motor windings. Schottky diodes have a smaller forward voltage drop (0.25V) than other silicon diodes.

Resistors R1-R4 and capacitor C1 set the frequency of U4's output. To select a speed, you write a number from 1 to 15 to bits 0-3 of the output port. Each bit controls one of U3's switches. For example, when pin 2 of U2 is high, pins 1 and 2 of U3 connect, and R1 is one of U4's timing components. When pin 2 of U2 is low, pins 1 and 2 of U3 are open, and R1 has no effect on U4. When more than one switch is closed, the parallel combination of resistors forms the timing resistance. When all switches are open, U4's output is high and the motor stops.

In addition to the frequency of the step input, motor speed depends on the step angle of your motor and the mode selected at U5. A typical motor has a step angle of 18 degrees, which means that it requires 20 steps (360/18) for one full rotation. Using the resistor values shown and a motor with an 18-degree step angle, the motor speed will vary from 1 to 15 Hz in wave-drive or 1-phase mode.

For a different range of speeds, use the formula shown to select resistor and capacitor values. For speeds from 10 to 150 Hz, use 0.01 microfarad for C1, or decrease the values of R1-R4 by a factor of ten. The formula assumes that in the series R1-R4, each resistor is half the value of the preceding one. If you use a different resistor scaling, you'll have to calculate the values of the parallel combinations of resistors to find the resulting frequencies.

Bits 5 and 6 of the port select the operating mode. Wave-drive mode powers one phase at a time, while two-phase drive powers two phases at once, and half-step drive alternates

Listing 11-3. Controls a stepper motor.

```
10    REM A=address of output port
20    A=0E400H
30    DO
40    INPUT "Speed (1-15)? ",S
50    INPUT "Mode (1=wave, 2=2-phase, 3=1/2-step, 4=stop)?",M
60    INPUT "Direction (0=Clockwise, 1=Counterclockwise)? ",D
70    IF M=1 THEN X=4
80    IF M=2 THEN X=0
90    IF M=3 THEN X=2
100   IF M=4 THEN X=6
110   XBY(A)=S+(X+D)*10H
120   WHILE 1=1
130   END
```

powering one and two phases. Wave drive uses the least power, but with reduced torque compared to 2-phase drive. Half-step drive uses twice as many steps per revolution, and so offers finer control.

Bit 4 (pin 12 of U2) sets the direction of rotation.

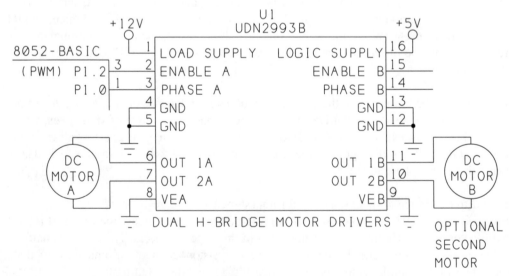

Figure 11-5. Using a UDN2993 to control a DC motor with pulse-width modulation.

The Microcontroller Idea Book

Listing   11-4.   Controls direction and speed of a DC motor with BASIC-52's PWM output.

```
10     PORT1=0FBH
20     T=1
30     INPUT "Direction (0 or 1)? ",D
40     INPUT "High (on) pulse width (25 to 0FFFFh)? ",H
50     INPUT "Low (off time) pulse width (25 to 0FFFFh)? ",L
60     IF D=0 THEN PORT1=PORT1.AND.0FEH ELSE PORT1=PORT1.OR.1
70     PRINT "Press any key to end program"
80     DO
90     PWM H,L,T
100    G=GET
110    UNTIL G<>0
120    PORT1=PORT1.AND.0FBH
130    END
```

You can stop the motor in any of three ways. You can bring bits 0-3 of the port low to stop the timer. You can bring bit 7 high, which removes power from U4's outputs. Or, you can bring pins 9 and 10 of U5 high, which continues to apply power to the motor, but ignores the step input.

Listing 11-3 prompts you for a motor speed, mode of operation, and direction, and then runs the motor as requested. You can stop the program, and the motor will continue to run, as long as it remains connected to the port and you don't write anything else to it.

Speed Control of a Continuous DC Motor

If you prefer ordinary continuous dc motors to steppers, Figure 11-5 shows a circuit that uses BASIC-52's PWM output to control motor speed.

This circuit uses another Allegro chip, the UDN2993B (U1). Pins 1 and 8 of U1 connect to the motor's power supply, which can range from 10 to 40V. Pins 6 and 7 connect to the motor. Pin 5 is the +5V logic supply, and pins 4, 5, 12, and 13 are additional grounds. At pins 10, 11, 14, and 15, you can connect and control a second motor.

Pin 3 of U1 controls motor direction, and connects to bit 0 of Port 1 (P1.0) on the 8052-BASIC. Pin 2 of U1 switches power to the motor, with a logic low shutting the motor off, and a logic high allowing current to flow. This pin connects to Port1, bit 2 (P1.2) of the 8052-BASIC, which is the PWM output.

BASIC-52's PWM expression causes a series of pulses to appear at P1.2, with this syntax:

PWM *high pulse width, low pulse width, number of cycles*

Listing 11-4 uses the PWM output to control motor speed. The program prompts you for motor direction and the width of the high and low PWM pulses. For faster speeds, use large values for the high pulses (H) and small values for the low pulses (L). This results in a waveform with a high duty cycle, or ratio of the width of a high pulse to the width of a complete cycle (consisting of 1 high and 1 low pulse). With a high duty cycle, power is applied to the motor for a large proportion of the total time. For slower speeds, do the reverse: select small values for the high pulses and large values for the low ones, for a low duty cycle.

The actual pulse width equals the value in the PWM statement multiplied by 12, divided by the frequency of the 8052-BASIC's timing crystal. So, with a 12-Megahertz crystal, if H=1000 and L=10,000, high pulses will be 1000 microseconds, or 1 millisecond, wide, and

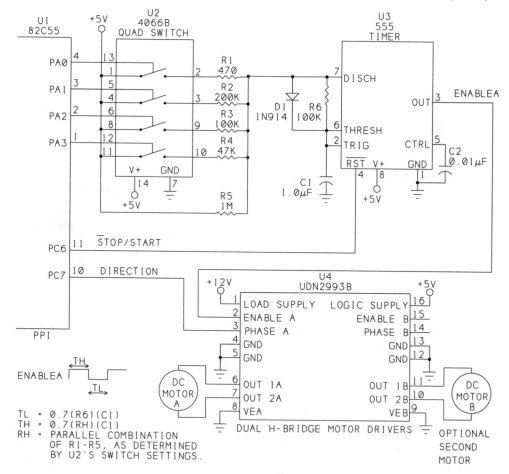

Figure 11-6. A 4066B quad switch and 555 timer enable you to select up to 16 motor speeds, with four port bits.

Listing 11-5. Controls direction and speed of Figure 11-6's DC motor.

```
10    REM A=base address of 82C55
20    A=0FC00H
30    REM configure 8255 for all outputs
40    XBY(A+3)=80H
50    INPUT "Direction (0 or 1)? ",D
60    IF D=0 THEN XBY(A+3)=0EH ELSE XBY(A+3)=0FH
70    INPUT "Speed (0-15)? ",S
80    XBY(A)=S
90    REM bring 555's Reset (PC.6) high (off)
100   XBY(A+3)=0DH
110   XBY(A)=S
120   G=GET
130   DO  : G=GET :  UNTIL G<>0
140   REM Remove 555's Reset
150   XBY(A+3)=0CH
160   END
```

low pulses will be 10,000 microseconds, or 10 milliseconds, wide. For accurate time calculations, set XTAL to match your crystal's frequency.

In Listing 11-4, the number of cycles is 1, so the PWM statement results in one low pulse followed by one high pulse. Lines 100-110 then use a GET operator to check to see if the user has pressed a key and if not, the PWM output repeats. Checking for a key press enables you to stop the program, since BASIC-52 ignores CONTROL+C keypresses while a PWM statement is executing.

The DO loop in the program results in a delay between each PWM statement. During the delay, P1.2 is high, so the motor is powered. Because of the delay, with a 12-Megahertz crystal, if L=1200h and H=25, P1.2 will have equal on and off times of about 5 milliseconds. Increasing L will lower the motor's speed, and decreasing L or increasing H will raise it.

Although you can control a second motor with the '2993B, you get only one PWM output on the 8052-BASIC, so it's not feasible to control two motors independently in this way.

Figure 11-6 shows another way to control the speed of a DC motor. As in Figure 11-4, the circuit uses a 4066B quad analog switch to select a timing resistance for a 555 timer. Varying the timing resistance varies the duty cycle of the 555's output, and thus the motor's speed.

You can select timing resistances that result in the motor speeds you want. The values shown will vary the duty cycle from about 90 to 20 percent.

Chapter 11

Four output bits of an 82C55 set the motor speed. Additional bits set the direction of rotation and turn the motor on and off by controlling the 555's RESET input. You can use any output port bits to control the motor, but logic high inputs at the 4066B must be at least 3.5V, so if you use NMOS or TTL outputs, add a 10K pull-up resistor from +5V to each port output that connects to the 4066B.

Listing 11-5 asks you for a motor speed and direction, then causes the motor to spin as directed.

12

Wireless Links

Wires and cables are by far the most common way to connect one circuit to another, but wireless links are another option. Sometimes a wireless connection is more flexible, convenient, or practical, because you don't have to string wires from point to point.

On an 8052-BASIC system, you can use a wireless link to send commands to devices that recognize and act on them. Or, in the other direction, the devices might transmit to an 8052-BASIC system that acts on the information received. Or you can have two 8052-BA-SIC systems that communicate with each other over the wireless link.

This chapter describes ways to do these, using infrared energy or radio waves as the transmitting medium.

Infrared Links

Over short distances and at lower speeds, infrared is a good choice for wireless links. Figures 12-1 and 12-2 show a link whose transmitter sends 4-bit messages to one or more receivers. Each receiver has a 5-bit address, which enables the transmitter to send a message to a selected receiver, while other receivers will ignore it.

These circuits are independent modules controlled by manual switches or jumpers, rather than by a microcontroller. This is a good way to get the link up and running. When that's

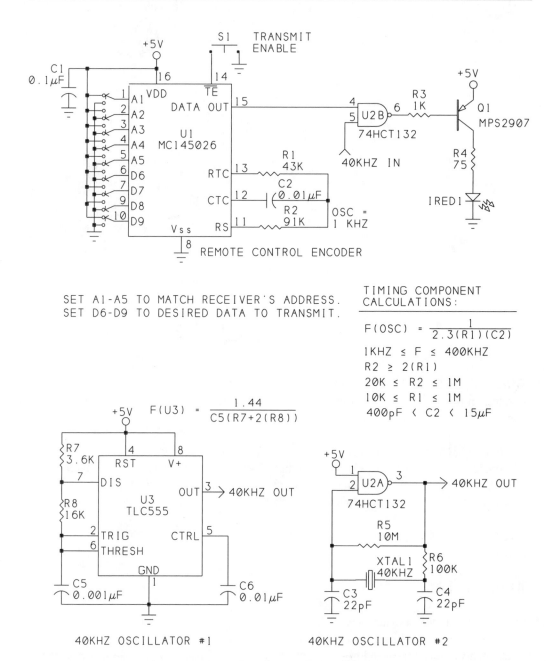

Figure 12-1. This infrared transmitter sends 4 bits of data to a receiver identified by a 5-bit address. The transmitted pulses are modulated at 40 kilohertz, using either a 555 timer or 40-kHz crystal to generate the frequency.

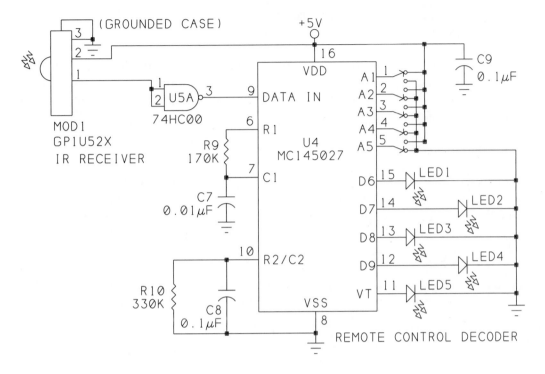

SET A1-A5 TO DESIRED ADDRESS.
LEDS 1-4 INDICATE RECEIVED DATA: ON = 1
OFF = 0

LED5 INDICATES VALID TRANSMISSION RECEIVED.

TIMING COMPONENT
CALCULATIONS:

$(R9)(C7) = 3.95(R1)(C2)$
$(R10)(C8) = 77(R1)(C2)$
(R1 & C2 ARE IN TRANSMIT CIRCUIT)
$R9 \geq 10K$
$R10 \geq 100K$
$C7 \geq 400pF$
$C8 \geq 700pF$

Figure 12-2. This infrared receiver identifies the transmissions intended for it, and makes the received data available at D6-D9.

accomplished, you can replace the manual switches with computer control of the transmitter, receiver, or both.

The circuit uses some specialized components that do a lot of the work of detecting, filtering, encoding, decoding, and error-checking of the transmissions. Two of these are Motorola's MC145026 and MC145027 encoder/decoder pair, which are low-cost chips intended for remote-control applications.

Transmitter Circuits

Figure 12-1 is the infrared transmitter, which has three main functions. It converts four bits of parallel data into a serial stream. It then modulates the resulting signal by chopping it at 40 kilohertz. And, it causes one or more infrared-emitting diodes to transmit the encoded, modulated data to a receiver that is tuned to respond to 40-kilohertz signals.

The encoder chip. The encoder (U1) has five address inputs (A1-A5) and four data inputs (D6-D9). The logic states of these inputs determine the transmitted address and data. The encoder outputs a different code for each of three states that the inputs may have: *Logic 0* (1.5V or less), *Logic 1* (3.5V or greater), or *Open* (no connection). Figure 12-3 shows the transmissions that result for each of these states.

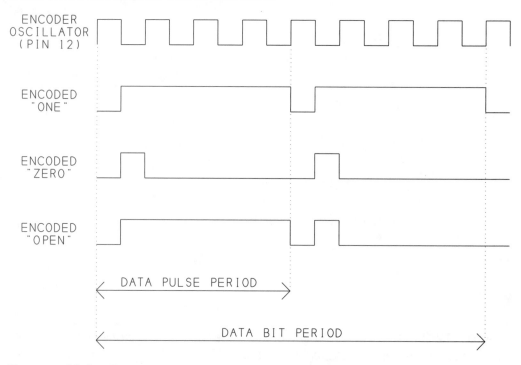

Figure   12-3.   Pulse patterns at DATA OUT of the MC145026 encoder.

Because there are three possible states, the information is trinary (as opposed to binary, with just two states). With five address inputs and three possible states for each, you can have as many as 243 receivers, each with its own address. Although data inputs D6-D9 also transmit in trinary form, the receiver decodes open inputs as logic 1's, so in effect the data bits are binary. For testing, you can use jumpers or switches to +5V or ground, or leave the pins open, to set the data and address inputs.

Transmit Enable ($\overline{TE}$) has an internal pullup, which turns off the transmitter when pin 14 is not connected. To enable transmitting, $\overline{TE}$ must pulse low for at least 65 nanoseconds. For manual operation, you can use a jumper or switch (S1) to bring $\overline{TE}$ low.

Components R1, R2, and C2 set the frequency of the on-chip oscillator. This in turn controls the width of the transmitted pulses. The figure shows the data sheet's formulas and recommendations for selecting values for these components. For best performance, use components with 5% or tighter tolerance.

With the values shown, the oscillator's frequency is 1 kilohertz, which is at the low end of Motorola's recommended range for the chip. With this frequency, the narrowest transmitted pulses are 500 microseconds wide. I chose this pulse width to be compatible with the requirements of the infrared module in the receiver circuit, which may not respond reliably at higher frequencies. If you have an oscilloscope or frequency counter, you can monitor the oscillator frequency at U1's pin 12.

For each transmission, the encoder sends all nine address and data bits in sequence, waits three data-bit times (24 milliseconds at 1 kHz), and then repeats the entire transmission. A complete transmission requires 182 milliseconds from the time that $\overline{TE}$ goes low. If you hold $\overline{TE}$ low, the encoder will transmit continuously. Otherwise, the transmission ends after sending the information twice.

The encoder's output drives infrared-emitting diode IRED1. Instead of directly driving the IRED with the encoder's output (DATA OUT), NAND gate U2B combines DATA OUT with a 40-kHz oscillator. The result is that the encoder's pulses transmit as bursts of 40-kHz pulses. As we'll see, the infrared receiver is designed to reject stray signals that don't pulse at 40 kilohertz. Pulsing the IRED also saves power, since the IRED is never on constantly.

Oscillator alternatives. I've included a choice of two designs for the 40-kHz oscillator. One has a stable, accurate output but requires a special timing crystal, while the other uses more common components but requires a constant power-supply voltage and accurate resistor and capacitor values for best stability and accuracy. You can choose whichever you prefer, and connect the output to pin 5 of U2.

The crystal-controlled oscillator uses a 40-kHz quartz crystal and an HCT132 Schmitt-trigger NAND gate (U2A) operated as an amplifier. If you substitute a different inverter, you may have to experiment with different component values. Some combinations might cause the oscillator to run at harmonics of two or more times the crystal frequency. Digi-Key is one source for the sometimes hard-to-find 40-kHz crystals. A ceramic resonator is another option for a 40-kHz source.

The other option is U3, which is a TLC555 timer configured as a 40-kHz oscillator. Components R7, R8 and C5 determine the output frequency, according to the formula shown. For accuracy and stability, use 5% or 1% tolerance values for these components. The timing error of the 555 can also add a few percent error to the output frequency.

For best accuracy, use a CMOS timer like the TLC555, rather than the bipolar 555. For an adjustable frequency, substitute a 50K potentiometer for R8. Connect the center tap and one other lead of the potentiometer in place of R8, and adjust the wiper for a 40-kHz output. If you have no way to monitor U3's frequency, you can adjust R8 later, by watching the receiver's response as you transmit.

The two inputs to NAND gate U2B are the 40-kHz oscillator and U1's pin 15 (DATA OUT). When DATA OUT is high, pin 6 of U2B pulses at 40 kilohertz. When DATA OUT is low, pin 6 of U2B is high. The result is a form of modulation, with the presence or absence of the 40-kHz signal representing the logic levels at the encoder's output.

When pin 6 of U2B is low, PNP transistor Q1 switches on, and current through IRED1 causes it to emit infrared energy. When pin 6 of U2B is high, Q1 and IRED1 are off. The result is that IRED1 pulses at 40 kilohertz when pin 15 of U1 is high, and IRED1 is off when DATA OUT is low. Resistor R3 limits Q1's base current. You can use any general-purpose or switching PNP transistor for Q1. Resistor R4 limits the current through IRED1 to about 50 milliamperes, which is high enough for basic testing. If necessary, you can increase the IRED's current later for increased range.

For best results, use an IRED with a high-power output. Radio Shack carries high-output IREDs. Digi-Key also has a selection, including Harris' F5D1QT and F5E1QT. Devices with outputs at 880 or 940 nanometers are acceptable. Look for a maximum continuous forward current of at least 100 milliamperes.

Receiver Circuits

The IRED transmits the encoded address and data. On the other end, you need to detect the transmitted signal, find out if the address matches, and if so, convert the received data into a usable format. Figure 12-2 shows a circuit that does these, using an infrared-receiver module and an MC145027 decoder that complements Figure 12-1's encoder.

The infrared-receiver module. MOD1 is a Sharp GP1U52X infrared-receiver module. Its circuits are enclosed in a metal cube about half an inch on each side. The module has just

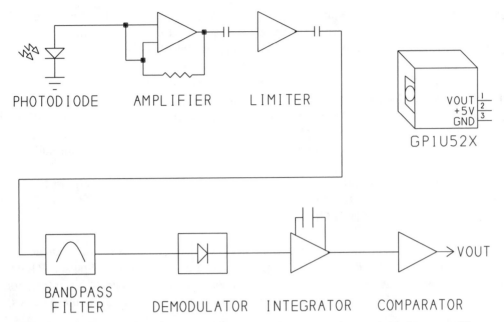

PHOTODIODE   AMPLIFIER   LIMITER

GP1U52X

VOUT
+5V
GND

1
2
3

BANDPASS
FILTER   DEMODULATOR   INTEGRATOR   COMPARATOR

→VOUT

Figure 12-4.   The GP1U52X infrared receiver contains a detector, amplifier, and filter. When the receiver detects infrared energy pulsed at 40kHz, VOUT goes low.

three connections, to +5V, ground, and VOUT. You can find this part at Radio Shack and other sources.

Another option for MOD1 is Lite-On's LTM-8834-2, carried by Digi-Key. It has a 32.7-kHz center frequency, rather than 40 kilohertz, so you'll have to adjust the oscillator, either by adjusting R8 or by changing XTAL1. Digi-Key has a 32.56-kHz crystal that's a good match for this receiver.

When MOD1 detects infrared energy that is pulsed at 40 kilohertz, its VOUT is low. Otherwise, VOUT is high. Figure 12-4 shows a block diagram of what's inside the module. The photodiode emits a current when it senses infrared energy in the range 880-1080 nanometers. An optical filter on the photodiode blocks visible light, to reduce responses to ambient light. The module amplifies the detected signal and limits the peaks. A bandpass filter centered on 40 kilohertz reduces the amplitude of signals outside of the range of 36-44 kilohertz. A demodulator filters out the 40-kHz oscillations and recreates the original pulse pattern generated by the encoder. An integrator and comparator help to ensure a clean output at VOUT.

The module does a good job of detecting transmitted infrared pulses at 40 kilohertz. Unfortunately, in spite of its optical filter, it also has some response to ambient light, which causes brief, random pulses to appear at VOUT even when an IRED isn't transmitting to the module. But as we'll see, these random pulses are rejected by the decoder chip, which looks for a specific pulse pattern to identify the transmissions intended for it.

To reduce false triggers on ambient light, you can ground MOD1's case by soldering a wire from pin 3 to the case. You can also add more optical filtering, though for this application, it shouldn't be necessary. Photographic film is a good, inexpensive filter that passes infrared and blocks visible light. Cover the photodiode's window with an exposed, developed scrap of color-print negative film, or an unexposed, developed scrap of (positive) color-slide film.

The signal at pin 1 of MOD1 is essentially the same as U1's DATA OUT in Figure 12-1, but inverted. U5A inverts MOD1's output so that pin 9 of U4 matches U1's DATA OUT. You can substitute just about any CMOS inverter.

The decoder chip. U4 requires timing components to match U1's oscillator frequency. R9 and C7 set the timing that discriminates between narrow and wide received pulses. R10 and C8 set the timing that detects the end of an encoded word and the end of a transmission. Figure 12-2 shows Motorola's formulas and recommendations for choosing these values.

U4 has five address lines (A1-A5), which must match A1-A5 on U1. As with U1, the inputs are trinary, and may be logic high, logic low, or open. For testing, you can set these with jumpers or switches.

When MOD1 transmits, U4 examines the incoming bits at its pin 9. If the five address bits received match U4's address, U4 stores the next four bits and compares them to the previous four data bits received. If the data bits don't match, D6-D9 don't change. If the data bits do match, the receiver latches the new data to D6-D9 and brings VT (pin 11) high to indicate that a valid transmission was received.

The receiver doesn't latch D6-D9 until it receives the same data twice in a row. This complements the behavior of U1, which automatically sends each transmission twice. Requiring the receiver to see the same data twice prevents the receiver from accepting data that was garbled in transmitting. The only way that an error can slip through is if the address transmits correctly both times, and the data contains the same error twice in a row—if a transmitted 0 shows up as a 1 at the receiver, for example. The chances of this are small, especially since the 40-kHz modulation adds another layer of rejection of unwanted signals.

The data at D6-D9 remains until it is replaced by new received data. VT remains high until an error is detected or until there is no input for four data-bit times (32 milliseconds at 1 kHz).

Figure 12-2 shows LEDs at D6-D9 and VT for monitoring these outputs during testing. Current-limiting resistors aren't required, since U4 sources only about 5 milliamperes through the LEDs. If you prefer an audible indicator to announce a valid transmission, you can replace LED5 with a piezoelectric buzzer. Instead of the LEDs, you can connect just about any digital inputs to D6-D9.

Power-supply Options

Figures 12-1 and 12-2 show the transmitter and receiver powered at +5 volts. Recommended supply voltages for U1 and U4 are 4.5 to 18V, for U2 and U5, 2 to 6V, for U3, 2 to 15V, and for MOD1, 4.7 to 5.3V. This means that usable supply voltages for the transmitter circuit are 4. 5 to 6V, and for the receiver circuit, 4.7 to 5.3V.

Each circuit draws only a few milliamperes, though the test LEDs add about 5 milliamperes each when on. Any regulated 5-volt supply that can output 100 milliamperes is suitable for the transmitter or receiver.

Chances are that you'll want to operate the transmitter, receiver, or both, from batteries. Four NiCad cells in series create a reasonably stable source at around 4.8V. Using unregulated alkaline cells is less desirable, since their voltage drops quite a bit as they discharge (from 1.5V to around 1V per cell), and there is no series combination of 1.5V cells that meets MOD1's supply-voltage recommendation.

A regulated supply is another option. When the supply voltage varies, U3's output frequency and MOD1's frequency response also vary slightly. A regulated supply eliminates these concerns.

Figure 12-5 shows a 5V supply that uses five or six NiCad or alkaline cells and National Semiconductor's 2931T-5.0 low-drop-out 5V regulator. The regulator requires an input of just 5.6V for a 5V output at 100 milliamperes. You can also use a 9V alkaline NiCad battery to power the regulator, but due to the low capacities of this type, you'll get fewer hours of use.

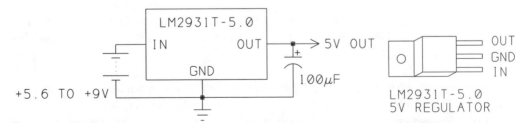

Figure 12-5. The LM2931T-5.0 voltage regulator creates a stable +5V supply with an input of 5.6V or greater.

Basic tests

When you have the circuits built and tested, if you have an oscilloscope or frequency counter, you can measure the frequency at pin 3 of U3 or pin 3 of U2A. If you're using U3, adjust R8 as needed for a 40-kHz output. You can also measure at pin 12 of U1 to verify that its oscillator is about 1 kilohertz.

To send a test transmission, set A1-A5 identically at U1 and U4, and set D6-D9 to the values you want to transmit. The schematics show the components set up to transmit the value *1000* to address *00001*.

Aim IRED1 so that it points to MOD1's photodiode window. To begin, place the transmitter and receiver a few feet apart. To transmit, press S1 momentarily to pulse pin 14 of U1 low. At U4, LED5 should flash to indicate that a valid transmission was received. At D6-D9, LED4 should be on and LEDs 1-3 should be off, to show that the value *1000* was received.

To change the data to be transmitted, move one or more jumpers or switches at U1's D6-D9. Press S1, and LEDs 1-4 should change to match. With these circuits, I was able to receive data from 12 feet away, with only casual aligning of the transmitter and receiver.

If you weren't able to measure and adjust U3's frequency, you can do so now. Jumper pin 12 of U1 to ground to cause the transmitter to continuously transmit. With IRED1 aimed at MOD1, slowly adjust potentiometer R8 until LED5 lights, continue to adjust until LED5 turns off, and then return R8 to about the middle of the range where LED5 is on. You can then keep the potentiometer, or replace it with a single resistor that matches the value you found experimentally.

To add a second receiver, build another circuit identical to Figure 12-2's, but with the address inputs set differently. In this way, you can transmit to a selected receiver by changing A1-A5 at the transmitter. Even if a receiver detects a transmission meant for another receiver, it will ignore it, since the address doesn't match.

Computer-controlled Transmitter

Figure 12-6 is a transmitter that is similar to 12-1, but with the manual controls replaced by outputs of an 82(C)55 PPI (from Chapter 6). Port A and bits 4-7 of Port C are configured as outputs.

The two halves, or 4-bit nibbles, of the 8255's Port A control the transmitted data and address. The high nibble controls data inputs D6-D9, and the low nibble controls address inputs A1-A4. The fifth address input, A5, is tied high, so you can control both the data and address with one 8-bit port. This reduces the number of decoders you can transmit to from 32 to 16, but this shouldn't be a problem in most applications.

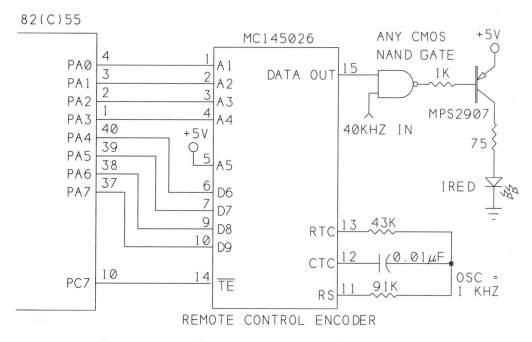

Figure   12-6. Using an 8255 to control an infrared transmitter.

The encoder's transmit enable ($\overline{\text{TE}}$) input connects to Port C, bit 7 on the 8255, which you can set and clear with the 8255's bit-control instructions.

Listing 12-1 shows a BASIC-52 program that causes the Figure 12-6's encoder to send a 4-bit value to Figure 12-2's decoder. The program asks for an address and data to transmit, writes the information to Port A, and then brings bit 7 of Port C low, then high, to cause the encoder to transmit the information. If the transmitted address matches the decoder's, the transmitted data appears at the decoder's data outputs, and its VT (valid transmission) output goes high. If the addresses do not match, or if the decoder detects an error in transmission, VT remains low and the decoder ignores the data.

If you want to do everything with a single 8-bit port, you can tie another of the encoder's address inputs high (or low, or leave it open), and use the additional bit on Port A to control $\overline{\text{TE}}$. If you do this, you'll have to use Boolean operators (AND, OR) to ensure that the data and address don't change when you toggle $\overline{\text{TE}}$. If you know you are going to transmit to only one address, you can hard-wire all of the encoder's address inputs and free up four bits on the 8255 for other uses.

Listing 12-1. Causes an encoder to transmit requested data.

```
10    REM 8255 mode set: Ports A,C = output, Port B = input
20    XBY(0FC03H)=82H
30    DO
40    INPUT "Enter the decoder's address (0-15): ",A
50    INPUT "Enter the data to send (0-15): ",D
60    REM Write the address and data information to Port A
70    XBY(0FC00H)=(D*10H+A)
80    REM Toggle TE (Port C, bit 7)
90    XBY(0FC03H)=0EH
100   XBY(0FC03H)=0FH
110   WHILE 1=1
120   END
```

Computer-controlled Receiver

Instead of, or in addition to, computer control of the transmitter, you can also add a computer interface at the receiver. For example, a data logger might accept data from a remote transmitter and process the data or store it for later use. Figure 12-7 shows a receiver similar to Figure 12-2's, with the manual controls replaced by port bits of an 82(C)55.

The circuit uses different port bits from Figure 12-6's circuit, so you can connect both a transmitter and a receiver to one 8255 if you wish. The low nibble of Port C is configured as an output, and sets A1-A4 on the decoder. As in the previous circuit, A5 is tied high so you can set the address with 4 bits. Port B is configured as an input, and its bits 4-7 store the data received at the decoder's D6-D9. VT is inverted and then connects to the 8052's $\overline{INT1}$ (pin 13). You can use any CMOS inverter.

Listing 12-2 is a BASIC-52 program that sets up the 8255 to receive data at port B, in Mode 0. The program writes an address to the decoder's address inputs, and also turns off $\overline{TE}$ (PC.7 in Figure 12-6, to ensure that the encoder on this end (if connected) isn't transmitting while the decoder is receiving. The program uses an edge-detecting interrupt to ensure that the program won't re-interrupt if VT is still low when the interrupt routine ends.

The main program is a do-nothing loop that waits for an interrupt. When VT goes high, indicating that a valid transmission has been received, the 8052-BASIC executes an interrupt routine that reads the data at bits 4-7 of Port B and displays it on the host computer.

Using VT to generate an interrupt is a handy way to detect when new data has arrived, but you don't have to use interrupts. If you don't enable interrupt 1, you can read Port 3's bit 3 periodically to find out if a new transmission has arrived. Or, you can leave VT unconnected

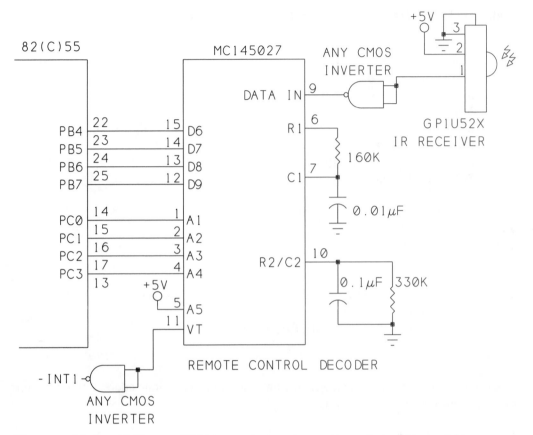

Figure   12-7.   Using an 8255 to control and access an infrared receiver.

and just read Port B once a minute, or on user request, or trigger the reading by some other factor under program control.

As with the encoder circuit, you don't have to use an 8255 to read and write to the decoder. Any latched port outputs will do for A1-A4, and any port inputs will do for D6-D9. Because the decoder latches the data, you don't need additional input latches. If the circuit will receive data from only one address, you can hardwire the decoder's A1-A5 and free up four bits on the 8255 for other uses.

You can transmit to Figure 12-7's circuit with either a manual or computer-controlled transmitter. Set the transmitter's address inputs to match the receiver's address, select the data you want to send, transmit, and view the received data on the 8052-BASIC system's host display.

Listing   12-2.   Reads received data at the decoder.

```
10    REM 8255 mode set: Ports A,C = output; Port B = input
20    XBY(0FC03H)=82H
30    REM     A=decoder address (0-15)
40    A=2
50    REM Write address to Port C, turn TE (PC.7) off (high)
60    XBY(0FC02H)=80H+A.OR.XBY(0FC02H)
70    REM Use edge-triggered interrupt
80    TCON=TCON.OR.4
90    DO
100   REM Wait for interrupt
110   ONEX1 500
120   WHILE 1=1
130   END

480   REM On interrupt 1, print received data
490   REM Data is at Port B, bits 4-7
500   PH0.(XBY(0FC01H).AND.0F0H)/10H
510   RETI
```

You can have more than one receiver in a link. If each has a unique address, it will accept only the transmissions meant for it.

Increasing the Distance

When you have your link up and running, one of the first challenges is to see how far you can reliably transmit. Two ways to increase the length of the link are by increasing the power of the transmitted signal, and by focusing the signal more precisely on the receiver.

About Infrared Energy

But first, some basics about infrared. Like visible light, infrared energy is a form of electromagnetic radiation. *Infra* means below, and infrared frequencies are just below those of red light. Infrared frequencies are invisible, or beyond the range detected by the human eye. Since wavelength is the inverse of frequency, infrared wavelengths are longer than those of visible light. Visible light covers the range 400-700 nm (nanometers), while infrared includes 700 nm through 1 million nm. (400 nanometers is 0.4 micron, or 4000 angstroms.)

Infrared-emitting diodes, or IREDs, are low-cost, widely available sources of infrared energy. An IRED is a semiconductor diode that emits infrared energy when a forward current passes through it, much as an LED emits visible light.

IREDs emit energy at specific wavelengths. Two popular types are GaAs (gallium arsenide), at 940 nm, and GaAlAs (gallium aluminum arsenide), at 880 nm. These are both in the range known as *near infrared,* to signify that their wavelengths are close to the visible spectrum.

Infrared detectors are also specific in the wavelengths they detect, although most will respond over a range. For example, the Sharp GP1U52X receiver module is most sensitive at 980 nm, but will also respond to the longer-wavelength emissions from GaAs and GaAlAs IREDs. Although the GaAs IREDs are a closer match at 940 nm, the GaAlAs IREDs tend

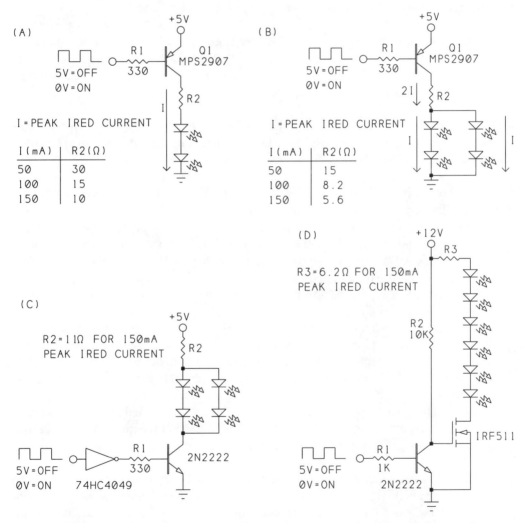

Figure 12-8. Circuits to increase the power and transmitting distance of an infrared link: (A) IREDs in series, (B) IREDs in parallel with PNP transistor driver, (C) IREDs in parallel with NPN transistor driver, and (D) MOSFET driver.

to be more efficient, so they may work as well even though 880 nm isn't as good a match with the detector.

Alternate Drive Circuits for IREDs

You can increase the strength of an infrared signal in two ways: by increasing the current through the IREDs, or by increasing the number of IREDs. Figure 12-8 shows both options, in a variety of circuits. All connect to the output of the NAND gate that combines the encoder's output and the 40-kilohertz oscillator in Figures 12-1 and 12-5.

Series drive. A simple way to double the power is to use two IREDs in series, as Figure 12-8A shows. With about 1.7 volts across each IRED, the series combination drops 3.4 volts. Instead of wasting energy by dropping 3 volts across a resistor, more of the current does useful work by powering a second IRED.

The maximum possible current through the IREDs is determined by the transistor's base current and gain. Outputs in the 74HC logic family can sink up to 25 milliamperes (absolute maximum), and are a good choice for driving the base.

Resistor R2 controls the amount of current through the IREDs. To determine a safe current through an IRED, you need to know the specifications of the IRED you are using, as well as how you plan to use the IRED in your circuit. The data sheet for any IRED should include an absolute maximum rating for continuous current. This is the maximum current that the device can withstand without damage. For example, for Harris' F5D1, this value is 100 milliamperes. When the IRED is powered continuously, the current through it shouldn't exceed this value. Since this is an absolute maximum, it's a good idea to stay well below it.

The infrared transmitter doesn't require the IRED to be on continuously, however. Instead, it pulses the IRED at 40 kilohertz. In non-continuous, or pulsed, operation, the IRED can handle much greater currents. The amount of allowable current depends on the pulse's duty cycle, which equals the width of a pulse divided by the width of a complete on-and-off cycle.

Unfortunately, the data sheets often do not say how to determine the limits for a particular pulse width and repetition rate. Occasionally, you get a graph of maximum forward current versus pulse width and duty cycle. Other data sheets just offer a few examples.

The F5D1's data sheet includes just two ratings for pulsed operation. For 10-microsecond pulses repeating at 100 Hz, the IRED's maximum peak current is 3 amperes, or 30 times the continuous rating. And for even shorter 1-microsecond pulses, repeating at 200 Hz, the maximum is 10 amperes. But neither of these describes the situation for the infrared transmitter.

In the infrared link, the amount of time the IRED is on depends on what information it is sending, and how often it transmits. When the IRED is pulsed at 40 kilohertz, it is on for just half of each 25-microsecond cycle. But the IRED pulses only when transmitting logic high outputs from the encoder. For logic low outputs, and when no data is transmitting, the IRED is off.

With the encoder chip clocked at 1 kilohertz, an encoded "1" contains two 3.5-millisecond high pulses and two 0.5-millisecond low pulses. This means that the IRED is pulsing almost 90 percent of the total time. If the 40-kilohertz oscillator has a 50-percent duty cycle, the IRED is on for half of this time, or 45 percent of each transmission. If you send a lot of 0's (if the receiver's address is 00, for example), or if you send only occasional, short transmissions, the average current will be much less.

In Figure 12-8A, with R2 at 30 ohms, the peak current through the IREDs is about 50 milliamperes, and the average current is under 25 milliamperes, well below the 100-milliampere limit. Even at a peak current of 150 milliamperes, the average over each transmission cycle will be under 70 milliamperes, still a safe level.

If you do pulse the IRED at 100 milliamperes or more, you have to be very careful to design your circuit so that the IRED never comes on continuously. When not transmitting data, the IRED should be off. At higher currents, it's a good idea to use a current-limiting resistor with a 1/2-watt or greater power rating.

Parallel drive. If two IREDs aren't enough, you can add two more in parallel, as Figure 12-8B shows. The value of the current-limiting resistor is smaller because it has twice the current through it, but the same voltage drop across it. Figure 12-8C shows four IREDs powered by an NPN transistor. A 74HC4049 inverter controls the transistor's base current. With multiples of this circuit, you can have as many IREDs as your power supply can support.

12V drive. And finally, if you have a 12-volt supply available, you can add up to six IREDs in series, as Figure 12-8D shows. The IRF511 MOSFET turns on when a voltage is applied to its gate. To turn on fully, the MOSFET requires a gate voltage greater than 5 volts.

For more powerful transmissions to a specific receiver, you can mount multiple IREDs in a cluster, all pointing at the receiver. If you want to transmit to multiple receivers, or if a receiver's exact location is unknown, you can mount the IREDs so that they transmit across a wider path.

Using Lenses

Another way to increase the range of a link is with optical lenses that focus or spread the transmitted energy.

Some IREDs are manufactured with integral lenses that focus the output into a beam. For example, Harris' F5D1 and F5E1 IREDs are identical, except that the F5D1 has a lens that aims the energy in a narrow beam, while the F5E1 has a flat window and wider beam angle. An IRED with an integral lens is an easy, low-cost option, if it can do the job. A flat-window package is useful if you want to add an external lens, or if you want a wider beam, to reach multiple receivers around a room, for example.

If you're interested in experimenting with lenses, Edmund Scientific has a huge selection, including inexpensive educational-grade lenses, lens mounts, optical benches, and books on optics.

Although infrared links are most often thought of as line-of-sight paths—for transmitting across a room, for example—optics can also overcome this limitation. For example, with mirrors, you can transmit around corners.

Radio Links

Another possibility for wireless links is to use radio frequencies. Radio transmissions consist of high-frequency electromagnetic waves that travel through the atmosphere. Most radio waves will also pass through windows, walls, and other solid objects. This makes radio useful where a direct line-of-sight between transmitter and receiver isn't available. Radio can also be a good choice for outdoor links, where daylight may interfere with infrared transmissions and wired links are inconvenient.

Radio circuits require special construction techniques, and radio transmissions must not violate regulations of agencies such as the Federal Communications Commission (FCC). For these reasons, the easiest option is to buy the transmitters and receivers for your link, rather than build them yourself.

One source of low-cost radio-frequency transmitter and receiver circuits is Electronics 123. The links transmit in the range 300-315 Megahertz, a frequency band used by many garage-door openers and alarm systems. The boards come with complete schematics and instructions for use.

The circuits are similar to the infrared-transmitting circuits described earlier. The transmitter sends 4-bit codes to a receiver identified by an 8-bit address. The transmitter and receiver use Holtek's HT-12E encoder and HT-12D or HT-12F decoder chips, also available separately from Electronics 123 and Digi-Key. The chips are similar in operation to Motorola's 146026/7 encoder and decoder, and you can in fact use them in infrared links as well. The encoder and decoder each require just one resistor to set the oscillator frequency.

13

Calling Assembly-language Routines

Although BASIC-52 is a convenient programming language that can do a lot, sometimes it's just not fast enough for what you need. A line in a BASIC-52 program can take many milliseconds to execute, and for some applications, this is just too long.

One way to speed things up is to use assembly language. This doesn't mean that you have to give up on BASIC-52 entirely. You can continue to use it for the parts of your programs that aren't time-critical, and call assembly-language routines only for those parts that have to be fast. BASIC-52 can also serve as a convenient development system for loading and testing assembly-language routines in RAM, and even for programming the routines into NV memory.

Calling routines from BASIC-52 is a good way to become familiar with assembly-language programming. Plus, through experimenting, you can learn a lot about the internal workings of the 8052 chip and how the BASIC-52 interpreter works.

This chapter explores how and when to interface assembly-language routines to BASIC-52 programs. An example project connects a digital-to-analog converter to the 8052-BASIC. Programs in BASIC-52 and assembly language cause a sine wave to appear at the converter's output. There's also a section on how to use your BASIC-52 system as a general-purpose

EPROM programmer, for storing assembly-language routines or anything else you want to program into an EPROM, for use on an 8052-BASIC system or another device.

Assembly-language Basics

The bare 8052 chip understands just one language: the binary machine codes that make up the chip's instruction set. The 8052's data book describes the function of each of the machine codes.

You can, of course, write programs without having to look up binary codes, by using a programming language. The language that is closest to the machine codes is assembly language, where a mnemonic, or abbreviation, represents each of the codes.

The assembly-language program that you write is called a *source file*. After you write a source file, you must use an assembler to translate the source file into an *object file,* which contains the machine codes that the chip will execute. You also must have a way of storing the object file in the 8052-BASIC system's memory, where the 8052-BASIC chip can access it.

The BASIC-52 interpreter is itself an assembled program that the 8052 runs on boot-up. The interpreter reads your BASIC-52 programs from memory and translates them into machine codes for the 8052 to execute. It does the same for the BASIC-52 commands that you type at the keyboard. The interpreter program includes many modular routines that BASIC-52 uses, such as reading a character from the serial port or comparing two values.

BASIC-52 programs are slow for two reasons. One is that the interpreter must translate each line of code every time it executes it. With assembly language, the assembler translates the program only once, and the 8052 then reads and executes the binary codes directly from memory. The other reason for the slowness of BASIC-52 programs is that the nterpreter program's translation from BASIC-52 to machine code doesn't result in the most efficient code. Programming directly in assembly language gives you much greater control over the final code that the 8052 will execute.

Incidentally, assembly language isn't the only way to get faster execution times. Other options include using a BASIC or C compiler or using a faster crystal to clock the 8052. But as a rule, these approaches will not speed up programs as dramatically as assembly language.

What You Need

To add assembly-language routines to your BASIC-52 programs, you need several items: a programming reference with details about the 8052's assembly language, a text editor for writing the source files, an assembler to create the executable files, memory in the 8052-BASIC system for storing your programs, and a way to transfer your executable files into memory in the 8052-BASIC system. The following sections describe each of these in more detail.

Programming Reference

This book concentrates on BASIC-52 programming. I've included enough information about assembly language to get you started programming, plus what you need to know to interface assembly-language routines to BASIC-52. But there is much more to assembly-language programming than I can cover here.

If you are an experienced assembly-language programmer, Intel's *Embedded Microcontrollers* handbook, or a similar reference from another 8052 vendor, may be all you need as a reference. The handbook includes a programmer's guide and describes each of the 8052's instructions.

If you're just starting out with assembly language, you might want to invest in a more complete text that includes examples and explanations of how to put together a program. Examples can be extremely useful for seeing how to do common tasks like generating a timing delay or handling an interrupt. Appendix A lists several books on the 8051 family that include programming examples and tutorials.

Text Editor

The text editor is the software that you use to create your source files. The editor program must be able to create files in straight ASCII format, without adding any formatting codes. Just about all word processors have this ability, as do simpler text editors like MS-DOS's *EDIT*.

Assembler

The assembler is the program that creates an object, or executable, file from your source file. If you write assembly-language programs for your personal computer, you use an assembler, such as MASM for 80x86 microprocessors. MASM creates files that will execute on 80x86 systems, using the 80x86's instruction set.

To assemble a program for an 8052 microcontroller, you need a special type of assembler called a *cross assembler*. The cross assembler runs on your personal, or host, computer, but creates programs to run on a different chip, such as the 8052. Assemblers for 8051-family chips, which you can use for 8052 programming, are widely available. Appendix A lists vendors of assemblers and BBS's from which you can download free and shareware assemblers.

Most 8051-family cross-assemblers create files in Intel Hex format, which is convenient for EPROM programming and uploading to RAM. During the assembly process, if the assembler encounters a program line that is incomplete or not understandable, it will display an error message describing the problem. The assembler will also create a *listing file* that shows each line of your source file alongside the addresses and machine codes of the object file and any error messages generated.

Memory for Program Storage

On your BASIC-52 system, you'll need room in external memory for storing your assembly-language routines. Remember that the 8052 has separate control signals for accessing code and data memory. For uploading into RAM and testing, you must use combined code/data memory, since you need data memory's $\overline{WR}$ signal to write the routine into memory, and code memory's $\overline{PSEN}$ to enable the 8052 to execute the routine.

You can upload routines into any unused combined code/data memory from 2000h to FFFFh. Code memory from 0 to 1FFFh is not available, because the 8052-BASIC chip uses these locations for the BASIC-52 interpreter. If you have a 32K RAM addressed at 0 in combined code/data memory, you can use the area above 1FFFh for storing and testing assembly-language routines. For combined data/code memory in Figure 3-1's circuit, move the connection at pin 22 of U7 from pin 17 of U2 ($\overline{READ}$) to pin 3 of U3A ($\overline{RDANY}$). With this setup, however, if you upload your programs into ordinary RAM, you'll lose them when you power down.

For more permanent storage, there are several options. You can use a 32K NV RAM, such as Dallas Semiconductor's DS1235, or a Dallas 1213C SmartSocket and 62256 SRAM, in place of ordinary RAM at 0. Although you don't need battery backup for data memory from 0 to 1FFFh, it does no harm. Again, you must connect $\overline{RDANY}$, not $\overline{READ}$, to pin 22 of the NVRAM.

To prevent overwriting your assembly-language routines in RAM when you reboot, set MTOP to 1FFFh, or another value that is lower than the beginning of your routines, and execute BASIC-52's PROG3 command, as described in Chapter 3. (You must have NV memory at 8000h to save MTOP.)

If you use a 32K NV RAM from 0 to 7FFFh, you should be aware that BASIC-52 reserves two areas of code memory for optional additions and enhancements. One area, from 2001h to 2091h, stores information that tells BASIC-52 about custom reset routines, keywords and other language extensions. Another area, from from 4003h to 41FFh, stores information about user-defined assembly-language interrupt routines.

If you won't be using these abilities, you can use these areas of memory for other purposes. However, if at all possible, it's a good idea to avoid writing to locations 2001h, 2002h, and

2048h in code memory. This is because BASIC-52 checks these locations on bootup to determine what additions have been made to BASIC-52. If you by chance have certain data stored at these locations, BASIC-52 will look for the additions it thinks you have, and crash when it doesn't find them.

If you have an EPROM addressed at 8000h, and you don't need the entire EPROM for BASIC-52 programs, you can store your assembly-language routines in the unused area. BASIC-52's (F) PROG command stores programs in sequence beginning at 8010h, so to leave the most room for BASIC programs, you should place your assembly-language routines in the EPROM's highest addresses.

You can also add NVRAM or EPROM in any unused area of combined code/data memory. For example, you could add an 8K NVRAM addressed from 2000h to 3FFFh, or a 16K EPROM from 4000h to 7FFFh.

Software for Uploading

You'll also need a way to load your routines from your personal computer into your 8052-BASIC system's memory. All that's required here are your host computer's communications software and a BASIC-52 program that reads and stores the uploaded file.

Appendix B contains two such programs. Listing B-1, HEX2RAM.BAS, loads Intel Hex files from your personal computer into RAM, including NVRAM, in a BASIC-52 system. Listing B-2, HEXLOAD.BAS, does the same, and also offers the options of loading into EPROM or EEPROM.

On your host computer, you can the same communications software that you use to upload BASIC-52 programs, as described in Chapter 3.

Another option for loading routines from your host computer into memory is to program an EPROM or other device with a device programmer, and then insert the programmed device into your BASIC-52 system. If you use this method, you can access the chip as code-only memory, rather than combined code/data memory, since you don't need to write to it when it's installed in the 8052-BASIC system.

Loading a Routine

When you have the necessary tools, you're ready to write an assembly-language routine and assemble, upload, and call, or run, it. As a first try, we'll begin with a very simple routine, just to verify that the circuits and techniques are working.

Listing 13-1 has just one function: it toggles pin 1 (Port 1, bit 0) of the 8052. An *ORG* directive tells the assembler the address at which to begin loading the routine. Listing 13-1

Listing   13-1.   Source file for a simple program to test assembly-language interfacing with BASIC-52.

```
        org    3000h           ;location where program will
                               ;load in RAM
        cpl    p1.0            ;complement Port 1, bit 0
                               ;(pin 1)
        ret                    ;return to BASIC-52

        end
```

specifies 3000h. You can change the address to match whatever locations you have available in your system.

The program body's single instruction complements bit 0 of Port 1, changing it from high to low or low to high. A *ret* instruction then returns control to BASIC-52.

To create and test the routine, do the following:

Use a text editor to create a file containing Listing 13-1.
Use your assembler to assemble the file. A typical command line looks like this:

```
    A51 bittog.asm -L bittog.lst -O bittog.hex
```

The above command tells the assembler to create two files: the listing file *bittog.lst* (shown in Listing 13-2) and the object file *bittog.hex*, in Intel hex format (shown in Listing 13-3).

File Formats for Assembly-language Routines

This is a good time to look at Intel Hex and other file formats in greater detail. Most EPROM programmers are able to program EPROMs directly from the files created by assemblers and compilers, but the file must be in a format that the programmer recognizes. Three

Listing   13-2.   Listing file created by assembling the source file in Listing 13-1.

```
3000 org  3000h               ;location where program will
                              ;load in RAM

3000      b2 90    cpl p1.0   ;complement Port 1, bit 0
                              ;(pin 1)
3002      22       ret        ;return to BASIC-52
```

Figure   13-1.   Examples of a byte expressed in binary, hexadecimal, and the ASCII codes representing the Hex characters.

Binary value	1100	0101
Hex equivalent	C	5
ASCII code for Hex character	43	35

common formats are binary, ASCII Hex, and Intel Hex. Intel Hex is also the format required for programs that you upload using Listings B-1 and B-2. Figure 13-1 shows a byte expressed in binary, hexadecimal, and ASCII hex.

Binary

A binary file is the most primitive or unadorned type. It consists of a sequence of bytes that exactly corresponds to the bytes to be programmed. The file contains no addressing information for loading or programming, and no error-checking.

To view or edit a binary file on a personal computer, you need a special file-viewing utility. This is because conventional file-viewing techniques, such as MS-DOS's TYPE command, will interpret the bytes as ASCII codes and will display the ASCII characters that the codes represent. For example, the value "1" in a binary file appears on-screen as a happy-face character.

ASCII Hex

In ASCII Hex, or pure Hex, format, each byte is expressed as a 2-character hexadecimal number, with each character represented by its ASCII code. ASCII Hex files contain only these 16 codes: 30h through 39h (for numerals 0 through 9) and 41h through 46h (for capital letters A through F).

You can easily view and edit ASCII Hex files on a personal computer, because the computer displays the ASCII characters that the codes represent. However, the EPROM programmer or uploading program must translate the codes into binary data before it writes the codes into the device to be programmed.

Because each byte to be programmed requires two codes, an ASCII Hex file is twice as long as the resulting file that is programmed into the EPROM.

Listing   13-3.   Intel Hex file created by assembling the source file in Listing 13-1.

```
:03300000B2902269
:00000001FF
```

Intel Hex

Like ASCII Hex, Intel Hex format stores bytes as ASCII codes representing hexadecimal characters. But Intel Hex adds addressing and error-checking information for more flexible programming and more reliable file transfer.

Each Intel Hex file consists of a series of records. Table 13-1 has more details about the records and what they contain. You don't have to understand everything about Intel Hex format in order to use it, but the information can be useful if you run into problems and want to examine the contents of a file.

Assembling a Program

When you assemble a program, the message *Assembly Successful,* or something similar, means that the assembler found no errors that prevented it from creating the object file. If you do see error messages, you'll have to find out what's wrong before continuing. The listing file also includes the error messages, and these should help you track down any problems.

Table 13-1. An Intel Hex file consists of a series of records , each of which contains the the six elements below.

Name	# Chars	Description
Record Mark	1	Each record begins with a colon (:).
Record Length	2	Number of data bytes in the record.
Address Field	2	In data records, the address where the first data byte is to be stored, with following bytes in sequence. In other record types, 0000.
Record type	2	There are four record types: 00 Data 01 End of File 02 Extended address 03 Start address
Data Field	varies	Contents depends on the record type: 00 Data to be programmed 01 Not used (empty) 02 Segment. For address fields larger than 64K, data is stored beginning at (segment+10h)+address field. 03 Start address of program. Often unused.
Checksum	2	To calculate the checksum: (1) Add the values of all of the bytes in a record. (2) Take the 2's complement of the result (Complement all bits and add 1.) (3) The checksum is the low byte of the result.

Successful assembly is a good sign, but it doesn't mean that the program is error-free. As in any programming language, a line of code may contain instructions that are valid, but that do not do what you intended. It's a good idea to at least scan the listing created by the assembler before you try to run a routine, to look for obvious errors.

Different assemblers may have slightly different syntax rules. For example, some require *org* and *end* to have a leading period (*.org, .end*). Check your assembler's documentation for the specifics.

Uploading a Program

When you're ready to load the program into RAM, boot your 8052-BASIC system, connect the serial link to your personal computer, and run your communications software. Use the software to upload Listing B-1 or B-2, in the same way that you upload any BASIC-52 program from disk.

For loading Intel hex files, you can set up your host computer's software so that it waits to receive the BASIC-52 ">" prompt (ASCII code 62) after each uploaded line. This will ensure that BASIC-52 has enough time to process each line before the next one arrives. Use this method only with Intel Hex files, not BASIC-52 programs. If a BASIC-52 program contains any ">" (greater than) operators, the software will think that these indicate the end of a program line. Intel Hex files contain no ">" characters, so there is no problem.

If you want to wait for the ">" character, in *Procomm Plus*, from the Setup menu, select Terminal Options, then Protocol Options, ASCII Options, and set the pace character to 62. Character pacing and line pacing can be 0. In the *Windows* terminal, select Settings, then Text Transfers, One Line at a Time, and enter ">" under Wait for Prompt String. Other software should have similar abilities.

If you wish, you can use BASIC-52's (F) PROG command to store the program in NV memory so it's available without having to upload each time.

To use Listing B-1 or B-2, run the program and, at the prompt, use your communications software to upload your object file. The file will load into the locations specified by your source file. The program will display error messages if it has problems with the uploading. For proper calculation of the programming-pulse width in Listing B-2, set BASIC-52's XTAL operator to match your crystal's frequency.

If the file loads successfully, you're ready to test it. Connect a logic probe to pin 1 on the 8052, or set a voltmeter to measure the voltage from pin 1 to pin 20 (ground) on the chip. To call your subroutine, enter and run this BASIC-52 program:

```
10 CALL 3000h
20 END
```

If necessary, change the address in line 10 to match the value in your routine's *org* directive.

Each time you run the program, you should see pin 1 on the 8052 change from high to low or low to high. The routine should then return you to the BASIC-52 prompt.

If the program crashes and does not return you to BASIC-52, you need to re-examine your listing file to see what went wrong. Remember that the address in BASIC-52's CALL

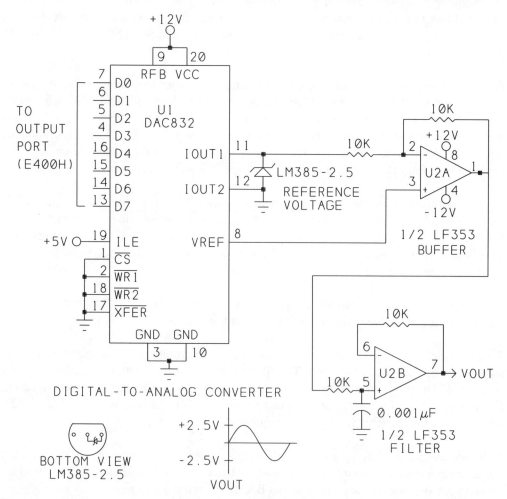

Figure **13-2.** By writing the appropriate values to an output port, you can cause a sine wave to appear at **VOUT**.

statement must match the address in your file's *org* directive. A missing *ret* instruction in the routine will also cause the system to crash.

Example: Creating a Sine Wave

When you have the simple routine working, you're ready to move on to bigger things. For the sine-wave project, we'll begin by generating a sine wave entirely with BASIC-52 statements. This way, we can first test the added circuits as well as the algorithm, or sequence of steps, that we plan to use to generate the sine wave. It also illustrates the speed limits of BASIC-52.

The Circuits

Figure 13-2 shows the circuit that interfaces to the 8052. I adapted the circuit from an example in National Semiconductor's data sheet for the DAC0832.

U1 is a DAC0832 digital-to-analog converter, or DAC, which converts data inputs D0-D7 into an analog voltage. D0-D7 are controlled by an output port at E400h. You may change this address to match any output port on your system.

Listing   13-4.   Sine-wave generator for Figure 13-2's circuit.

```
10    REM Begins by calculating and storing sine values
20    REM for 256 locations along a sine wave.
30    REM Line 100 converts a position in the sine wave
40    REM (0-255) to the radians required by the sine
50    REM operator: (0.0246 = 2*PI/256). Adding 1 to the
60    REM sines makes all values positive, from 0 to +2.
70    REM Multiplying by 127.5 results in values that
80    REM range from 0 to 255.
90    FOR I=0 TO 255
100   XBY(3000H+I)=INT((SIN(I*.0246)+1)*127.5+.5)
110   NEXT I
120   PRINT "Sine values are stored in RAM (3000h-30FFh)"
130   PRINT "Press Control+C to quit"
140   REM Write the values in sequence to E400h
150   DO
160   FOR I=3000H TO 30FFH
170   XBY(0E400H)=XBY(I)
180   NEXT I
190   WHILE 1=1
200   END
```

The DAC is configured in its flow-through and voltage-switching modes. In flow-through mode, the analog output continuously reflects the data inputs. The chip has several control signals for latching inputs and outputs, but these aren't needed by our circuit.

In voltage-switching mode, the analog output is a voltage proportional to the value of the byte formed by D0-D7. An LM385 2.5-volt reference is applied across current output terminals IOUT1 and IOUT2, and the output appears at VREF. (This configuration is the inverse of the device's current-switching mode, where VREF is an input and IOUT1 and IOUT2 are outputs, as their names suggest.)

Op amp U2A buffers the output, and U2B is a low-pass filter that helps to smooth VOUT.

A BASIC Program

Listing 13-4 causes a sine wave to appear at VOUT. The sine wave represents the value of the trigonometric sine function for an angle that varies continuously from 0 to 360 degrees, or 0 to 6.28 (2*PI) radians. Lines 90-110 are a loop that selects 256 equally-spaced points along one cycle of the sine wave, calculates the sine for each, and stores the values in RAM. The program uses BASIC-52's SIN operator in calculating the values. Sine values normally vary from +1 to -1, but line 100 adjusts the values so that they vary from 0 to 255, which is the range of inputs accepted by the 8-bit DAC. Using these values, 0 is the negative peak, 255 is the positive peak, and the zero crossing occurs midway between points 127 and 128.

To generate the sine wave, Lines 150-180 are a loop that reads each value in sequence from RAM and writes it to an output port at E400h. After writing a complete cycle, the program loops back and begins another. The sine wave repeats endlessly, until the user presses CONTROL+C.

Listing 13-4 creates a perfectly good sine wave, but at a very low frequency. Using 12-Megahertz crystal to clock the 8052, the frequency is only about 0.7 Hertz, or 1.5 seconds per cycle.

Adding Assembly Language

To speed things up, Listing 13-5 is an assembly-language routine that performs the functions of lines 150-180 in Listing 13-4. As in the original program, Listing 13-5 copies values in sequence from RAM to E400h, repeating the sequence after 256 writes. The routine illustrates a couple of major differences between BASIC and assembly-language programming.

One is that assembly language has no built-in FOR, DO, or WHILE loops. Instead, you have to create loop structures from the instructions available. Listing 13-5 creates a 256-step

Listing   13-5.   Assembly-language sine-wave routine for Figure 13-2's circuit..

```
;Reads and copies values in sequence from locations 3000h
;to 30FFh to E400h. A DAC0832 generates a sine wave from
;the values.
;A keypress terminates the routine and returns to BASIC-52.

org          3100h                   ;load routine above the
                                     ;stored values
OutputPort   equ   0e400h            ;address of port to write
                                     ;sine values to

;Begin generating the sine wave:
nextcycle    mov   20h,#0ffh         ;store initial count at 20h
                                     ;in internal
                                     ;data memory
nextvalue    mov   dph,#30h          ;put high byte of sine wave
                                     ;address (30h)
                                     ;in dptr
             mov   dpl,20h           ;copy low byte of sine wave
                                     ;address from 20h to dptr
             movx  a,@dptr           ;place sine wave value in
                                     ;acc.
             mov   dptr,#OutputPort       ;copy port address
                                     ;to dptr
             movx  @dptr,a           ;copy sine wave value to
                                     ;output port
             djnz  20h,nextvalue ;do another if count > 0
             jb    ri,return         ;after writing one complete
                                     ;cycle, check serial receive
                                     ;flag and quit if set
             sjmp  nextcycle         ;if serial flag not set,
                                     ;begin another cycle

;Return to BASIC-52:
return       clr   ri                ;clear serial receive flag
             ret                     ;return to BASIC

             end
```

FOR loop by loading FFh into register *dpl* (the lower byte of *dptr*), and decrementing *dpl* repeatedly until it equals zero.

In assembly language, you also do not have built-in conveniences like BASIC-52's ability to terminate a program on CONTROL+C. You have to add these features yourself. In Listing 13-5, after each complete cycle of the sine wave, the program checks the serial port's receive flag. If the flag is set, it means that the user has pressed a key, and the program returns to the BASIC-52 prompt. Otherwise, the program begins another cycle of the sine wave.

To run Listing 13-5, create a source file with your text editor, assemble it, and upload it to RAM as before. Edit Listing 13-4 by removing lines 150-180 and adding this line:

```
150   CALL 3100h
```

Now when you run Listing 13-4, you should again see a sine wave at VOUT, but at a much higher frequency.

With a 12-Megahertz crystal, the sine wave should be around 350 Hertz, or 2.8 milliseconds per cycle. You can verify this by consulting the 8052's data book, which tells the number of machine cycles required to execute each instruction. At 12 Megahertz, each machine cycle is 1 microsecond, and one complete cycle requires 11 microseconds multiplied by 255 points on the wave, plus 6 microseconds to test the serial flag, or 2811 microseconds total.

With different crystal frequencies, the output frequency will vary in direct proportion. For example, with a 6-Megahertz crystal, the sine wave will be half as fast.

To slow down the sine wave, you can add "do-nothing" instructions to the code. For example adding a *nop* (no operation) instruction in the main loop will add 1 microsecond to the time between points on the wave, for a frequency of 326 Hertz. For long delays, you can insert a timing loop that executes after each point in the wave.

Listing 13-5 still relies on BASIC-52 to calculate the sine values and store them in RAM. Although you can also write these parts in assembly language, doing so in BASIC is much easier, and doesn't affect the frequency of the sine wave that results. Even if you later decide to write this part in assembly language, with BASIC-52 you can test each section of the code as you go along.

When you have your assembly-language routine in the form you want it, you can use Listing B-2 or an EPROM programmer to store the code in EPROM. If your EPROM has different addressing than the RAM you used to test the code, you must change the ORG directive in the source file to match the new location, and reassemble the file before you program it into the EPROM.

Avoiding Program Crashes

It's very easy to write an assembly-language program that crashes the system and forces you to reboot. To prevent this, you have to take care that your routines do not interfere with each other, or with BASIC-52. Remember that BASIC-52 is a program in itself, and it uses many of the registers and other memory locations, both inside and outside of the 8052, for its own purposes.

For example, BASIC-52 uses locations 13h and 14h in internal RAM to store the starting address of the current BASIC program in external RAM. If you overwrite these values, BASIC-52 will no longer be able to find your program.

The BASIC-52 programming manuals list the registers and other memory addresses used by BASIC. In general, you should avoid writing to these locations, unless you know what you're doing and how to deal with the results.

Often, an assembly-language routine will alter some of the 8052's registers. You are responsible for seeing that all critical values are unchanged when the routine returns control to the program that called it, whether it's BASIC-52 or another assembly-language program.

The *stack* is a convenient way to preserve values on entering a routine, and to restore them on exiting. The stack is a special area of memory with a last-in, first-out structure, which means that you read values from the stack in the reverse order that you wrote them. Storing values in the stack area is called *pushing*, or placing, values on the stack. Retrieving values from the stack area is called *popping* them off the stack.

Assembly language has *push* and *pop* instructions for accessing the stack. (BASIC-52's PUSH and POP instructions access a separate area called the argument stack.)

You can also preserve values by selecting a unique register bank for use by a routine. The 8052 has 32 registers arranged in four banks of eight, from 0 to 1Fh in internal data memory. You can access the registers by specifying the address, or by selecting a register bank and specifying a register from R0 to R7 within the bank. For example, if bank 0 is selected, R0 is location 00h, but if bank 1 is selected, R0 is location 08h.

BASIC-52 uses banks 0, 1, and 2, but uses bank 3 only with the PGM instruction, so this bank is usually free for other uses. Bits 3 and 4 of the 8052's program status word (*psw*) select the register bank. When you call an assembly-language routine, BASIC-52 automatically selects register bank 0. To select bank 3, add this to the beginning of your routine:

```
push      psw              ;save program status word
orl       psw,#18h         ;select register bank 3
```

Listing   13-6.   This assembly-language routine is similar to Listing 13-1, except that external interrupt 1 causes the routine to run.

```
;On external interrupt 1, Port 1, bit 0 is complemented

          org    4013h          ;vector for external
                                 ;interrupt 1
          cpl    p1.0           ;complement Port 1, bit 0
                                 ;(pin 1)
          pop    psw            ;push psw was automatic on
                                 ;interrupt,
                                 ;but pop psw must be added
          reti
          end
```

and add this to the end, before returning to BASIC-52:

```
          pop    psw                 ;restore program status word
```

Your routine can then write to registers R0-R7 without worrying about conflicting with BASIC.

Interrupts

BASIC-52 also includes a way of adding assembly-language routines that respond to interrupts. Normally, the 8052 stores its interrupt vectors (the locations where the program jumps on interrupts) from 03h to 2Bh in code memory. Since these locations are in ROM in the 8052-BASIC, your programs can't change their contents. But built into BASIC-52 is the ability to place alternate interrupt routines from 4003h to 402Bh.

To illustrate, Listing 13-6 is an assembly-language interrupt routine. The routine's origin is 4013h, which is BASIC-52's alternate vector for external interrupt 1. The interrupt routine has the same function as Listing 13-1. It toggles bit 0 of Port 1, then returns to BASIC-52.

These are a few things of note about Listing 13-6:

• You must have code memory at 4013h, since BASIC-52 specifies that this location must contain either the interrupt routine or a jump to a longer routine. If the routine is longer than 8 bytes, use a jump instruction, such as *sjmp 4033h*, to prevent overwriting any interrupt vectors that follow.

- BASIC-52's ON EX1 instruction will also respond to external interrupt 1, but the response time will be much slower. ON EX1 has priority, however, and Listing 13-6 will not execute if an ON EX1 statement has executed in BASIC-52.

- When BASIC-52 jumps to an assembly-language interrupt routine, it automatically pushes *psw* on the stack. But popping *psw* on returning from the interrupt routine is not automatic, so the interrupt routine must include an instruction to do so.

- Unlike other subroutines, which end with *ret*, interrupt routines must end with *reti*.

To test Listing 13-6, upload it to RAM at 4013h, and execute these two lines of BASIC-52 code, to ensure that the interrupt is enabled:

```
IE=IE.OR.84h
TCON=TCON.OR.04h
```

Now, each time pin 13 goes low, pin 1 should toggle, as it did with Listing 13-1.

Adding Custom Commands and Instructions

Another feature of BASIC-52 is the ability to add up to 16 custom keywords representing commands or instructions that you define with assembly-language routines. Listing 13-7 is an example program for doing so.

To add custom keywords, you must have code memory from 2000h to 2071h, because BASIC-52 looks for special information at several addresses in this area.

On bootup, BASIC-52 examines the data at address 2048h. If bit 5 is set, BASIC-52 assumes that you have added custom keywords, and it looks for additional information in a token table and vector table.

At 2078h, BASIC-52 expects to find the starting address of a token table, which lists your new keywords. At 2070h, it expects the starting address of a vector table, which lists the assembly-language routines that the new keywords execute.

You may upload both tables to any free area of combined code/data memory. If you're using an external EPROM programmer, you can use code-only memory in the 8052-BASIC system.

In the token table, each new keyword is assigned a number, in sequence from 10h to 1Fh. The name of the keyword is surrounded by quotation marks, and a 0 indicates the end of the token. The final keyword in the list ends in 0FFh, to signify the end of the list of tokens. Listing 13-7 adds three keywords, which toggle, set, and clear bit 0 of Port 1.

Listing   13-7. (page 1 of 2)   Creates instructions to set, clear, and toggle Port 1, bit 0 in BASIC-52.

```
;example program for creating custom commands and instruc-
tions in BASIC-52
;system must contain code memory from 2000h-2079h

tokentable   equ    2100h             ;start address, token table
vectortable  equ    2200h             ;start address, vector table

             org    2002h             ;5Ah at 2002h tells BASIC-52
             db     5ah               ;to call 2048h (see below)

             org    2048h             ;Set bit 45 to tell BASIC-52
                                      ;that custom commands or
             setb   45                ;instructions have been
             ret                      ;added

             org    2078h             ;stores starting address of
             mov    dptr,#tokentable      token table
             ret

             org    2070h             ;stores starting address of
             mov    dptr,#vectortable     vector table
             ret

             org    tokentable        ;token table start address
             db     10h               ;first user-defined token
             db     "TGGP10"          ;command or instruction name
                                      ;(must use all capital
                                      ;letters, beginning
                                      ;combination of letters
                                      ;must be unique)

             db     0                 ;end of token indicator

             db     11h               ;2nd user-defined token
             db     "SETP10"          ;command or instruction name
             db     0                 ;end of token indicator

             db     12h               ;final user-defined token
             db     "CLRP10"          ;command or instruction name
             db     0ffh              ;end of list indicator
```

Listing   13-7. (page 2 of 2)

```
                 ;can add up to 1Fh tokens
                 ;final token must end with 0ffh

                 org    vectortable    ;vector table address
                 dw       tggp10       ;label to branch to on
                                       ;TGGP10 command
                 dw       setp10       ;label to branch to on
                                       ;SETP10 command
                 dw       clrp10       ;label to branch to on
                                       ;CLRP10 command

tggp10   org 3000h    ;use any available address
         cpl    p1.0             ;complement Port 1, bit 0
                                 ;(pin 1)
         ret                     ;return to BASIC-52

setp10   org 3010h    ;use any available address
         setb   p1.0             ;set Port 1, bit 0 (pin 1)
         ret                     ;return to BASIC-52

clrp10   org 3020h    ;use any available address
         clr    p1.0             ;clear Port 1, bit 0 (pin 1)
         ret                     ;return to BASIC-52

         end
```

The vector table consists of a list of labels corresponding to the beginning of each assembly-language routine.

In addition to the tables, you must store the assembly-language routines themselves, again using any free code/data or code memory.

To use Listing 13-7, you must assemble it and upload the resulting Intel Hex file into NV memory that will be preserved on powering down or rebooting. Reboot, and you can use the new keywords TGGP10, SETP10, and CLRP10 to control bit 0 of Port 1. (Notice that the "bit-toggle" keyword is TGGP10, rather than TOGP10, which contains the keyword TO and so won't work.)

Listing 13-8. (page 1 of 2) Copies data from external memory into EPROM, EEPROM, or NV RAM.

```
10    PRINT "enter device type: "
20    PRINT "EPROM 50-msec       1"
30    PRINT "EPROM Intelligent   2"
40    PRINT "EEPROM or NV RAM     3"
50    PRINT "quit                 4"
60    INPUT T

70    REM set pulse width for device type
80    REM W = pulse width in milliseconds
90    IF T=1 THEN W=.05
100   IF T=2 THEN W=.001
110   IF T=3 THEN W=.0005
120   IF T=4 THEN GOTO 470

130   REM calculate and store pulse width
140   B=(65536-(W*XTAL/12)) :  GOSUB 500
150   DBY(40H)=BH : DBY(41H)=BL

160   REM set up for intelligent programming or not
170   I=DBY(26H)
180   IF W=.001 THEN DBY(26H)=I.OR.8 ELSE DBY(26H)=I.AND.0F7H

190   INPUT "starting address of data to copy (source)? ",S
200   IF S<200H OR S>0FFFFH THEN  GOTO 190

210   INPUT "ending address of data to copy (source)? ",E
220   IF E<S OR E>0FFFFH THEN GOTO 210

230   INPUT "starting address to program (destination)? ",P
240   IF P<MTOP OR P>0FFFFH THEN  GOTO 230

250   REM calculate and store number of bytes to program
260   B=(E-S)+1 :  GOSUB 500 : DBY(1FH)=BH : DBY(1EH)=BL

270   REM store starting address of destination-1
280   B=P-1 :  GOSUB 500 : DBY(1AH)=BH : DBY(18H)=BL
290   PH0. "eprom low = ",BL
300   PH0. "eprom high = ",BH
```

Listing   13-8. (page 2 of 2)

```
310   REM store starting address of source
320   B=S :  GOSUB 500 : DBY(1BH)=BH : DBY(19H)=BL
330   PH0. "ram low = ",BL
340   PH0. "ram high = ",BH

350   PRINT "press ENTER to begin programming"
360   X=GET :  IF X<>0DH THEN 360

370   REM program the EPROM
380   PRINT "programming in progress..."
390   PGM

400   REM check for errors
410   IF (DBY(1EH).OR.DBY(1FH))=0 THEN PRINT "programming OK"
      :  GOTO 470
420   REM on error, calculate address that failed to program
430   DC=DBY(19H)+256*DBY(1BH)-1
440   PH0. "ERROR: Source address      ",DC," = ",XBY(DC)
450   DP=DBY(18H)+256*DBY(1AH)
460   PH0. "        Destination address ",DP," = ",XBY(DP)
470   END

500   REM separate B into high (BH) and low (BL) bytes
510   BL=(B.AND.0FFH)
520   BH=INT(B/256)
530   RETURN
```

A General-purpose EPROM Programmer

With Listing B-2, you can use an 8052-BASIC system as a general-purpose programmer for EPROM, EEPROM, or NV RAM. The program will read any file in Intel Hex format, and store it at the addresses specified in the file.

For example, you can add a socket for an 8K EPROM, EEPROM, or NV RAM addressed at A000h-BFFFh in combined code/data memory. For EEPROM or NVRAM, wire the socket exactly like U8 in Figure 4-3, except wire pin 1 of U9 to chip-select A000h (pin 10 of U6 in Figure 3-1) instead of to 8000h. For EPROM programming, also connect Figure 4-5's circuits to pins 1 and 28 of the EPROM, for the programming voltages.

With these added components and Listing B-2, you can program a DS1225 NV RAM, a 28(C)64 EEPROM, or a 27(C)64 EPROM with an Intel Hex file.

One use would be to program an EPROM for a non-BASIC-52 system, where $\overline{EA}$ is tied low and on bootup, the 8052 runs a program beginning at 0 in external code memory, instead of running the BASIC-52 interpreter in internal ROM. For this use, you must add A000h to the values given in all *ORG* directives. For example, you would change *ORG 0* to *ORG A000h*, and change *ORG 200h* to *ORG A200h*. You can then use Listing B-2 to copy the program into the EPROM at A000h, remove the EPROM and install it at 0 in code memory in your non-BASIC-52 system. On bootup, the 8052 will run the program in EPROM.

Another Way to Program EPROMs

Listing 13-8 is another program that you can use to copy information from external data memory into an EPROM, EEPROM, or NVRAM. To use this program, you must specify the locations to copy (the source), the locations to copy to (the destination), and the device type to copy to. The program does the rest. With this program, you can copy information directly from RAM or other memory to another device, without uploading or translating to Intel Hex format.

The program prompts you for and stores information about the programming algorithm and addresses to program and copy from. BASIC-52's PGM instruction then uses this information to program the selected locations.

14

Running BASIC-52 from External Memory

Most BASIC-52 circuits use the 8052-BASIC chip with the BASIC-52 interpreter in internal ROM. This is convenient, but another option is to place BASIC-52 in external EPROM, EEPROM, or NV RAM. Two reasons for doing so are to save money and to enable you to customize BASIC-52 by modifying and reassembling BASIC-52's source file.

For those who want to experiment with BASIC-52 in external memory, this chapter shows how to copy the BASIC-52 interpreter from ROM into NV RAM, and how to design and use a system with BASIC-52 in external memory.

Reasons

Placing BASIC-52 in external memory can save money, although as prices for the 8052-BASIC chip have dropped, the savings have become minimal. Still, if you find a good deal on 8032s or 8052s and 8K EPROMs, you might find it worthwhile to build systems with these rather than using the single-chip 8052-BASIC. In your calculations, though, remember that sockets and board space add cost, not to mention the extra time involved in wiring or laying out a printed-circuit board for the added component.

For experienced assembly-language programmers, another reason for placing BASIC-52 in external memory is so that you can modify the source file for BASIC-52. You then can reassemble your modified source file and use the new version in your projects. In this way, you can add functions or make other changes to BASIC-52 itself. To do this, you must have a copy of BASIC-52's source code, which has been available on Intel's and Philips' BBS's, plus Intel's ASM51 or a compatible 8051-family assembler.

Iota Systems is one vendor that has customized BASIC-52 in this way, with an expanded BASIC-52 PLUS that runs from external EPROM on Iota's 8052-BASIC boards. BASIC-52 PLUS includes commands for uploading and downloading Intel Hex files, as well as other enhancements and bug fixes.

Copying BASIC-52

To copy BASIC-52 from ROM to NVRAM, you can use the same circuits shown in Figures 3-1 and 4-3. Use a DS1225 8K NV RAM at U8. Listing 14-1 is a program that copies the 8052-BASIC's ROM from 0 to 1FFFh in internal code memory to U8 at 8000-9FFFh in external data or code/data memory. Boot up your system, enter or upload Listing 14-1 and run it. Then power down and remove the NV RAM at U8, which now contains a copy of BASIC-52.

If you prefer, you can use a 28(C)64 8K EEPROM instead of NV RAM at U8. Because the write-cycle time of EEPROMs is often 2 to 10 milliseconds, you may have to slow Listing

---

Listing 14-1. Copies the BASIC-52 interpreter program from ROM to NVRAM.

```
10    PRINT "copying BASIC-52 from ROM to RAM at 8000h..."
20    FOR I=0 TO 1FFFH
30    XBY(I+8000H)=CBY(I)
40    NEXT I
50    PRINT "verifying..."
60    X=0
70    FOR I=0 TO 1FFFH
80    IF XBY(I+8000H)<>CBY(I) THEN  GOSUB 120
90    NEXT I
100   IF X=0 THEN  PRINT "Copy successful"
110   END
120   PH0. "Error at location ",I
130   X=1
140   RETURN
```

14-1 for longer delays between writes. To do so, between lines 30 and 40, add this or a similar "do-nothing" loop: FOR J=1 to 10:NEXT J.

For EPROM storage, you can copy the ROM into RAM and then use Listing 13-8 to program an EPROM. For this method, use a 32K RAM at U7 in Figure 3-1. You'll also need an unprogrammed 8K EPROM accessed as data or code/data memory. Set MTOP to 5FFFh or lower to ensure that BASIC-52 won't overwrite the area from 6000h to 7FFFh. In Listing 14-1, lines 10, 30, and 80, change 8000h to 6000h. Run the revised program to copy the 8052-BASIC's ROM into RAM at 6000h-7FFFh. You then can upload or enter Listing 13-8 to copy BASIC-52 into your EPROM, at the starting address you specify.

Another option is to use an EPROM programmer to copy BASIC-52. If your programmer has an adapter for 8051s, you can copy the 8052-BASIC's ROM directly into the programmer's buffer and then program an EPROM, EEPROM, or NV RAM with the buffer's contents. If you don't have an adapter, you can use the technique described above to copy BASIC-52 into NV RAM or EEPROM, and then read the device into your programmer.

To read a DS1225 into an EPROM programmer's buffer, configure the programmer for a DS1225 or 2764 EPROM, since the pinouts for reading these devices are the same. Place the DS1225 in the programming socket and read the contents into the programmer's buffer. Be sure not to subject the DS1225 to any EPROM programming voltages (by trying to program the device as an EPROM, for example), since this could be lethal to it.

After reading the DS1225, insert a 2764 EPROM into the programming socket, and program the EPROM with the buffer's contents. You now have an EPROM with the same contents as your NV RAM.

System Requirements

To run BASIC-52 from external memory, your circuit must include the following:

- Any 8052, 8032, 80C52, or 80C32 chip, with pin 31 tied low.
- BASIC-52 stored in non-volatile memory (NVRAM, EEPROM, or EPROM), beginning at 0 in code memory.
- At least 1K of read/write memory (RAM), beginning at 0 in data memory (required for all BASIC-52 systems).
- For permanent storage of BASIC-52 programs, non-volatile memory beginning at 8000h in data or code/data memory.

One limitation to running BASIC-52 from external memory is that you can't use PROG, FPROG, or PGM. This is because during programming, BASIC-52 accesses the address bus as ports, but when BASIC-52 runs from external memory, the 8032 needs the address bus to access BASIC-52. But you can store programs in NV RAM or EEPROM, using a BASIC-52 program presented later in this chapter.

For the external-BASIC-52 system, you can use the same circuits as in Figures 3-1 and 4-3, plus Figure 14-1, which adds the chip containing BASIC-52.

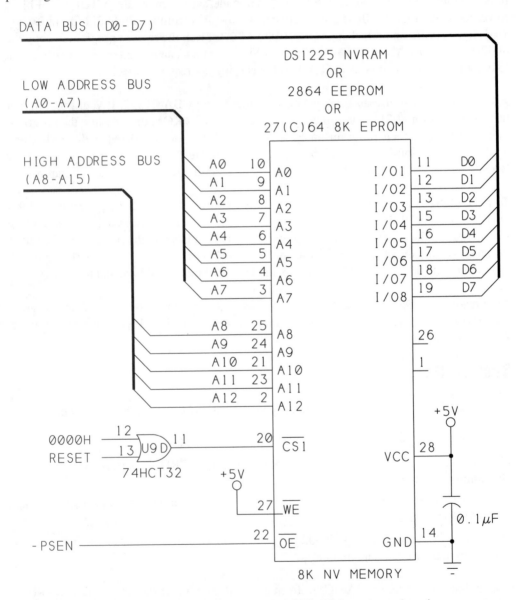

Figure 14-1. Added circuits for storing BASIC-52 in external code memory.

The Microcontroller Idea Book

In Figure 3-1, tie pin 31 of U2 ($\overline{EA}$) to ground instead of +5V, so that the 8032 boots to external memory instead of internal ROM.

Since you aren't using the programming functions, you can eliminate some components and free up three port pins for other uses. First, you don't need an AND gate to combine ALE and $\overline{ALEDIS}$, so you can wire ALE (U2, pin 30) directly to LE (U4, pin 11). You can also eliminate R2-R9. Plus, in Figure 4-3, you can eliminate AND gate U3C, and wire $\overline{WRITE}$ (U2, pin 16) directly to $\overline{WE}$ (U8, pin 27).

If you make these changes, bits 4 and 5 of Port 1 are free for any use you want. And, since NVRAM requires no programming voltage, bit 3 of Port 1 is also free for other uses. If you don't make the changes, you can still run BASIC-52 from external memory, but if you try to use PROG, FPROG, or PGM, the system will crash. (You can also make these changes in a circuit that uses an 8052-BASIC, to free up some port pins if you use the program described below instead of the programming commands.)

U2 can be any 80(C)32 or 80(C)52. U7 can be an 8K or 32K static RAM, addressed beginning at 0 in data memory.

Figure 14-1 shows the wiring for NVRAM, EPROM, or EEPROM that contains BASIC-52. This chip is accessed from 0 to 1FFFh in external code memory.

U8 is NVRAM accessed from 8000h to 9FFFh in combined code/data memory, for storing BASIC-52 programs and assembly-language routines.

Storing BASIC-52 Programs

With BASIC-52 in external memory, you can't use the built-in programming functions, but there is another way to store programs. Using the circuits described above, write and test your BASIC-52 programs as usual. When you want to store a program permanently, append the code in Listing 14-2 to your program. The code is shown beginning at line 9000, but it can begin at any line number after the END statement in the program you want to save.

To store a program in U8, type GOTO 9000, where 9000 is the line number where Listing 14-2 begins, and follow the on-screen instructions.

Listing 14-2 has all of the abilities of PROG1 – PROG6, including auto-execute on power-up, setting the baud rate, and saving MTOP. Line 8990 indicates the end of the program you want to save. Lines 9000-9040 prompt you to press *P* to copy the current BASIC-52 program to NVRAM at U8, or press *Q* to quit. Line 9050 writes 55h to NVRAM, which indicates to the interpreter that a BASIC program follows. Lines 9060-9080 copy the current BASIC-52 program, which is stored beginning at 200h in external data memory (U7), to NVRAM (U8) beginning at 8011h. Listing 14-2 is also copied as part of the current program. Lines

Listing 14-2. Simulates BASIC-52's PROG and PROG1-6 commands, for systems with BASIC-52 in external memory or systems that do not use the $\overline{\text{PGM}}$ $\overline{\text{PULSE}}$ signal. Adapted and reprinted with permission from Micromint.

```
8990  END
9000  PRINT "Press 'P' to copy the current BASIC program to
      RAM at 8000h."
9010  PRINT "Press 'Q' to quit."
9020  G=GET
9030  G=GET :  IF G=0 THEN 9030
9040  IF (G<>80.AND.G<>112) THEN  END
9050  XBY(8010H)=55H
9060  FOR X=200H TO (200H+LEN)
9070  XBY(X+7E11H)=XBY(X)
9080  NEXT X
9090  PRINT "Press a number from 1 to 6 to do PROG1-PROG6."
9100  PRINT "Press 'Q' to quit."
9110  G=GET
9120  G=GET :  IF G=0 THEN 9120
9130  IF (G<49.OR.G>54) THEN END
9140  XBY(8000H)=G
9150  XBY(8001H)=INT(RCAP2/256)
9160  XBY(8002H)=RCAP2-(XBY(8001H)*256)
9170  IF G<50 THEN  END
9180  XBY(8003H)=INT(MTOP/256)
9190  XBY(8004H)=MTOP-(XBY(8003H)*256)
9200  END
```

9090-9130 prompt you to press a number from 1 to 6 to simulate a PROG1-PROG6 command, or to press Q to quit. Lines 9140-9190 store the PROG value (1-6), RCAP2 (for saving the baud rate), and MTOP, as requested.

Listing 14-2 stores only the current program, not multiple programs like the PROG command. But you can store a new program whenever you wish by writing over the previously stored program. And you don't have to worry about removing and erasing an EPROM when it's filled.

If you have a 32K RAM at 0, remember to set MTOP to 7FFFh and use Listing 14-2 to execute a PROG3, to ensure that your NV RAM won't be overwritten on bootup.

You can use EEPROM with Listing 14-2, if you add a delay loop after each write operation using XBY, as described for Listing 14-1.

15

Related Products

Because of the popularity of the 8052-BASIC chip, many companies have developed products to simplify the tasks of designing, building, and testing BASIC-52 systems. This chapter describes some of the offerings in these areas.

Enhanced BASIC-52

The BASIC-52 interpreter contained in the original 8052-BASIC is a good, full-featured and easy-to-use programming language. However, Intel hasn't updated the program since version 1.1. Fortunately, other programmers have taken on the task of improving and enhancing the language.

MDL Labs' MDL-BASIC is an EPROM that contains an enhanced version of BASIC-52. It includes new operators that set and clear individual bits in memory, increment and decrement values, and return the remainder in integer division. MDL-BASIC also has improvements for faster loading and running of programs, and fixes many of BASIC-52's bugs, such as the problem with variable names beginning with F (see Chapter 5). It requires a system that can operate with BASIC in external memory, as described in Chapter 14.

Other vendors, including Blue Earth Research and Micromint, have improved and added to the BASIC-52 interpreter as well.

BASIC compilers

A BASIC compiler offers a middle ground between the BASIC-52 interpreter and assembly-language programming. With a BASIC compiler, you write your programs using the familiar keywords and syntax rules of BASIC, but the compiled programs run on their own, without requiring the BASIC-52 interpreter. Binary Technology, Systronix, and Blue Earth are three vendors of BASIC compilers for the 8052.

As with assembly language, to use a BASIC compiler, you first write a source file, using any text editor. But instead of using assembly-language mnemonics, you write the source file using the BASIC compiler's keywords and conventions. When the program is complete, the compiler program translates your program lines into the machine codes required by the 8052 chip. The compilers will create an object file, usually in Intel Hex format, for uploading or programming into EPROM, plus a listing file for documentation and debugging use. When the object file is stored in the 8052's code memory, the 8052 can run the program directly, without having to use the BASIC-52 interpreter.

Using a compiler has several advantages:

- Unlike with assembly language, the syntax used with BASIC compilers is similar to BASIC-52. This means that you don't have to learn a new programming language. In fact, you can usually use the BASIC-52 interpreter to test your code before you compile it. You can also use BASIC-52 for loading and debugging your compiled programs, as described in Chapter 13.
- A compiled BASIC program will run faster than an interpreted BASIC-52 program. The speed increase depends on the program, but programs that run 20 to 50 percent faster are typical.
- Because a compiler doesn't limit you to the 8052-BASIC chip, you can develop programs for other members of the 8051 family. For example, Systronix's BASIC compiler has optional language extensions for Dallas Semiconductor's DS5000 8051-compatible microcontroller.

A disadvantage to using a compiler rather than an interpreter is that you have the extra steps of compiling and uploading programs before you can run them. But because the BASIC-52 language is so similar to the compilers, you can do a lot of your testing with the interpreter, and use the compiled version for final testing only.

There's also the added expense of buying the compiler. But if you develop many different projects, or if you need many copies of a single project, the compiler can end up saving you money, since you can use 8032 chips instead of the more expensive 8052-BASICs.

Finally, a compiled BASIC program usually requires more memory than an interpreted one, but you do gain 8 kilobytes of code memory because you no longer need the BASIC-52 interpreter.

Programming Environments

If you like the convenience of the BASIC-52 interpreter, but would like features that make it easier to write, edit, and store your programs, there are alternatives here as well.

MDL Labs and MicroFuture are two sources for development environments, which are programs that typically include communications and program-editing abilities. Most run on IBM-compatible host computers. Figure 15-1 shows a typical screen.

The environments include features like these:

- Block editing, or the ability to move, delete, or copy blocks of text in one operation.
- The ability to refer to subroutines by name, rather than by line number.

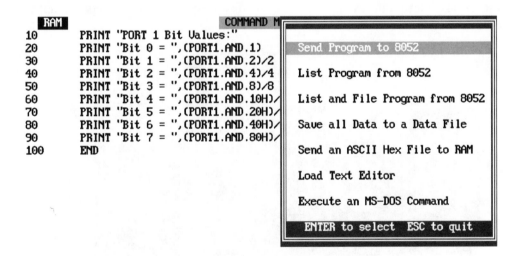

Figure 15-1. MDL Labs' Basikit includes communications and program-editing abilities.

- Elimination of the need to use line numbers at all.

- Automatic stripping of comments, to save memory and execution time in uploaded programs.

- On-line help for BASIC-52.

- Debugging tools, such as setting of breakpoints or watch variables for program testing.

- Conversion of BASIC-52 programs to hex files for EPROM programming.

- Screening of variable names for duplicates or embedded keywords.

Pc Boards

If you'd rather not build your own 8052-BASIC system from scratch, a variety of sources are ready to help here as well, with fabricated pc boards ready for use with the 8052-BASIC chip. The boards contain all of the components required to get an 8052-BASIC system up and running. Most come with complete schematics, to make it easy to add to the included circuits. A few boards are available as kits or bare boards, if you'd rather build your own.

I'll describe just a few of the available products here; see Appendix A for a more complete listing of sources.

Figure   15-2. Prologic's BASCOM1 is available as a low-cost bare pc board with an instruction manual for construction and use.

Figure 15-3. Blue Earth's Micro440 board has BASIC-52 and a monitor program in a tiny package.

Micromint offers a variety of 8052-BASIC boards and other products. Both the BCC52 and RTC52 are single-board systems that can also serve as the base of an expanded system. The BCC52 uses edge connectors and a backplane, while the RTC52 is a stackable design. A variety of expansion boards are available, including interfaces to displays, keypads, relays, infrared control, and A/D converters. The BRUTE-52 is a single board with many expansion options on-board.

Micromint's Domino is a complete Basic-52 system in a 20-pin encapsulated package that's about the size and shape of a domino. It has a surface-mount 80C52-BASIC chip, 32 kilobytes each of RAM and EEPROM, and twelve I/O pins, two of which may be analog inputs. The Domino's BASIC-52 interpreter adds functions for measuring frequency and period and for reading the analog inputs.

Prologic Designs offers an inexpensive bare pc board (Figure 15-2) and detailed manual for 8052-BASIC systems, for those who prefer building their own.

Blue Earth Research's Micro-440e is a complete system on a tiny pc board, just 1.9" x 2.25" (Figure 15-3). The system uses a surface-mount 83C51FB chip with both Blue Earth's version of BASIC-52 and a monitor program in ROM. A case and expansion boards are also available. The Micro-485 adds an analog-to-digital converter, clock and calendar, and an RS-485 interface for networking.

To speed up program execution, you can use Dallas Semiconductor's DS80C520 high-speed microcontrollers, which are compatible with the 8051 family. MDL Labs and Photronics Research offer variations of BASIC-52 designed for use with these chips.

BASIC-52 Source Code

If you're interested in seeing the source code for the BASIC-52 interpreter, look for it on Intel's or Philips' BBS or on the Internet (Appendix A). To modify the code, you'll need Intel's ASM51 or a compatible 8051 assembler.

Appendix A

Sources

This Appendix lists a variety of sources to help you in your 8052-BASIC projects, including books, on-line BBS's, and companies who offer products related to the topics in this book.

Books

Here is a selection of books about BASIC-52, the 8051/2 microcontroller family, and related topics:

BASIC-52 Essentials

These are the essential hardware and software manuals for working with the 8052-BASIC. You'll need either Intel's or Systronix's programming manual, and a data book from Intel or another 8052 vendor. See the Product Vendors section for addresses and phone numbers.

BASIC-52 Programming
Systronix
$20 postpaid
Complete reference to the BASIC-52 programming language. Includes many program examples and handy back-cover index.

BASIC-52 User's Manual (Intel #270010-004
$15
Complete reference to the BASIC-52 programming language. Includes some circuit schematics.

Embedded Microcontrollers Handbook (Intel)
$22.95
Intel's handbook, or data book, has hardware details and an assembly-languuage reference for the 8052 and 80C52 (and much more), but nothing specifically about the 8052-BASIC chip. Intel updates the data books yearly, so the exact title and price may vary. Ask for the data book that covers 8-bit embedded controllers. Philips, Siemens, and other manufacturers also publish data books for their 8052 and 80C52 chips.

8051/2 Microcontrollers

These are some additional books about the 8051 family of microcontrollers. The Product Vendors list has addresses and phone numbers for many of the publishers. Local bookstores can order the others, which are from major publishers.

Assembly Language Programming (L.S. Electronic Systems, 190 pages, $33.00). For the 8051 family.

C and the 8051: Programming and Multitasking, by Thomas W. Schultz (Prentice Hall, 1993, $52). Discusses using an operating system to handle multiple tasks. Examples include solenoid cyclers, a pulse generator, envelope detector, and motor speed control, using the C programming language.

The 8051 Family of Microcontrollers by Richard H. Barnett (Prentice Hall, 1995, 164 pages, $49)

T*he 8051 Microcontroller, 2nd edition,* I. Scott MacKenzie (Macmillan, 1994, 356 pages, $58). Includes schematics for a single-board computer, assembly-language source code for a monitor program, and interfaces to a keypad, LEDs, and loudspeaker.

The 8051 Microcontroller: Architecture, Programming, and Applications, Kenneth J. Ayala (West Publishing Company, 1991, 241 pages, $49). Includes disk with assembler and simulator.

The 8051 Microcontroller: Hardware, Software, and Interfacing, James W. Stewart (Regents/Prentice Hall, 1993, $27.50, 273 pages). Includes many interfacing examples, such as switches, solenoids, relays, shaft encoders, displays, motors, and A/D converters, and a chapter on top-down design method.

Programming and Interfacing the 8051 Microcontroller by Sencer Yeralan and Ashutosh Ahluwalia (Addison-Wesley, 1995, $40, 328 pages)

Programming and Interfacing with Microcontrollers–Experimenting with the 8031 Family of Microcontrollers (Rigel Corporation).

Data Books

Data books are where to look for specific, detailed information about a particular IC. They're also a good source for application examples. National Semiconductor has a good selection of books covering most types of integrated circuits. The exact titles and prices change from year to year, but this is a typical selection:

CMOS Logic (including HCMOS, HCTMOS, 4000 series, 74C series)
TTL Logic (including LSTTL)
Linear Devices (A/D, D/A, temperature sensors, voltage references)
Op Amps
Power ICs (voltage regulators, peripheral drivers)

You can request data books directly from the manufacturers. Digi-Key and other component vendors also offer a selection. For a small charge, many suppliers will include data sheets for individual components that you order.

Related Topics

These are some other books that you may find useful in designing, building, and working with microcontroller circuits:

The Art of Electronics, second edition by Paul Horowitz and Winfield Hill (Cambridge University Press, 1989, $59.95). A complete and readable reference on electronic circuits of all types.

Gordon McComb's Tips and Techniques for the Electronics Hobbyist by Gordon McComb (TAB-McGraw Hill, 1991). A good introduction to building, testing, and understanding electronic circuits.

Making Printed Circuit Boards by Jan Axelson (TAB-McGraw Hill, 1993, $19.95). How to design and make pc boards, with a chapter on wire-wrapping and other construction methods.

BBS's

Use your personal computer and communications software to explore these BBS's (on-line bulletin boards), which are good sources for files relating to the 8051/2, including the 8052-BASIC.

BBS Name	Phone Number	Available Files
Circuit Cellar	203-871-1988	8052 programming tools, programs
Intel Applications	503-264-7999	BASIC-52 source code
Philips Semiconductor	1-800-451-6644	BASIC-52 source code
Systronix	801-487-2778	HEX2RAM.BAS, HEXLOAD.BAS

Internet

Many of the vendors listed here now have information available on the World Wide Web. Lakeview Research's Web site includes a BASIC-52 page with links to product vendors and updates to the information in this book. You can also save yourself some typing by downloading a file containing all of the code listings in the book.

You can find Lakeview Research on the Internet at: *http://www.lvr.com*

Product Vendors

The following companies offer products related to microcontroller applications. Many are mentioned as sources for particular products in this book.

Airpax Company   stepper motors
604 West Johnson Avenue
P.O. Box 590
Chesire, CT 06410
203-271-6000

Allegro Microsystems   motor-control chips
115 Northeast Cutoff, Box 15036
Worcester, MA 01615
508-853-5000

All Electronics Corp.   surplus components
P.O. Box 567
Van Nuys, CA 91408-0567
1-800-826-5432

Allen Systems   8051 assembler
2346 Brandon Road
Columbus, OH 43221
614-488-7122

Anywhere Engineering   8051 assembler
920 Eighth Street
Boulder, CO 80302
303-442-0556

Amperex/Philips Sales Corporation   LCD modules, manual (publication #238)
Providence Pike
Slatersville, RI 02876
401-762-9000

Basicon, Inc.   80C52-BASIC chip, systems, related products
14273 NW Science Park Drive
Portland, OR 97229
503-626-1012

Binary Technology
PO Box 67
Meriden, NH 03770
603-469-3232

BASIC compiler, 8052-BASIC systems, related products

Blue Earth Research
165 W. Lind Ct.
Mankato, MN 56001
507-387-4001

8052-BASIC systems, related products

Blue Ridge Micros
2505 Plymouth Road
Johnson City, TN 37601
615-335-6696

8052-BASIC board

Dallas Semiconductor
4350 South Beltwood Parkway
Dallas, TX 75244-3292
214-450-0400
1-800-336-6933

NV RAM, real-time clocks

Digi-Key Corporation
701 Brooks Ave. South
P.O. Box 677
Thief River Falls, MN 56701-0677
1-800-344-4539

electronic components

Dunfield Development Systems
P.O. Box 31044
Nepean, Ontario K2B 8S8
Canada
613-256-5820

8051 assembler

Edmund Scientific Company
101 E. Gloucester Pike
Barrington, N.J. 08007-1380
609-573-6250

lenses, optical components, other scientific equipment

Electronics 123
17921 Rowland Street
City of Industry, CA 91748
1-800-669-4406
818-913-6735

products for wireless communications

F.C. Kuechmann
8113 NE 25th Ave.
Vancouver, WA 98665

BASIC-52 development software

Harris Semiconductor
P.O. Box 883
Melbourne, FL 32902-0883
407-724-3000

display-control chips

Hitachi America, Ltd.
Semiconductor and IC Division
Hitachi Plaza
2000 Sierra Point Parkway
Brisbane, CA 94005-1819
1-800-448-2244

HD44780 LCD controller data

Hosfelt Electronics, Inc.
2700 Sunset Boulevard
Steubenville, OH 43952-1158
1-800-524-6464
614-264-6464

surplus components

Intel Corporation
3065 Bowers Ave.
Santa Clara, CA 95051
408-765-8080
1-800-548-4725

8052 data book

Jameco
1355 Shoreway Road
Belmont, CA 94002
1-800-831-4242
415-592-8097

8052-BASIC chip, electronic components

JDR Microdevices
2233 Samaritan Drive
San Jose, CA 95124
1-800-538-5000
408-559-1200

electronic components

Lite-On
720 S. Hillview Dr.
Milpitas, CA 95035
408-946-4873

infrared detectors

L.S. Electronic Systems Design
2280 Camilla Rd.
Mississauga, ON L5A 2J8
Canada
905-277-4893

8051 programming book

Marlin Jones & Associates
P.O. Box 12685
Lake Park, FL 33403-0685
407-848-8236

surplus components

Maxim Integrated Products
120 San Gabriel Drive
Sunnyvale, CA 94086
408-737-7600

RS232 interface, power-supply monitor ICs

MDL Labs
1073 Limberlost Ct.
Columbus, OH 43235
614-431-2675

BASIC-52 programming environment,
enhanced BASIC-52

Micro Computer Control
P.O. Box 275
17 Model Avenue
Hopewell, NJ 08525
609-466-1751

8051 assembler

Microcomputer Systems
1814 Ryder Drive
Baton Rouge, LA 70808
504-769-2154

BASIC-52 systems

The Microcontroller Idea Book

Micro Future 40944 Cascado Place Fremont, CA 94539 510-657-0264	BASIC-52 programming environment
Micromint 4 Park Street Vernon, CT 06066 203-871-6170	80C52-BASIC chip, systems, related products
Midwest Micro-tek 2308 E. 6th St. Brookings, SD 57006 605-697-8521	8052-Basic boards
Mitel Semiconductor P.O. Box 13089 Kanata, Ontario K2K 1X3 Canada 1-800-267-6244 613-592-2122	switch-matrix chips
National Semiconductor Corporation 2900 Semiconductor Drive P.O. Box 58090 Santa Clara, CA 95052-8090 408-721-5000 1-800-272-9959	linear, digital ICs
Newark Electronics 4801 N. Ravenswood Ave. Chicago, IL 60640-4496 312-784-5100	electronic components
Omega Engineering One Omega Drive Box 4047 Stamford, CT 06907 1-800-826-6342	sensors

Optek Technology
1215 West Crosby Rd.
Carrollton, TX 75006
214-323-2200

optoelectronic components

Philips Components/Signetics
811 East Arques Ave.
P.O. Box 3409
Sunnyvale, CA 94088
408-991-2000

8052 chips, data books

Photronics Research
109 Camille St.
Amite, LA 70422
504-748-7090

high-speed BASIC-52 in Dallas DS87C520

Prologic
P.O. Box 19026
Baltimore, MD 21204
410-661-5950

8052-BASIC pc board, kit

PseudoCorp
716 Thimble Shoals Blvd., Suite E
Newport News, VA 23606
804-873-1947

8051 assembler

Rigel Corporation
P.O. Box 90040
Gainesville, FL 32607
904-373-4629

8051 book

Sensors Magazine
Helmers Publishing, Inc.
174 Concord St.
P.O. Box 874
Peterborough, NH 03458-0874
603-924-9631

Sensors Buyer's Guide

Sharp Electronics
Microelectronics Group
5700 NW Pacific Rim Blvd., M/S 20
Camas, WA 98607
206-834-2500

optoelectronic components

Siemens Components
2191 Laurelwood Rd.
Santa Clara, CA 95054
408-980-4500

8052 chips, data books

Siemens Components
Optoelectronics Division
19000 Homestead Rd.
Cupertino, CA 95014
408-257-7910

optoelectronic components

Sil-Walker
880 Calle Plano, Unit #N
Camarillo, CA 93012
805-389-8100
FAX: 805-484-3311

keypad kits

Suncoast Technologies
PO Box 5835
Spring Hill, FL 34606
Voice/FAX: 352-596-7599

8052-BASIC board

Systronix
555 South 300 East
Salt Lake City, UT 84111
801-534-1017
FAX: 801-534-1019
BBS 801-487-2778

BASIC compiler, BASIC-52 programming
manual

TAB-McGraw Hill
P.O. Box 0850
Blue Ridge Summit, PA 17294-0850
1-800-262-4729

book publisher

Timeline, Inc.
1490 W. Artesia Blvd.
Gardena, CA 90247
1-800-872-8878

surplus LCD modules

Unicorn Electronics
10010 Canoga Ave. Unit B-8
Chatsworth, CA 91311
1-800-824-3432

8052-BASIC chip, electronic components

Universal Cross Assemblers
P.O. Box 6158
Saint John, NB E2L 4R6
Canada
506-847-0681

8051 assembler

Appendix B

Programs for Loading Files

This appendix contains the BASIC-52 programs HEX2RAM.BAS and HEXLOAD.BAS described in Chapter 13. Use HEX2RAM.BAS to load an Intel Hex file from your host computer to RAM, including battery-backed (NV) RAM. The HEXLOAD.BAS program does the same, but also allows you to load the file into EEPROM or EPROM. HEX2RAM uses XBY, while HEXLOAD uses PGM, and is slower.

Listing B-1 (page 1 of 2). HEX2RAM.BAS loads Intel Hex files from a host computer to memory in the 8052-BASIC system. Reprinted with permission from Systronix.

```
10    STRING 82, 80 : DIM HI (70) : DIM LOW (70)
15    FOR I=48 TO 57 : HI(I) = (I - 48) * 16 : LOW(I) = I - 48
      : NEXT
25    FOR I=65 TO 70 : HI(I) = (I - 55) * 16 : LOW(I) = I - 55
      : NEXT
35    PRINT TAB(19),"INTEL HEX FILE TO RAM LOADING PROGRAM V1.1'
45    PRINT TAB(14), "Copyright 1991 Systronix Inc. All rights
      reserved." : PRINT
55    PRINT TAB(8),"This program accepts as input an Intel hex
      file and stores"
65    PRINT TAB(8),"it in external RAM at the addresses speci-
      fied in the HEX file.":PRINT
75    PRINT TAB(8),"Ready to receive the input file one line at
      a time. Set your"
85    PRINT TAB(8),"communication software to send a line when
      when it receives"
95    PRINT TAB(8),"the '>' prompt." : PRINT

100   LINE=LINE+1 : INPUT ">",$(0) : PRINT"Validating and stor-
      ing...",
105   C = ASC($(0),1) : IF C<>58 THEN GOTO 500

REM Get the byte count and save it in the variable COUNT
115   I = 2 : GOSUB 700 : COUNT = CH

REM Get the starting address for this record's data
125   FOR I = 4 TO 7 STEP 2 : GOSUB 700 : ADDR = (ADDR * 256)
      + CH : NEXT
REM Get the record type (we only understand types 0 and 1)
135   I = 8 : GOSUB 700 : IF (CH <>0 .AND. CH <>1) THEN GOTO
      510
145   RECORD = CH
REM The initial checksum calculation
155   CHECK=(ADDR/256)+(ADDR.AND.0FFH)+COUNT+RECORD

REM Get the individual bytes, accumulate them in the check
      sum and store
REM them in memory at the appropriate destination
165   FOR I = 10 TO 10 + (COUNT * 2) STEP 2 : GOSUB 700
```

Listing B-1 (page 2 of 2).

```
REM Here we deal with the data bytes (not executed when RE-
    CORD is type 1)
175   CHECK=CHECK+CH
185   IF RECORD = 1 THEN GOTO 210

REM Store the data in RAM
195   XBY(ADDR)=CH
205   if CBY (ADDR) <>CH THEN GOTO 550 ELSE ADDR = ADDR + 1 :
      NEXT

210   CHECK=CHECK.AND.0FFH : IF CHECK<>0 THEN GOTO 520
215   IF RECORD = 1 THEN GOTO 640

REM Reset and continue
225   ADDR = 0 : PRINT CR : GOTO 100

REM Error messages and program termination
500   PRINT  CR, "Line ", LINE, ": Character", I, "unexpected"
      : GOTO 600
510   PRINT CR, "Line ", LINE, ": Unknown record type", CH :
      GOTO 600
520   PRINT CR, "Line ", LINE, ": Checksum failure. Expected",
525   PH0. ABS (CHECK-CH) : GOTO 600

550   PRINT CR, "Line", LINE, ": Verify error at address", :
      PH0. ADDR
555   PH0. "The byte at", addr, " is", CBY (ADDR)
565   PH0. "The byte should be", CH : GOTO 600

600   PRINT "Stop sending input file. Type a CONTROL+C to
      quit."
605   GOTO 605

REM Normal program exit point
640   PRINT CR, "Received an End record in line",LINE : END

REM Convert the ASCII text to numbers
700   C = ASC($(0),I) : CH = HI(C) : C = ASC($(0),I + 1) : CH
      = CH + LOW (C)
705   RETURN
```

Listing B-2 (page 1 of 4). HEXLOAD.BAS copies an Intel Hex file into RAM, EEPROM, or EPROM in an 8052-BASIC system.

```
1 STRING 82, 80
2 PRINT TAB(22),"HEX FILE LOADING PROGRAM 1.2"
3 PRINT TAB(14), "(C) 1990,1991 Systronix Inc. All rights
    reserved." : PRINT
4 PRINT "This program accepts as input, an Intel format hex
    file and stores"
5 PRINT "it in RAM, EPROM, or EEPROM at the addresses speci-
    fied." : PRINT
6 PRINT : PRINT "Select the destination device type:" :
    PRINT
7 PRINT TAB(10), "[1] RAM" : PRINT TAB(10), "[2] Timed
    EEPROM"
8 PRINT TAB(10), "[3] EPROM (Intelligent algorithm)"
9 PRINT TAB(10), "[4] EPROM (50mS algorithm)"
10 PRINT TAB(10), "[5] EEPROM (RDY/BUSY type)"
11 INPUT "Select Device Type (1, 2, 3, 4, 5) >> ", TYPE
12 IF (TYPE < 1) .OR. (TYPE  5) THEN PRINT CHR(7) : GOTO 11
20 TYPE=TYPE-1 : IF TYPE = 0 THEN GOTO 1300
21 if type = 1 then goto 22 else goto 30
22 INPUT "Delay between writes >> ", delay : goto 1300
30 ON (TYPE) GOSUB 2100, 2100, 2110, 2120, 2100
40 IF TYPE = 2 THEN DBY(38) = DBY(38) .OR. 8 ELSE DBY(38) =
    DBY(38) .AND. 0f7H
rem Calculate and store pulse width
50 WAIT = 65536-WAIT*XTAL/12 : DBY(40H) = WAIT/256 :
    DBY(41H) = WAIT.AND.0ffH

1300 PRINT "Ready to receive the input file one line at a
    time. Set your"
1310 PRINT "communication software to send a line when when
    it receives"
1320 PRINT "the '>' prompt." : PRINT

1330 SOURCE = MTOP - FREE + 1
1340 LINE = LINE + 1 : INPUT">", $(0) : PRINT "Validating
    input buffer ...",
1350 I = 1 : C = ASC($(0),1) : IF C<>58 THEN GOTO 3000 :
    REM if not ":"
```

Listing B-2 (page 2 of 4).

```
rem Get the byte count and save it in the variable COUNT
1360 I = 2 : GOSUB 2000 : COUNT = CH

rem Get the starting address for this record's data
1370 FOR I = 4 TO 7 STEP 2 : GOSUB 2000 : ADDR = (ADDR *
     256) + CH : NEXT
rem Get the record type (we only understand types 0 and 1)
1380 I = 8 : GOSUB 2000 : IF (CH <>0 .AND. CH <>1) THEN
     GOTO 3010
1385 IF TYPE <>0 .AND. ADDR <8000H .AND. CH = 0 THEN GOTO
     3040
1390 RECORD = CH

rem Get the individual bytes, accumulate them in the check
     sum and store
rem them in memory
1400 INDEX = SOURCE : FOR I = 10 TO 10 + (COUNT * 2) STEP 2
     : GOSUB 2000

rem Here we deal with the data bytes (not executed when RE-
     CORD is type 1)
1410 CHECK=CHECK+CH
1420 IF RECORD = 1 THEN GOTO 1440
1430 XBY(INDEX)=CH : INDEX = INDEX + 1 : NEXT

rem Calculate the checksum
1440 CHECK=(CHECK+(ADDR/256)+(ADDR.AND.0FFH)+COUNT+RE-
     CORD).AND.0FFH
1450 IF CHECK<>0 THEN GOTO 3020

1460 IF RECORD = 1 THEN GOTO 3030
1470 PRINT CR, "Storing a Data record of", COUNT, "bytes
     at", : PH0. ADDR

rem Retreive the data from memory and store them in the
     proper addresses
1480 on type gosub 1500, 1570, 1520, 1520, 1520

rem Restore our variables and continue
1490 ADDR = 0 : CHECK=0 : GOTO 1340
```

Listing B-2 (page 3 of 4).

```
rem Store the data in RAM
1500 FOR I=SOURCE TO SOURCE + COUNT-1 : XBY(ADDR)=XBY(I)

rem Now verify that stored data is readable as code
1505 if XBY(I) <> CBY(ADDR) THEN GOTO 3130
1508 ADDR = ADDR+1 : NEXT
1510 RETURN

rem Store the data in EPROM or RDY/BUSY EEPROM
rem First load the source address registers
1520 DBY (1BH) = SOURCE/256 : DBY (19H) = SOURCE .AND. 0FFH

rem Now load the destination address registers
1530 DBY (1AH) = (ADDR-1)/256 : DBY (18H) = (ADDR - 1)
     .AND. 0FFH

rem Now load the number of bytes to program
1540 DBY (1Fh) = COUNT/256 : DBY (1Eh) = COUNT .AND. 0FFh

rem Program the data into the part
1550 PGM : IF DBY (1Fh) .OR. DBY (1Eh) <>0 THEN GOTO 3060
1560 RETURN

1570 FOR I=SOURCE TO SOURCE + COUNT-1 : XBY (ADDR) = XBY
     (I)
1580 time = 0 : dby (47h) = 0 : clock1 : do : until time >=
     delay
1590 if xby (addr) <>xby (i) goto 3100
1600 addr = addr + 1: clock0 : next : clock0 : return

rem Convert the ASCII text to numbers
2000 C = ASC($(0),I) : IF (C<=70 .AND. C>=65) THEN C = C -
     55 ELSE C = C - 48
2020 CH = C * 16 : C = ASC($(0),I + 1)
2040 IF (C<=70 .AND. C>=65) THEN C = C - 55 ELSE C = C - 48
2050 CH = CH + C : RETURN

rem Here when we are going to load the data into EEPROM.
2100 WAIT = 0.0005 : RETURN
rem Here for Intelligent programming
2110 WAIT = 0.001 : RETURN
```

Listing B-2 (page 4 of 4).

```
rem Error messages and program termination
3000 PRINT  CR ,"Line ",LINE," EXPECTED ':', FOUND
     '",CHR(C),"'" :   END
3010 PRINT CR, "Line ", LINE, ": Unknown record type", CH :
     END
3020 PRINT CR, "Line ", LINE, ": Checksum failure. Ex-
     pected",
3025 PH0. ABS (CHECK - CH) : END
rem Normal program exit point
3030 PRINT CR, "Received an End record in line",LINE : END
3040 PRINT CR, "Line", LINE, ": Illegal EPROM/EEPROM ad-
     dress :",
3050 PH0. ADDR : END
3060 PRINT CR, "Line", LINE, ": PGM error at address",
3070 ADDR = DBY (1AH) * 256 + DBY (18h) : PH0. ADDR
3080 PH0. "The byte at", address, " is", XBY(ADDRESS)
3090 PH0. "The byte should be",DBY (28) : END
3100 PH0. CR, "Line", LINE, ": Error writing at address",
     ADDR
3110 PH0. "The byte at", addr, " is", XBY(ADDR)
3120 PH0. "The byte should be", XBY (I) : END
REM verify CBY() read in RAM failed:
3130 PH0. "The byte at",addr," failed a verify with CBY" :
     END
```

The Microcontroller Idea Book

Appendix C

Number Systems

Designing and programming microcontroller circuits often involves working with different number systems, including hexadecimal and binary as well as familiar decimal numbers. Hexadecimal and binary systems are useful because they offer an easy-to-interpret way of expressing the bit- and byte-oriented values that computers use. This appendix is a review of these number systems.

About Number Systems

A number system provides a way to express numerical information. Each of the number systems described below varies in the number, or quantity, on which it is based (10, 2, or 16). This determines, among other things, how many characters you need to express a given quantity.

Decimal Numbers

In the decimal number system used in everyday (non-computer) life, there are ten digits (0-9). Each digit in a number represents a value raised to a power of 10.

This table shows the value of each digit in the decimal number *193*:

Decimal digit	1	9	3
Digit multiplier	10^2	10^1	10^0
Digit value	100	90	3

Binary Numbers

In the binary number system, each digit represents a value raised to a power of 2. The numbers use only two of the ten decimal digits (0 and 1).

Binary representations are useful when you need to quickly see the value of each bit in a byte. For example, you might want to set, clear, toggle, or read a bit in one of the 8052's special function registers (TCON, PCON, and so on). Or, in a control circuit, individual bits might control switches or relays. BASIC-52's logical operators offer a way to control and display individual bit values.

This table shows the value of each digit in *1100 0001,* which is the binary representation of the decimal number *193*:

Binary bit	1	1	0	0	0	0	0	1
Bit multiplier	2^7	2^6	2^5	2^4	2^3	2^2	2^1	2^0
Bit value (decimal)	128	64	0	0	0	0	0	1

Hexadecimal Numbers

In the hexadecimal (or hex) number system, each character represents a value raised to a power of 16. There are 16 characters, with the letters *A* through *F* representing the decimal values 10 through 15.

Because each character in a hex number represents 4 bits, hex numbers are a convenient, compact way to express 8-bit or 16-bit numbers. In BASIC-52, you enter hex values at the host system's keyboard by adding a trailing *h* to the number. (Example: 1Fh.) If the first character is in the range A-F, you must also add a leading 0. (Example: 0E9h.) BASIC-52's PH0. and PH1. operators display numbers in hex format on the host computer's screen.

The Microcontroller Idea Book

This table shows the value of each character in *C1h*, which is the hexadecimal representation of the decimal number *193*:

Hex character	C	1
Character multiplier	16^1	16^0
Character value (decimal)	192	1

Binary-coded Decimal Numbers

Binary-coded decimal, or BCD, is yet another way of expressing numbers. It allows easy translation of binary bits to decimal values. Chapter 10 has more on this number system.

Kilobytes and Megabytes

Two other popular terms for dealing with quantities in the computer world are *kilobyte* and *Megabyte.*

In the metric system of measurement, kilo means 1000, but in the computer world, it commonly refers to 1024 (2^{10}, or 400h in hexadecimal). So, an 8-kilobyte RAM chip actually stores 8192 bytes, not 8000. "K" is short for kilobyte: 8K equals 8 kilobytes.

In an similar way, in the metric system, Mega means a million, but in the computer world, it commonly refers to 1,048,576 (2^{20}, or 1000h in hexadecimal). One Megabyte equals 1024 kilobytes. "M" is short for Megabyte: 8M equals 8 Megabytes.

The Microcontroller Idea Book

Index

57